PAOLO VERONESE

☞ Books in the RENAISSANCE LIVES series explore and illustrate the life histories and achievements of significant artists, rulers, intellectuals and scientists in the early modern world. They delve into literature, philosophy, the history of art, science and natural history and cover narratives of exploration, statecraft and technology.

Series Editor: François Quiviger

Already published

Albrecht Dürer: Art and Autobiography *David Ekserdjian*
Aldus Manutius: The Invention of the Publisher *Oren Margolis*
Andreas Vesalius: Anatomy and the World of Books *Sashiko Kusukawa*
Artemisia Gentileschi and Feminism in Early Modern Europe *Mary D. Garrard*
Benvenuto Cellini and the Embodiment of the Modern Artist *Andreas Beyer*
Bernard Palissy and the Arts of the Earth *François Quiviger*
Blaise Pascal: Miracles and Reason *Mary Ann Caws*
Botticelli: Artist and Designer *Ana Debenedetti*
Caravaggio and the Creation of Modernity *Troy Thomas*
Descartes: The Renewal of Philosophy *Steven Nadler*
Domenico Ghirlandaio: An Elite Artisan and His World *Jean K. Cadogan*
Donatello and the Dawn of Renaissance Art *A. Victor Coonin*
Erasmus of Rotterdam: The Spirit of a Scholar *William Barker*
Filippino Lippi: An Abundance of Invention *Jonathan K. Nelson*
Francis I: The Knight-King *Glenn Richardson*
Francisco de Zurbarán and the Fabric of the World *Jeremy Robbins*
Giorgione's Ambiguity *Tom Nichols*
Hans Holbein: The Artist in a Changing World *Jeanne Nuechterlein*
Hans Memling and the Merchants *Mitzi Kirkland-Ives*
Hieronymus Bosch: Visions and Nightmares *Nils Büttner*
Isaac Newton and Natural Philosophy *Niccolò Guicciardini*
Jan van Eyck within His Art *Alfred Acres*
John Donne: In the Shadow of Religion *Andrew Hadfield*
John Evelyn: A Life of Domesticity *John Dixon Hunt*
Leon Battista Alberti: The Chameleon's Eye *Caspar Pearson*
Leonardo da Vinci: Self, Art and Nature *François Quiviger*
Lorenzo Ghiberti: Designer *Scott Nethersole*
Lucas Cranach: From German Myth to Reformation *Jennifer Nelson*
Machiavelli: From Radical to Reactionary *Robert Black*
Michelangelo and the Viewer in His Time *Bernadine Barnes*
Paolo Veronese and the Nobility of Painting *Tom Nichols*
Paracelsus: An Alchemical Life *Bruce T. Moran*
Petrarch: Everywhere a Wanderer *Christopher S. Celenza*
Piero della Francesca and the Invention of the Artist *Machtelt Brüggen Israëls*
Piero di Cosimo: Eccentricity and Delight *Sarah Blake McHam*
Pieter Bruegel and the Idea of Human Nature *Elizabeth Alice Honig*
Raphael and the Antique *Claudia La Malfa*
Rembrandt's Holland *Larry Silver*
Robert Hooke's Experimental Philosophy *Felicity Henderson*
Rubens's Spirit: From Ingenuity to Genius *Alexander Marr*
Rudolf II: The Life and Legend of the Mad Emperor *Thomas DaCosta Kaufmann*
Salvator Rosa: Paint and Performance *Helen Langdon*
Thomas Nashe and Late Elizabethan Writing *Andrew Hadfield*
Titian's Touch: Art, Magic and Philosophy *Maria H. Loh*
Tycho Brahe and the Measure of the Heavens *John Robert Christianson*
Ulisse Aldrovandi: Naturalist and Collector *Peter Mason*

PAOLO VERONESE

and the Nobility of Painting

TOM NICHOLS

REAKTION BOOKS

To my mother, Mary Nichols (1931–2023), who had a natural affinity with Paolo's presiding love of lavish stuffs and materials

Published by Reaktion Books Ltd
2–4 Sebastian Street
London EC1V 0HE, UK
www.reaktionbooks.co.uk

First published 2026

Published with support from The Gladys Krieble Delmas Foundation

EU GPSR Authorised Representative
Logos Europe, 9 rue Nicolas Poussin, 17000, La Rochelle, France
email: contact@logoseurope.eu

Printed and bound in India by Replika Press Pvt. Ltd

A catalogue record for this book is available from the British Library

ISBN 978 1 83639 192 0

COVER: Paolo Veronese, *Lucretia*, *c.* 1583–5, oil on canvas. Kunsthistorisches Museum, Vienna, photo akg-images/Erich Lessing.

CONTENTS

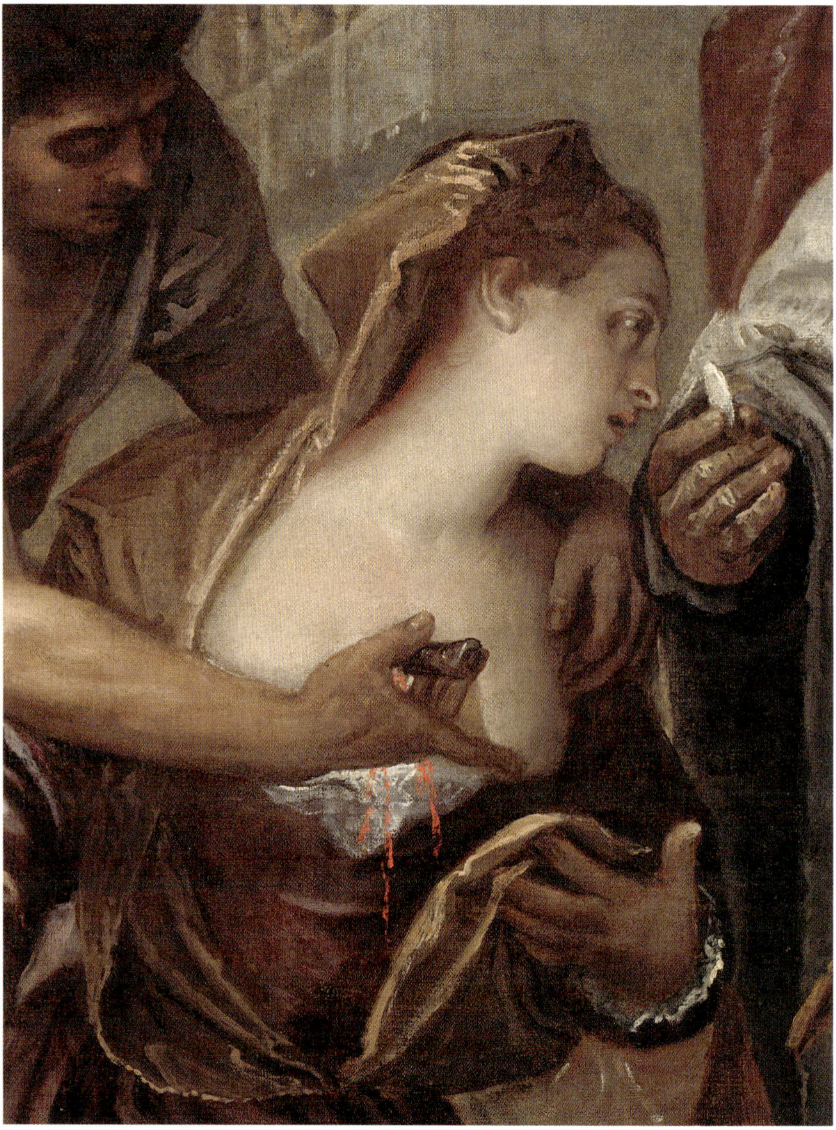

Introduction

Whether Veronese tells or shows has been one of the key questions asked about his paintings over the centuries. Does he convey the story, generating profound meanings, or does he resist it, substituting a playful visuality for all deeper significations? Is he a great narrative painter or one unconcerned with meanings derived from beyond the realm of the picture itself? For Veronese's contemporaries in the sixteenth century such questions were of less significance, although they certainly underpinned the Inquisition's interview with the painter on 18 July 1573, during which he was interrogated about the obscurity of a religious painting he had recently completed for the main Dominican church in Venice (illus. 44). Many of Veronese's patrons, however, were very happy with his approach to painting, enjoying and encouraging the visual flair and flamboyance that typically took him beyond the narrower dictates of his given subject. It was only much later, in the context of learned theoretical debate in the new art academies of France and Britain in the seventeenth and eighteenth centuries, that Veronese's richly elaborated approach to pictorial composition began to appear problematic from their intellectualizing point of view. In a telling echo of the concerns of the inquisitors several centuries earlier, the academicians expressed doubts that Veronese had paid due attention to the high moral values embodied in the historical, biblical and mythological stories he depicted.

1 Paolo Veronese, *Martyrdom and Last Communion of St Lucy*, c. 1585–6, detail.

When Sir Joshua Reynolds, the first president of the Royal Academy in London, identified Veronese 'as an ornamental Painter' whose intention was 'solely to produce an effect of light and shadow', he drew on more than a century of doubts about the artist.[1] In Reynolds's view, Veronese was visually excessive: more interested in the vainglorious display of his pictorial skills than with the typically heroic meanings of the narratives he painted. In this way, he fell short of 'the Great Style' developed by the Renaissance artists of Florence and Rome that the academicians most admired. While the authority of Reynolds's moral idealism regarding painting gradually ebbed away in the following centuries under the successive impacts of Romanticism, Realism and Modernism, the idea that Veronese's art was too showy, or trivial in content, persisted. In his *Italian Hours* of 1909, Henry James made Veronese serve as a sensuous and frivolous foil to the deeply spiritual Tintoretto (1518/19–1594), who 'never drew a line that was not . . . a moral line'. Veronese, by implication, never drew one that *was*. The maker of the *Rape of Europa* (illus. 48), James noted, was, 'pictorially speaking, no greater casuist than any other genius of supreme good taste'.[2] The Bloomsbury art critic Roger Fry noted in 1934 that Veronese 'doesn't care a damn about anything but his [artistic] opportunities', though given that Fry was planning to write a book on the painter it is unclear whether he felt this to be a weakness or a strength.[3] The dismissal of Veronese as a serious painter more certainly underpins Michael Levey's description of him as a 'negative personality' in a book review of 1967. When measured against a Bellini or a Titian, Levey remarked, Veronese's paintings can be considered little more than 'effective, agreeable decoration'.[4]

VERONESE AND THE LANGUAGE OF PAINTERS

Such views have since stimulated earnest attempts to revive Veronese's critical reputation by emphasizing the depth and meaning of his works. In this view, the painter is understood to have been much more closely concerned with the important subjects that he painted than had hitherto been allowed. He is seen as a painter who responded profoundly to the new ethical demands of the Catholic Counter-Reformation in the later decades of the sixteenth century; or, more broadly, as an avid iconographer, especially attentive to the exposition of the texts that he illustrated.[5] His portraits and drawings have also been reinterpreted along these lines: the former seen as containing deeper symbolic meanings and the latter as deployed to establish core motifs of ethical life subsequently used in his paintings.[6] Although the more recent arguments for Veronese's seriousness dispute the earlier stress on his superficiality, they nonetheless accept one assumption implicit in the older view: that the deep meanings conveyed through art are superior to a mere concern with sensually perceived surfaces and pictorially generated effects. Yet that assumption is potentially anachronistic from a historical point of view. The insistence on a hierarchical, ethically freighted division between surface and depth in art owes more to the much later rationalistic Enlightenment criticisms noted above than it does to the sixteenth century. In Veronese's time, the display of richly sensuous materials was often taken as a sign of the presence of high spiritual or ethical values, rather than as necessarily obscuring or occluding them.[7]

Although the Reynoldsian criticisms may have been mistaken in their evaluation of Veronese's paintings as of low moral value, they can nonetheless be taken as accurate enough insofar as they recognize that this painter was especially – perhaps even fundamentally – concerned with generating a pleasurable effect of opulent and expansive visuality. He sometimes flirted with illusionistic and iconographic obscurity, and even with semantic irreverence and mockery, or the taboo of non-meaning. In this he might be more typical of his age, given that a press towards individualistic style was common enough in the work of many Renaissance artists of the Cinquecento. In Venice, leading painters had especially reserved the right to invent in pictorial terms, improvising in their favoured medium of oil, which encouraged such freedoms. Veronese, as one of his responses to the inquisitors in 1573 tells us, understood the licence to invent as the basic right of a leading picture-maker in the city. Like Giovanni Bellini (*c.* 1430–1516) before him, Veronese preferred 'to wander at will' in his art, rather than to be closely confined by the prescriptions of a given client or subject-matter.[8] And this seems to have been widely respected by his patrons and supporters. His contract with the Benedictine monks of San Giorgio Maggiore of 6 June 1562, for example, stipulates that the subject depicted must be the supper 'where Christ performed his miracle at Cana' (illus. 43). But the wording of the contract makes no further prescriptions, merely inviting Veronese to make 'that quantity of figures that can be comfortably accommodated' within the space allotted for the painting.[9] Veronese's patrons seem to have actively encouraged the painter to multiply figures as he saw fit. They expected him to exercise his impressive armoury of visual effects beyond the promptings of the given story that they commissioned him to depict.

Does an artist's attention to meaning always or necessarily secure the depth of his work? Or, conversely, does a presiding concern with ever-varying coloured surfaces of forms mean that the work is necessarily superficial? Certain more recent writers on Veronese have intelligently departed from the usual two-sided critical debate by arguing that the painter's profundity lies precisely in the acute attention he pays to surfaces.[10] It is no longer necessary to make excuses for Veronese's special concern with the appearances of flesh, fabrics and textiles, or to criticize his emphasis on jewellery and carved stone. His interest in the complex and arbitrary twists and turns of tightly knotted figural clusters, and his placement of these groupings within spatial and architectural contexts that are never quite the stable, objective or understandable domains that they appear to be, can be seen as the product of powerfully independent artistic decision, rather than of triviality or solipsism. One lesson that Veronese's paintings might teach us is that a preoccupation with such visual aspects – what Reynolds criticized as an undue display of 'the language of painters' – is legitimate enough. Indeed, Veronese's sensual pictorialism is recoverable as a dynamic mental and intellectual practice.[11]

I will argue in this book for the lasting value of Veronese's 'ornamental' approach, laying emphasis on his defining sense of the primacy of his pictures themselves. I will revive the older emphasis on Veronese's essential decorativeness while also suggesting that this can be seen as a positive attribute: less an issue of his shallowness of mind than a signal of his sharp visual intelligence. I will question, too, the binary or oppositional nature of the main strands of Veronese criticism introduced above. This painter's defining commitment to 'the pictorial vision', as Bernard Berenson once described it, does not, after all, mean that he took no notice of his subject-matter, or ignored its wider moral or allegorical implications.[12] In many works by Veronese, the subject depicted is not in question and his attention to it is careful and adroit. Even when the iconography is unproblematic, though, the narrative is subtly woven into the visual fabric of the picture, becoming one element within its wider realization. In paintings from the last decade or so of his life Veronese's engagement with his given subject-matter certainly intensified. But these sometimes tragic late works continue to deploy elements of the deflecting, digressive and occluding approach that he had championed in earlier decades. Veronese's late style drew him closer to the other leading masters of Venetian painting, especially to Tintoretto and Jacopo Bassano (*c.* 1510–1592). But across the preceding decades Veronese had pursued a different path, avoiding the darker grounds and paint tonalities of his contemporaries in favour of luminous colouristic harmonies, glowing in the full light of day. He filled his works with exotic figure types dressed in lavish costumes and other digressive details that boldly lead the viewer's eye around his picture surface. He often avoided the representation of the narrative climax or denouement altogether so that in some works the precise textual passage represented becomes difficult to determine.[13]

The remarkable consistency of Veronese's style across the four decades or so of his career, like his relative lack of attention to precise viewing angles, picture types or media, indicate the visual autonomy he preserved when fulfilling a commission. In making a painting, Veronese powerfully translated extraneous ideas from the world beyond the frame into his own idiom, altering them in the process. If this meant compromising their purely imitative or indexical qualities, then it also allowed him to maintain an underlying sense of the independent authority of his work, which enjoyed an adventurous and non-inductive relationship to everything outside itself. In taking this approach, Veronese certainly drew on the existing approach to oil painting practised in Venice known as *colorito*, which encouraged the active manipulation of pigments on the picture surface at the point of execution, to some extent above and beyond the control of the underlying idea or 'design' for the work.[14] Veronese's relatively elaborate preparatory approach when making a painting owed more, though, to his training in Verona than it did to Venetian examples. Technical analysis of his finished works has revealed that they include far fewer *pentimenti* or changes at the painting stage than is the case with the other leading masters in Venice. Veronese's pictorialism cannot finally be interpreted as a matter of his technique, his painterly touch, or of his 'Venetianness' (*venezianità*). Nonetheless, if this master typically took the given text as his starting point, it did not usually determine his point of arrival. In the chapters to come, careful attention to a selection of Veronese's most important paintings will help to reveal how he made the given themes over into his own singular and inimitable style. In a Veronese painting, the intentions of a master picture-maker tend, in the end, to win out.

THE MAKING OF AN ARISTOCRATIC PAINTER

Laying emphasis on Veronese's pictorialism might risk isolating him too much from the wider mores of his time and place.[15] It should be acknowledged that Veronese's sense of painting as an independent entity did not necessarily represent a departure from the wider cultural and aesthetic understandings of his period. The primacy of artistry over content was typical enough in this sophisticated and ornate phase of visual culture in Italy and elsewhere. By the mid-sixteenth century, leading artists were more-or-less expected to develop carefully differentiated or 'stylish styles' against more normative or self-suppressing values.[16] There are good grounds for thinking of Veronese as a knowing Late Renaissance *maniera* painter, acutely aware of the art of the past, and thus ever ready to sacrifice direct imitation of nature for the artistic emulation of the great works of his forebears and contemporaries. Veronese's elaborate approach was anyway commensurate with his social and professional identity, which was carefully fashioned or composed, like one of his paintings. To understand this more clearly, we need to consider the close attention that the young painter paid to the production of himself on the public stage of Venetian artistic culture, where he first appeared in the early 1550s, as the high-born purveyor of an aristocratic style.

Even the earliest sources on Veronese do not take us much beyond this carefully manicured professional persona: it is hard to find the 'true Veronese' beyond the idealizing image of him as the perfect gentleman artist. Veronese is mentioned positively – but briefly – by the contemporary Florentine writers Giorgio Vasari and Raffaello Borghini. The first extended 'Life of Veronese' was published in 1648 by Carlo Ridolfi: a Vicenza-born painter who had trained with one of Veronese's pupils and knew his grandson. Ridolfi's detailed account presents Veronese's personality as supremely well-mannered and polite, equitable to his professional colleagues and prudent and caring regarding his growing family. Ridolfi took care to contrast Veronese with his rival, Tintoretto, who constantly clamoured and pushed for commissions, sometimes undertaking low tricks to secure them. Veronese, by contrast, stood back, his reticence reflecting his noble virtues, waited for his patrons to come and ask him to paint for them. In a subsequently influential anecdote, we hear that when the great Titian (*c.* 1488/90–1576) met the young artist in St Mark's Square he 'affectionately hugged him', saying 'that it made him happy to consider Paolo as uniting in his person the decorum and the nobility of painting'.[17] Whatever the truth about the overlap between Veronese's noble personality and his approach to painting that this implies, it seems that he half-invented his aristocratic identity. Born in 1528 as the son of Gabriele Bazaro, Paolo was, at least on his father's side, from relatively lowly stock: the offspring of a well-established family of stonecutters or masons whose workshop activities in Lugano and in the San Paolo area of Verona can be traced back over four generations.[18] He continued to identify with the traditional working world of these local craftsmen into the early 1550s, signing himself as 'Paullo spezapreda [stonecutter]' on a contract of 1553.[19] His decision to move to Venice in the following few years changed things. The ambitious young painter seems to have realized that a more active and distinguishing self-presentation would be necessary to secure professional lift-off in the arch-competitive artistic melting pot of Venice. By 1555 he referred to himself on contracts as 'Paolo Veronese', 'Paolo da Verona' or 'Paolo Caliaro Veronese'.[20] The new emphasis on his origins in Verona evident in these names paradoxically indicates that he was primarily working and/or resident away from his hometown. His use of 'Caliaro', which became increasingly frequent during his career, went further, asserting that he was a scion of the aristocratic Caliari family of Verona.

Becoming a Caliari meant exchanging his earlier allegiance to the wider artisanal culture of his stonecutter father for a connection to the forebears of his recently widowed mother, Caterina, who may have come to live with him in Venice following her husband's death between 1553 and 1555.[21] Paolo's new domestic and perhaps emotional closeness to his mother might have helped to stimulate his incorporation of aspects conventionally recognized as feminine into his painting style. His depictions of the beautiful Old Testament heroine Esther at San Sebastiano in 1555–6, for example, featuring an intensified interest in the depiction of lavish fabrics, fashionable dress and expensive jewellery, might be significant in this regard (illus. 17). Paolo's adoption of Caterina's aristocratic surname more certainly served to assert Paolo's fast-developing connection with a patrician clientele in Venice, suggesting that the young painter shared his new patrons' elite social status and their associated refinement in cultural and artistic values. Paolo was not, however, straightforwardly a Caliari. Although his mother was indeed the daughter of a nobleman – Antonio Caliari – she was also illegitimate. Caterina's own mother, Maddelena Dragina, was in all likelihood a courtesan, given that she went on to have a further child out of wedlock with the nobleman Leonardo Bevilacqua Lazise.[22] However this may be, Caterina's marriage to the artisan Bazaro indicates her somewhat déclassé or even outsider position vis-à-vis Veronese high society.

By assuming his maternal grandfather's noble name, Paolo did not seek to compete arrogantly with the high aristocratic status of his gathering posse of Venetian patrons. His earlier clients from the leading families – the Grimani, Giustiniani and Barbaro among them – would certainly have understood well enough that the young painter was not really a nobleman of similar rank to themselves. Paolo remained connected to the artisanal artistic culture within which he had grown up in Verona and continued to work in his hometown and in several other mainland centres, on and off, late into his career. As a 'Veronese' based in Venice he remained forever a *straniero*, falling outside the carefully defined social hierarchy in the city. Veronese would have been recognized as a loyal subject of the mainland empire – Verona had been under Venetian control since 1405 – but he had no chance of inclusion in the *Libro d'Oro* (Golden Book) of patrician family names so assiduously maintained by the locals; or even in the *Libro d'Argento* (Silver Book), the equivalent list of respectable non-noble citizen families.[23] Paolo's lowly social rank relative to those he typically worked for is clear from the fact that he rented houses (where his studios were presumably housed) from patricians in the working-class district of Cannaregio in Venice up until his marriage, rather than owning his own property. Even after 1566, when he moved to a more central and upmarket location at San Samuele, he continued to pay rent to the patrician Giacomo Federici and his heirs.[24]

Social position or identity in mid-Cinquecento Venice was not so fixed as this might make it appear, however, and it is likely that the crowded metropolis offered Paolo certain freedoms that would have been denied him had he remained in Verona. Venice was then one of the great entrepôts of Europe, centre of a frenzy of international and multinational exchange, trading silks, spices and other luxury goods from the East with wool and metals from the West. Populous home to an ever-changing, ethnically diverse population, it was, too, a centre of fervid cultural, intellectual and artistic production and innovation. It is no surprise that Paolo's move to this thriving metropolis stimulated the above-noted manipulation of his professional persona. If his upper-class credentials were questionable then so too, at least from the perspective of settled mainland aristocratic society, were those of the Venetian patricians that he now 'courted': especially as their leadership in the city was typically based on success in trade rather than on land ownership or military achievements. During the sixteenth century many Venetian patricians sought to alter or suppress their anomalous status as the kind of merchant-nobles who kept their saleable stock in the warehouse-like ground floors of their palazzi. Increasingly, they attempted to remodel their profile in accordance with the more conventional one of the country or estate-based gentleman, buying up vast tracts of farming land on the Venetian-owned inland territory known as the *terraferma*.[25] By highlighting his origins as an aristocrat from this much-favoured area, Paolo sought to mirror the concern of his new patrons among the patriciate to reshape their identity. Here was a young artist who appeared especially sympathetic to their increasingly westward-leaning social, cultural and economic values.[26] The sophisticated *all'antica* tone of Paolo's paintings reflected back to his clients just the kind of gentrifying values that they coveted.[27] Obeying an unspoken decorum, his 'noble' style made no direct reference to the reality of their ongoing trading activities or to the basis of their wealth in the mercantile exchange of goods for sale.

There could be a broad historical or subject-based justification for the inclusion of socially refined elements and settings in Veronese's paintings. In a paradigmatic work of his artistic maturity, the *Family of Darius before Alexander* from circa 1565–7, the tone of exotic courtliness was almost a requirement of the subject (illus. 2). Veronese was not the first master working in Republican Venice to fantasize the choreographed appearances, rituals and refined behavioural etiquette of a perfected royal court. In his St Ursula cycle of the 1490s, Vittore Carpaccio (*c.* 1460/65–1525/6) had imagined the different world of the medieval courts of Brittany, England and Rome, although the painter, who did not often leave Venice, also took care to model their appearances on the built environment and public ceremonials of his native city. Veronese was particularly alert to Carpaccio's penchant for showing moments of arrival and departure, in which high-ranking figures go down on their knees before seated rulers, in public and performative contexts, watched by elegantly dressed courtiers. Veronese also drew on the earlier painter's amalgamations of foreign, exotic and regal aspects with more local references. In the *Darius*, Veronese is careful to include elements that would have familiarized his imagery for a local audience. The main actors are, after all, easily recognizable as aristocratic Venetian contemporaries, even if they are dressed up as ancients.

Titian, long resident in Venice, then became one of the great propagandists in painting for court values in the first half of the sixteenth century across Italy and Europe, especially in his portraits and mythologies.[28] Veronese took careful note of these progressive supra-Republican and individualizing aspects of Titian's painting. But he typically served a more proximate clientele, and his works often reflect local values – especially their concern to improve their social standing. It was 'aristocratizing' rather than 'aristocracy' that he was most concerned with.[29] His *Darius* is the epitome of this particularly Venetian kind of aspirational courtliness, commissioned as it was by a prominent patrician, Francesco Pisani, for his lavish country villa on the *terraferma*.[30] As a leading landowner in the Montagnana area, Pisani would have been keen to build his identity as an estate-owning aristocrat. Veronese granted his patron a key role in the painting where he appears in the guise of an elderly courtier-advisor. Pisani introduces the wife and daughters of the defeated Darius to the victors, his delicate gesture counselling understanding and compassion on Alexander's part following the defeat of their husband and father, and their misidentification of the victorious emperor for his second-in-command, Hephaestus. Perhaps, too, the kneeling women are portraits of the commissioning family, who – along with the conquering heroes – play-act the ancient story, as if they were performing in a drama put on for the delight of guests at their country villa.[31] Veronese was especially careful to promote the head of the family, Francesco, placed centrally in the composition before an elaborately moulded pyramidal gateway that lends his considerate action a further triumphal quality. Pisani's paternal figure, as he ushers the women into the presence of the handsome young victors, embodies the twinned aristocratic values of magnificence and magnanimity: the display of rank on the one hand and its dissimulation or downplaying on the other.

The painting was intended to model an ideal of social manners for the patron and his family in their country residence. Berenson described Veronese as 'one of the few artists who helped to make the great of the earth aware of themselves and to live in ways worthy of their status'.[32] But 'the great of the earth' were, at this pivotal point in Venetian social and economic history, also keen to refashion and improve themselves, and the social didactics underpinning a work such as the *Darius* articulate their particular kind of cultural ambition. The strategic placement of Francesco's figure between the royal family of Darius and Emperor Alexander and his army recalls the age-old patriotic idea of Venice as a peacemaker between two powerful warring factions. It also gives visual form to the now coveted place of the urban mercantile

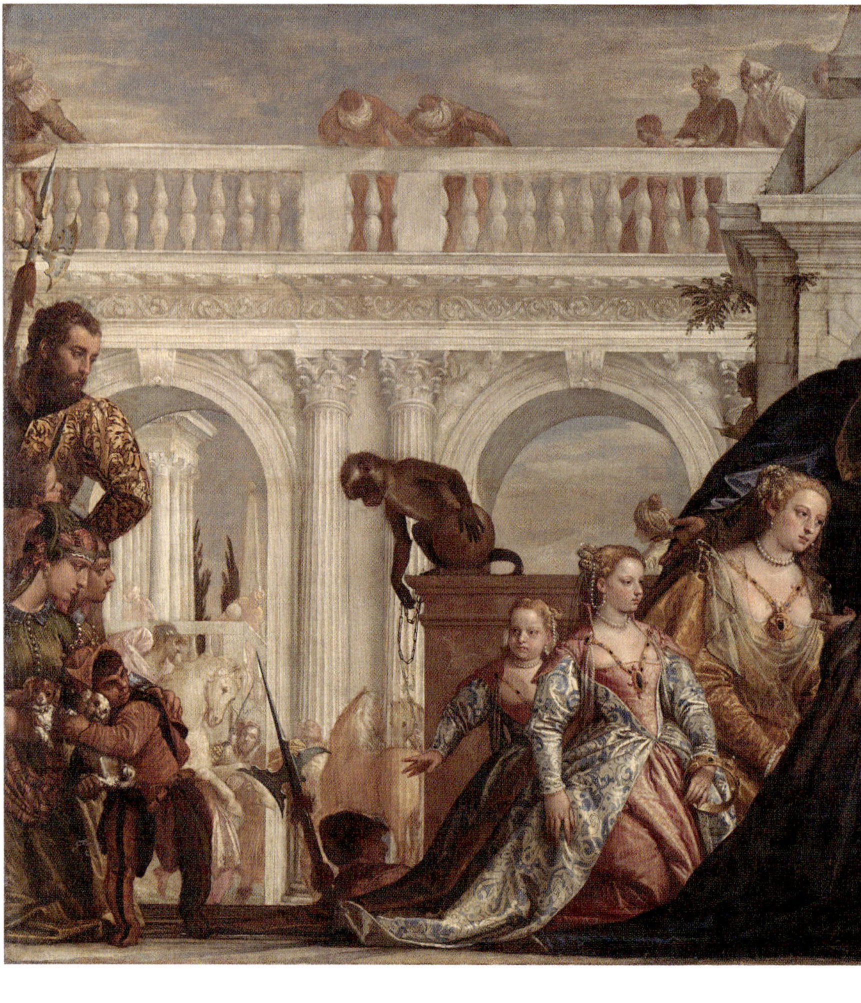

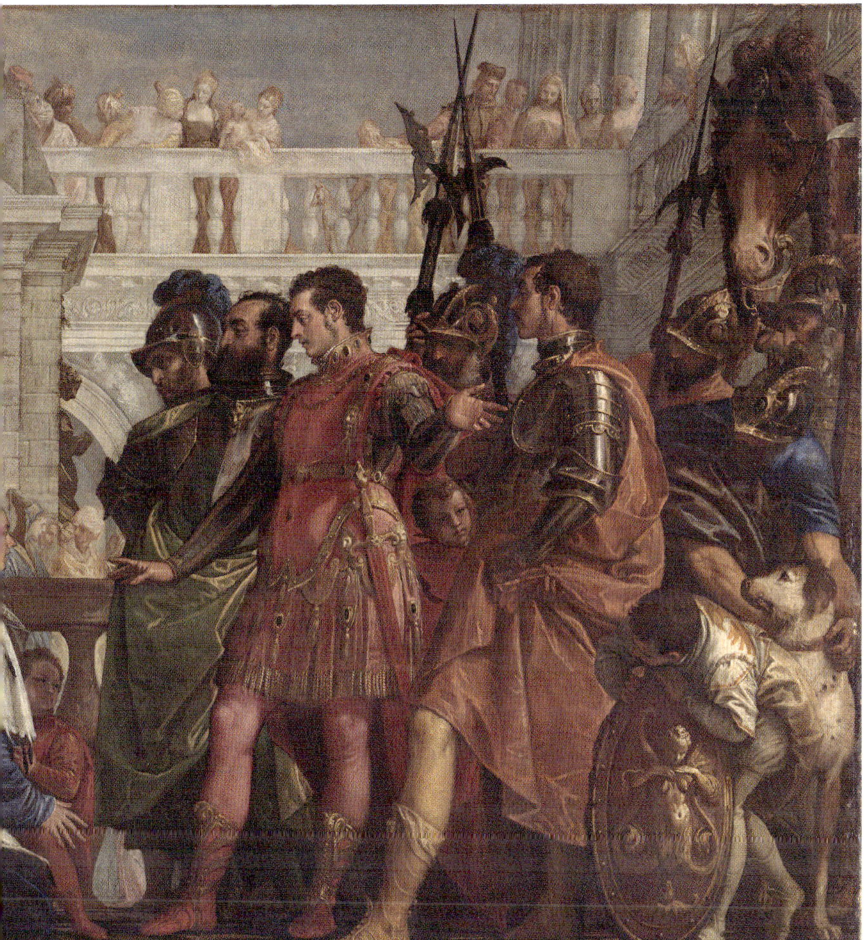

2 Veronese, *Family of Darius before Alexander*, c. 1565–7, oil on canvas.

patriciate at the top table of international aristocratic culture. It is a pity that the Francesco of historical reality did not live up to his ideal model in Veronese's painting, especially regarding the example of gracious behaviour towards vulnerable women promoted in that context. Instead, he disinherited his wife in favour of his cousin, Zan Mattio: an action that led (following Francesco's death in 1567) to her desperate attempt to remove the picture from the palace, and to a lawsuit against her husband's chosen heir.[33]

Veronese's paintings offered to fulfil his patrons' fantasies of life led on the wider elevated stage of European aristocratic culture. The earliest published response to his work in Venice indicates that his close fit with socially ambitious patrician patrons was quickly recognized and appreciated. In the first edition of his guidebook to Venice, Francesco Sansovino, writing under the pseudonym Anselmo Guisconi, admiringly described Paolo's recent paintings on a ceiling in the Ducal Palace as works of 'true design and gentility' (illus. 12).[34] The first of these terms allied the young painter's style with the dominant mainland tradition of Renaissance art, following the true principles of *disegno* (design) recently lauded in Vasari's *Lives of the Artists* (1550). The second made sure to connect it with models of aristocratic etiquette established in widely read manuals of courtly behaviour, such as Baldassare Castiglione's *Book of the Courtier* (1528). Guisconi/Sansovino's words give us an early indication of the underlying homologies between Veronese's persona, his patrons and his artistic style: the professional building blocks that secured his early and lasting success in Venice.

VELVET SLIPPERS: FROM *SPEZAPREDA* TO *SPREZZATURA*

Veronese's adoption of new names on his arrival in Venice represented a key moment in his self-definition within the competitive field of artistic culture in the city. Up until this point, he often worked alongside other young painters from Verona and elsewhere in a semi-communal fashion.[35] Now promoting himself as 'Paolo da Verona' or 'Paolo Veronese', he became more individualistic, asserting a new measure of artistic independence. His patrons among the Venetian patriciate should now consider him as *the* 'Veronese' rather than merely *a* Veronese. Paolo's honing of his professional profile in the direction of a putative noble identity must have been further encouraged by the rivalry in painting that he now entered into with the Venice-born favourite, Jacopo Tintoretto.[36] Jacopo's adopted professional persona as 'the little dyer' highlighted his identity as the proud son of a local artisan, and thus suggested his connection with the wider and typically non-noble working populace of Venice (among whom dyers were particularly respected and numerous).[37] If Veronese had continued as 'Paulo spezapreda' he would only have meekly followed Tintoretto's lead, though without the imprimatur of a local identity. But as 'Paolo Caliaro Veronese' he asserted a double distinction from his main competitor in painting, identifying himself as both non-local and non-artisan.

It would be easy to see the contrasting professional identities of Veronese and Tintoretto as passively reflecting fixed social or class realities. Their adopted personae were, instead, the product of calculated self-curation in relation to existing and potential areas of demand in the market for paintings. If Tintoretto had actively shaped his identity as local and non-elite, his younger rival sought to define himself in opposite terms. Paolo's new sobriquet made his difference from Tintoretto explicit to potential patrons in both a geographical and social sense. The success of both these contrasting gambits is evident from the way that the two masters – the Castor and Pollux of Venetian painting, as Ridolfi aptly described them – came to dominate in the field of painting in Venice from around 1550 onwards. If Tintoretto concentrated on patronage from the myriads of non-noble confraternities active in the city, then Veronese sought out commissions from its leading patrician families. But both painters worked frequently in the city's churches and decorated official buildings, and their concentration on specific markets did not preclude, on occasion, crossing over to work in the area dominated by the other painter. Despite their evident differences in style and approach, Veronese and Tintoretto shared a common aim: to increase the quantity of paintings commissioned and brought to completion in the city.[38]

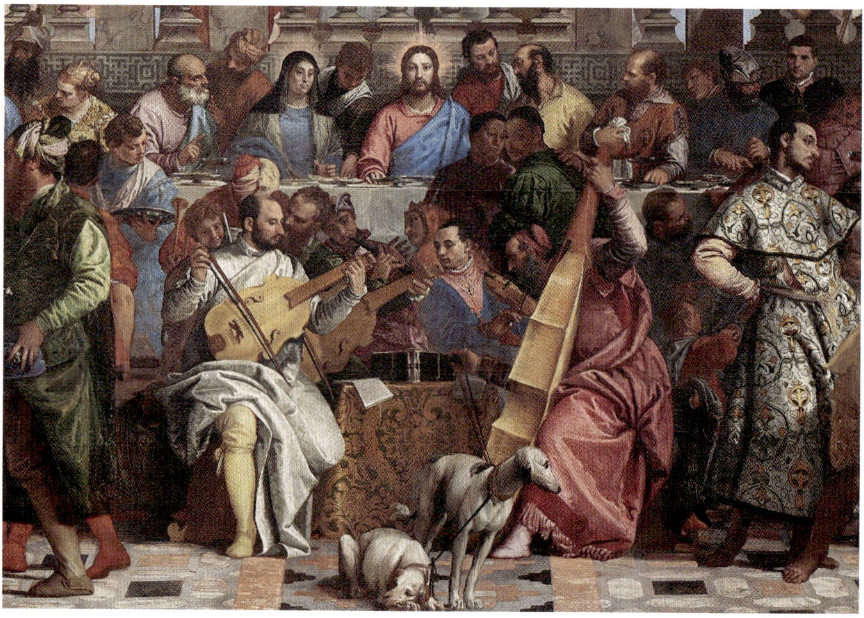

3 Veronese, *Marriage at Cana*, 1562–3, oil on canvas, detail of musicians.

However, in the building of a noble artistic persona certain defining appearances had to be maintained. Drawing on the testimony of Veronese's grandson, Giuseppe Caliari, Ridolfi tells us that Paolo always presented himself in the guise of a finely dressed aristocrat, wearing 'precious clothes and velvet slippers which are still kept by his heir'.[39] This recalls Leonardo's ideal image of the ultra-civilized Renaissance court painter who 'sits before his work, perfectly at ease and well-dressed', listening to poetry or music while he works.[40] Paolo seems to have shown himself in similar guise in a self-portrait as a musician included in his *Marriage at Cana* where he plays a tenor viol in accompaniment to Titian's *violone*, sporting silvery and lemon-coloured silken robes that might allude to the elegant acerbity of his preferred palette, while complementing Titian's sonorous reds (illus. 3).[41] If Leonardo imagined the painter 'enjoying the accompaniment of music', then Veronese shows himself *as* a musician: that is, as a higher servant at the aristocratic feast, rather than as an aristocrat per se. Even if he cuts a culturally refined figure, with elegant proportions and a distinguished-looking head, he remains no more than an entertainer, busy at his work rather than enjoying the leisure of the noble guests sat around the table. Veronese's placement of his self-image among those serving the guests indicates his acceptance of a middling supportive role in the service of his social superiors. Both he and possibly his younger painter-brother Benedetto (1538–1598), standing to the right of Titian, belong to the entourage of underlings at a grand occasion and are at home among the legions of accessories that populate many of his feast scenes and other crowded paintings.

It is, however, the elegance rather than the humility of this self-representation that is most striking. If the painter does not sport his velvet slippers, then the finely made silks and satins of his costume nonetheless display the great wealth he had accrued less than a decade following his arrival in Venice.[42] As a nouveau-riche outsider to Venice, who continued to labour with his hands in a rented workshop, Veronese could not realistically hope to join the social elite of his day. But he was nonetheless given the freedom to dignify himself as he saw fit in the fantasized domain of his paintings. His disguised self-portrait suggests his claim to artistic licence. It is, after all, a playful and knowing fiction beyond the strict demands of the text that he illustrates, given that musicians and painters do not appear in John's sparse gospel account of the marriage at Cana in the Bible. In the subsidiary areas of his compositions Veronese was used to taking liberties, inventing especially freely and at will, imagining the setting for the given narrative in the ways that he wanted. Picturing himself as a paid entertainer at a grand occasion, Veronese does not appear as the aristocrat-painter of Castiglione's imagining. He had, though, learned the lesson of elegant behavioural self-modelling that this author recommended. The elegant muscian-painter who appears in the *Cana* of 1562–3 can be taken as a measure of the rapidity and assurance of his social ascent from the artisan *spezapreda* to the high-ranking man of Castiglionesque *sprezzatura*: that nonchalance or ease in all social interactions that the carefully presented courtier must develop through experience and careful study. The underlying assumption in Castiglione's vastly influential book is that nobility, rather than being dependent on biological or genealogical givens, is a culturally defined quality that can be learned. And this historically contingent understanding is also indicative of the fluid social conditions in late Renaissance Venice that facilitated Veronese's rapid acquirement of his new identity.

ONE

Earlier Works

For centuries it was assumed that Veronese's painting simply belonged to Venice and its great Renaissance tradition, while his origins and training in Verona were ignored. Ridolfi went further still, claiming that Verona was a backward cultural 'wilderness' in which the young painter was actively held back, and from which he had to escape to win the recognition he deserved in glorious Venice. More recently, renewed emphasis has been laid on the formative input of Veronese's native city on his work, and his continuing engagement with its artistic culture.[1] Verona was a vibrant centre of Renaissance learning in the mid-sixteenth century, especially proud of its surviving Roman buildings that were unmatched in Venice. Its two ancient gateways, triumphal arch, arena and theatre were the subject of intense local interest, scholarly interpretation and attempted artistic revival. The painter's early commissions show that he was strongly backed by leading aristocratic families of Verona from the very outset of his career. Evidence of the impact of the appearances of contemporary Verona on the young painter are not difficult to find. In several early works, he quotes the recent *all'antica* buildings of the fashionable local-born architect Michele Sanmicheli (1484–1559).[2] In addition, his relatively elaborate preparatory process when making a painting clearly owed more to his early training in the workshops of Antonio Badile (*c.* 1518–1560) and Giovanni Caroto

(1480–1555) in Verona than to anything that he learned later in Venice.[3]

All this does not make Veronese wholly or just a product of his birthplace on the mainland. The appearance of his earliest known works of circa 1546 indicates his immediate close engagement with the 'painterly' Venetian approach, deploying rich and sonorous colour combinations that typically resist the definition of sharp contours and outlines. Veronese's early style might seem to make him a 'Venetian painter' after all. But as we have seen, Veronese carefully promoted his difference from local rivals such as Tintoretto, presenting himself as an incomer ready to introduce newly fashionable mainland and *all'antica* ideas and values to Venice. Rather than seeing this master as either Veronese or Venetian, we should note the way in which he maintained the dialectical aspects of his position between the two artistic centres he primarily worked in. Instead of trying to closely pin Paolo down in terms of his artistic origins, inheritance or geography, we might note instead the seamless way in which he adapted to the artistic milieux of Verona and Venice, without quite belonging to either. His approach to painting was non- or supra-local, at least insofar as it was not circumscribed by a defining attachment to a given cultural context. Veronese did not typically make too many concessions to 'place'. Even when he incorporated ideas drawn from one location or another, these were typically absorbed into his own unique manner of artistic realization. And similar observations can be made regarding the powerful consistency of his style across different visual media and picture types.

In accordance with this, Veronese's earliest works in Verona do not differ so greatly from those he completed following his move to Venice. This admittedly reflects the already well-established overlap between mainland and Venetian artistic taste and culture in the mid-sixteenth century. The young painter did not need to alter or vary his approach too much, whether he worked

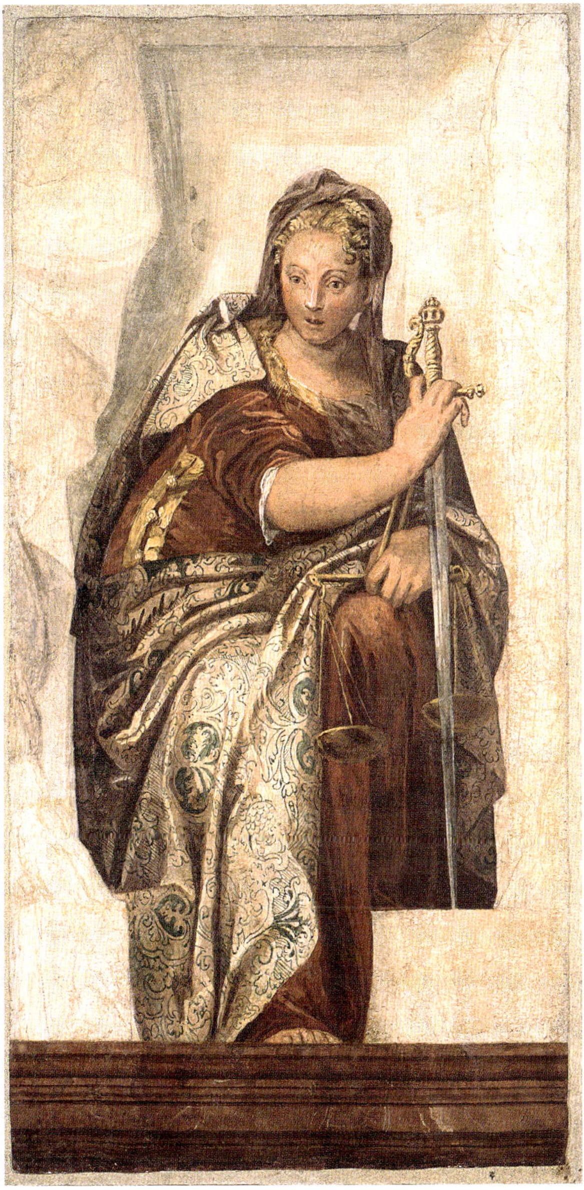

4 Veronese, *Justice*, 1551, fresco.

in one city or the other. The appearance of the surviving ceiling and wall frescoes that he painted for grand private residences in the first decade or so of his career indicate that his approach remained similar, whether he decorated a country villa on the *terraferma*, an urban palazzo in Verona or Vicenza or a patrician one in Venice.[4] Differences of picture-type, iconography or medium do not appear to have unduly disturbed the stability of his approach. For example, the damaged remains of the frescoes he painted for the villa La Soranza at Treville near Treviso in 1551 are more limited in figural or compositional terms than certain of his near-contemporary works for Venetian buildings. But the concern with richly worked surfaces characteristic of his oil paintings is equally apparent in these early frescoes. In his figure of *Justice*, for instance, the young master focuses our attention on swirling masses of complexly arranged, patterned drapery in a way that pushes against the high morality or severity of the allegorical meaning, as also against the limitations of his given medium (illus. 4).

Conversely, Veronese's preference for compressed, frieze-like formal arrangements in his oil paintings carries over certain aspects already evident in his frescoes, in which figures press towards the picture surface in narrow, niche-like spaces. Whether Veronese painted an altarpiece, a laterally shaped religious narrative painting, a domestically scaled devotional work, a portrait or a ceiling painting, in oil or in fresco, his approach remained in certain ways self-consistent and supra-medial. The overall design of Veronese's earliest altarpiece for a church in Verona already closely anticipates the one that he went on to paint some years later in Venice (illus. 7, 8). If, in his painted architecture, reference to Andrea Palladio (1508–1580) gradually supplanted that to Sanmicheli, then the overall pictorial effect of his pale, stone-built *all'antica* structures remained similar enough.[5] Veronese's style, which appeared all at once, as if fully fledged, in the mid-1540s, did not change so dramatically over the subsequent decades: an aspect that has caused great difficulties in establishing the chronology of his paintings.[6] As we will see, Veronese's extraordinary stylistic stability owed much to his systematic and internalized artistic process.

RAISING OF THE DAUGHTER OF JAIRUS

A surviving example of Veronese's very earliest work is the oil sketch for a lost religious narrative painting that once hung in a church chapel in Verona (illus. 5).[7] In this little painting, Veronese's strongly pictorialized presentation resists the clear expression of the narrative to some extent, and this effect might owe more to aesthetic decision than to artistic immaturity. It is admittedly easy enough to pick out Christ's figure as he grasps the left hand of the miraculously revived twelve-year-old daughter of Jairus, a leader of the Synagogue. As she awakens, Christ turns to look into the face of her father. The girl is propped up by her mother, while to the right of the composition we see John, Peter and James, the three disciples admitted to Jairus's house, as specified in the Bible (Mark 5:21). The foreground figures in this area cluster tightly together, generating an effect of formal overlapping or interchangeability that is very different to the other recent works for the same chapel by his two masters, Badile and Caroto.[8] Veronese's repeated use of sonorous reds, rose pinks and lime greens with pale highlights for the figures has the effect of obstructing the viewer's apprehension of specific bodies. St Peter's depiction offers a particular visual surprise, given the subjection of his figure to a radical formal ellipsis. We manage to glimpse some golden drapery, a left knee, hands and a head, while the rest of his body is hidden by that of St John. The exact position of Peter's limbs in space, and their interrelationship, is made hard to establish. Those that we are permitted to see appear like strange protuberances out of John's occluding figure.

If the foreshortened position of Jairus's daughter on the bed superficially recalls a famous example of Renaissance perspectivism by Andrea Mantegna (1431–1506), the *Lamentation of the Dead Christ* (*c.* 1480, Milan, Pinacoteca di Brera), then the effect of linear recession in this model has been dissolved by Veronese's crumbly form-obscuring brushwork. It becomes hard to establish where her legs and feet are, as surface values trump indications of depth. The expected contrasts between the conjoined foreground figures and the strolling players further back in space is downplayed, their pinkish and green draperies repeating the tones of those in the figures nearer to us, partially contradicting the idea of distance that their smaller scale implies. In similar fashion, the arcade, loosely derived from recent *all'antica* buildings by Sanmicheli in Verona, is reduced to diaphanous insubstantiality, its effect of contrasting distance undermined by the even colouration of the pavement linking it to the foreground.[9] Scale and colouration might have served the definition of a coherent perspectival space, but this is partially disintegrated by the pictorial handling. Similar visual effects are evident enough in other Veronese paintings of this early phase and subsequently became a common feature in many of his works in the decades that followed.

TWO EARLY ALTARPIECES

A further surviving Veronese oil sketch, also from circa 1546, indicates that the young master had learned to follow an elaborate approach in the preparation of his works (illus. 6). This kind of carefully designed *modello* was not typically made in Venetian workshops in the 1540s and must reflect Veronese's training in Verona in the workshops of Badile (from 1541) and Caroto (from 1544). The sketch is a very well-resolved study for the full-scale altarpiece that once hung in the chapel of the Bevilacqua Lazise

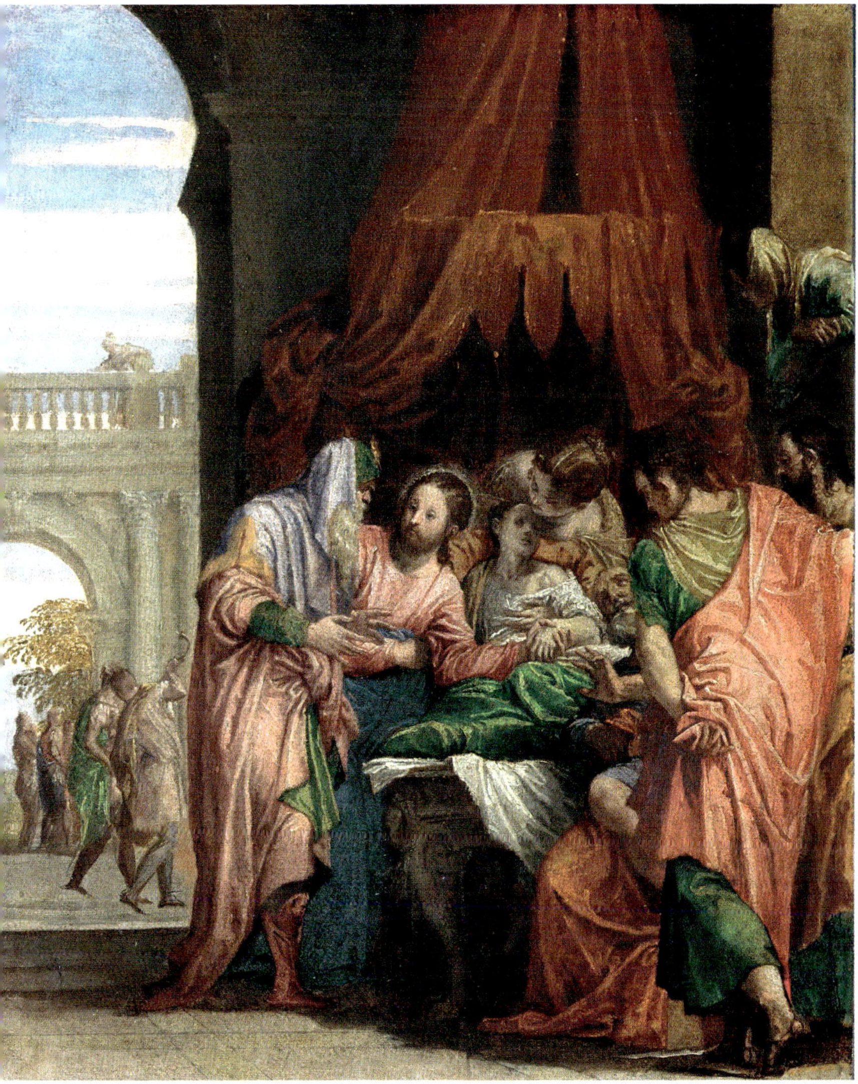

5 Veronese, *Raising of the Daughter of Jairus*, *c.* 1546, oil on paper, mounted on canvas.

in San Fermo Maggiore (illus. 7), a local family to whom Paolo was related through his mother. Comparison of the sketch with the finished work indicates their overall similarity rather than any major differences between them, and this despite the different people featured in the donor portraits included in a forward spatial plane at the bottom.[10] The compositional arrangement in the preparatory work is already fully articulated and is repeated in the altarpiece itself with only a few minor alterations, such as the change from blue to white in the Virgin's robe, the repositioning of St John's left arm, and the addition of a parrot (in this context probably symbolizing the Virgin as the 'nova Eva').[11] So much indicates that these sketches were made at a relatively late stage in Veronese's artistic process, probably following rapid studies in pen and ink, and more detailed ones in chalk, to establish in detail the positioning of the figures.[12] Veronese's careful preparatory procedures secured the impression of certainty and stability that underpin even these earliest works. And the evidence suggests that he did not deviate too much from this approach to picture-making following his move to Venice.

In the Bevilacqua Lazise altarpiece the teenaged Veronese immediately drew attention to the connection of his design with Titian's Pesaro altarpiece (1519–26, Venice, Santa Maria Gloriosa dei Frari): a painting that became a fundamental point of reference, especially in his subsequent works of this type for Venetian churches. Visual quotation was also simultaneous with an assertion of difference.[13] The setting of the figures against a vast column and base placed to the right of the picture, like the gestures of the two saints towards the patrons below, point back to Titian's painting. However, Veronese's saints are seated or crouched rather than standing, the zigzag internal dynamic of their limbs setting in motion horizontalized movements across the surface that contradict the overall verticality of the picture space. The Virgin and Child are enlarged and centralized, while the inclusion of musician angels to the left and a swath of green drapery above, along with omission of the spatially anchoring and depth-creating background column included in Titian's painting, serve to flatten or compress the pictorial space. The young Veronese was uncomfortable with the repeated indications of visual obliquity in Titian's prototype, reinstating elements of formal symmetry and spatial planarity that the older master had boldly dispensed with. While this might seem only to indicate the tentative conservatism of a very young master, the internal coherence of the modifications suggests something more ambitiously constructive.

The dynamic, crouching saints generate sharp internal bodily torsions that recall more recent experimental figures in non-Venetian *maniera* works by Giulio Romano (*c.* 1499–1546) and Parmigianino (1503–1540).[14] But this was not merely a case of updating one visual source by quoting another. The way in which the saints' limbs and draperies extend along the picture surface introduces an altogether more original visual theme that was destined to become much favoured in the Veronese idiom. The relation of Veronese's Bevilacqua altarpiece to a wide range of visual sources is already in line with the outwardly conventional style he would subsequently develop: one which draws attention to the works of famous precursors in ways that his visually sophisticated patrons would have enjoyed. Veronese shared this habit of visual quotation with many other painters in the mid-Cinquecento, and to this extent he can be considered a *maniera* artist whose productions were based on artistic emulation rather than the direct imitation of nature. This does not mean that Veronese was swamped by the renowned examples of the leading visual authorities to which he referred. Although he was closely aware of the art of the past, he does not seem to have been assailed by a debilitating sense of late coming within the powerful Renaissance tradition of painting, or by an anxiety of influence. The overt quotation of Titian's Pala Pesaro in his painting for the Bevilacqua Lazise

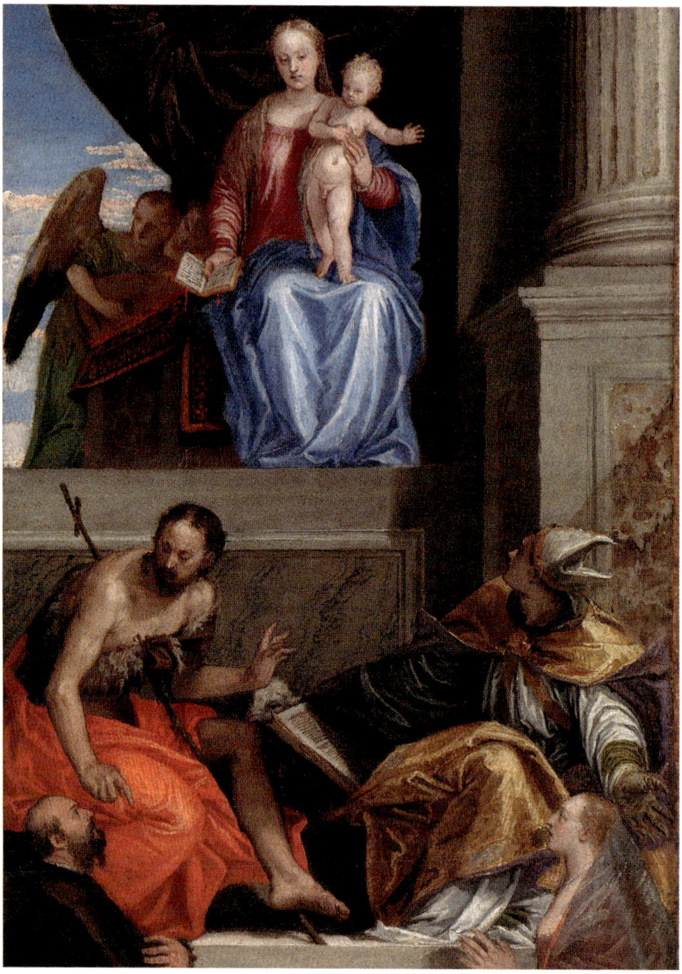

chapel was certainly meant to be registered by his knowing viewer: but so too was the extent to which he controlled, absorbed and appropriated his model.

In his first altarpiece for Venice completed in 1551 for the new church of San Francesco della Vigna by Jacopo Sansovino

6 Veronese, *Virgin and Child with Sts John the Baptist and Louis of Toulouse with Donors* (sketch for the Pala Bevilacqua Lazise), *c.* 1546, oil on paper, mounted on canvas.

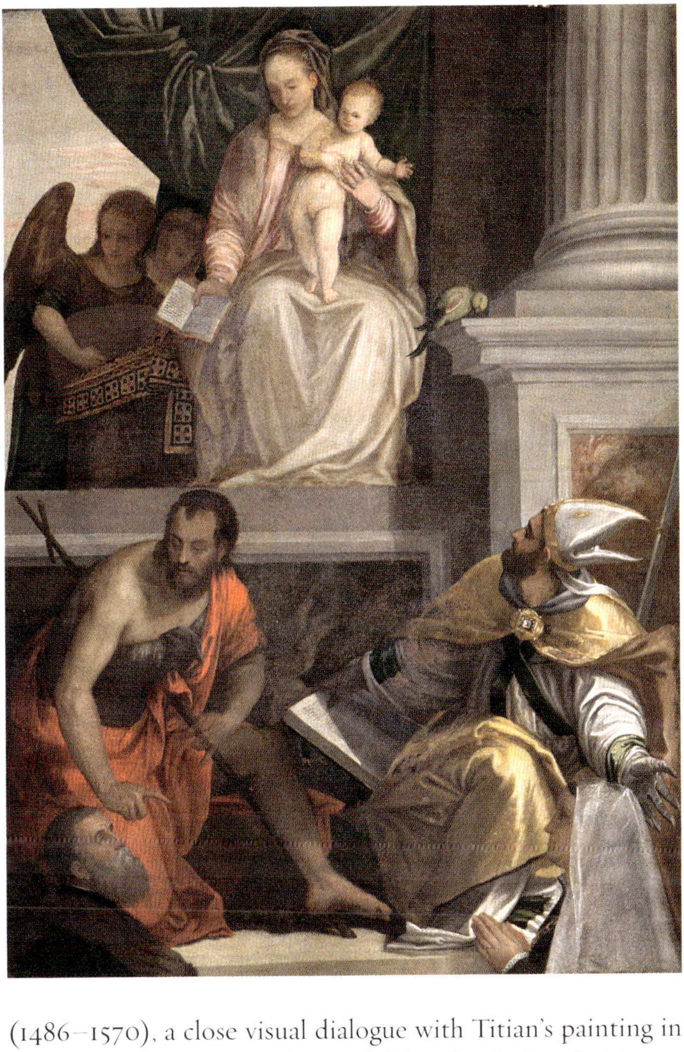

(1486–1570), a close visual dialogue with Titian's painting in the Frari is made more explicit still (illus. 8). The key decision to remove the entire 'donor zone' that dominated in Titian's painting may, in part, have been dictated by non-artistic or contextual factors. Veronese's painting was commissioned for the family

7 Veronese, *Virgin and Child with Sts John the Baptist and Louis of Toulouse and Donors* (the Pala Bevilacqua Lazise), *c.* 1546, oil on canvas.

chapel of the brothers Antonio and Lorenzo Giustiniani, taking its place alongside a sequence of new altarpieces donated by leading patrician families in a display of caste unity that discouraged individualizing donor portraits.[15] Veronese was subsequently very active in developing visually extended approaches to donor portraiture in his religious works. But at San Francesco, the cancellation of the lower 'life zone' seems also to have suited his aesthetic imperatives, given that it allowed him to close off the visually porous lower edges and forward planes of the composition, and by so doing make his picture appear more independent and self-contained. Veronese's painting is simplified in comparison with its prototype given that it features little more than half the number of figures, although these are now enlarged while the pictorial space is flattened or constricted. St Anthony Abbot's step upwards onto a broken fluted column has symbolic connotations. The once proud pagan architecture is pressed still further into the earth, its grandeur mocked by the sniffing of the pig, Anthony's special identifying attribute. As the saint pulls his dark cloak around him, his figure is extended beyond its bodily contours, an effect mirrored in the figure of St Catherine of Alexandra opposite, whose feminine presence immediately marks a difference from the strictly male-dominated lower foreground of Titian's painting.

Her twisting figure represents a further modernizing development of the Parmigianinesque seated St John the Baptist in the Bevilacqua altarpiece.[16] As Ridolfi noted, Catherine's internally complex figure, with bent knees and head twisted sharply away from her body, was immediately recognized by artists and connoisseurs in Venice as especially innovative; it was quickly imitated by Tintoretto in a controversial painting for another Venetian public building.[17] The figure's drapery folds draw attention to themselves with exaggeratedly sharp highlights and shadows, probably reflecting Veronese's study after the prints of Albrecht Dürer (1471–1528).[18] The cloth gathered around the Virgin's knees above indicates Veronese's early understanding of established naturalistic approaches to drapery painting, particularly evident in Italian painting from Leonardo onwards, and modelled to reveal the body shape beneath, and to demonstrate the downward pull of gravity. In contrast, Catherine's clothing leads the viewer's eye beyond her bodily contours, generating more complex and arbitrary patterns of drapery folds across the picture surface. In Veronese's paintings more generally, draperies often brilliantly suggest the three-dimensionality of the forms they cover, and their subjection to gravitational force. Just as often, however, they suggest a horizontalizing directionality, offering the viewer's eye a means of escape from the stricter dictates of anatomical accuracy, contour and perspective space.[19]

Although Catherine's figure introduces elements of instability, the overall effect of Veronese's composition is one of self-contained and four-square planarity that is supported by the arrangement of the architecture against which the saints are shown.[20] The eye's movement into depth is limited, given that we see little of the background sky; although angled views of columns and column bases are suggested, they are made secondary to other architectural mouldings that align with the picture surface. The decentred figures of the Virgin and Child come closer to Titian's model than in the Bevilacqua Lazise painting, but they appear almost equivalent in scale to the saints below, pressing forward to join them in a shared forward spatial plane. Veronese's abandonment of Titian's open-ended, oblique and mobile compositional arrangement was undoubtedly a response to the reality of the narrow and oblong space of the Giustiniani chapel itself at San Francesco. But his modifications are nonetheless representative of a wider tendency to assert the authority of the picture over its immediate viewing context. The initial impression of visual simplicity and clarity tends to dissolve, the closer one looks. The supporting architecture bears little or no

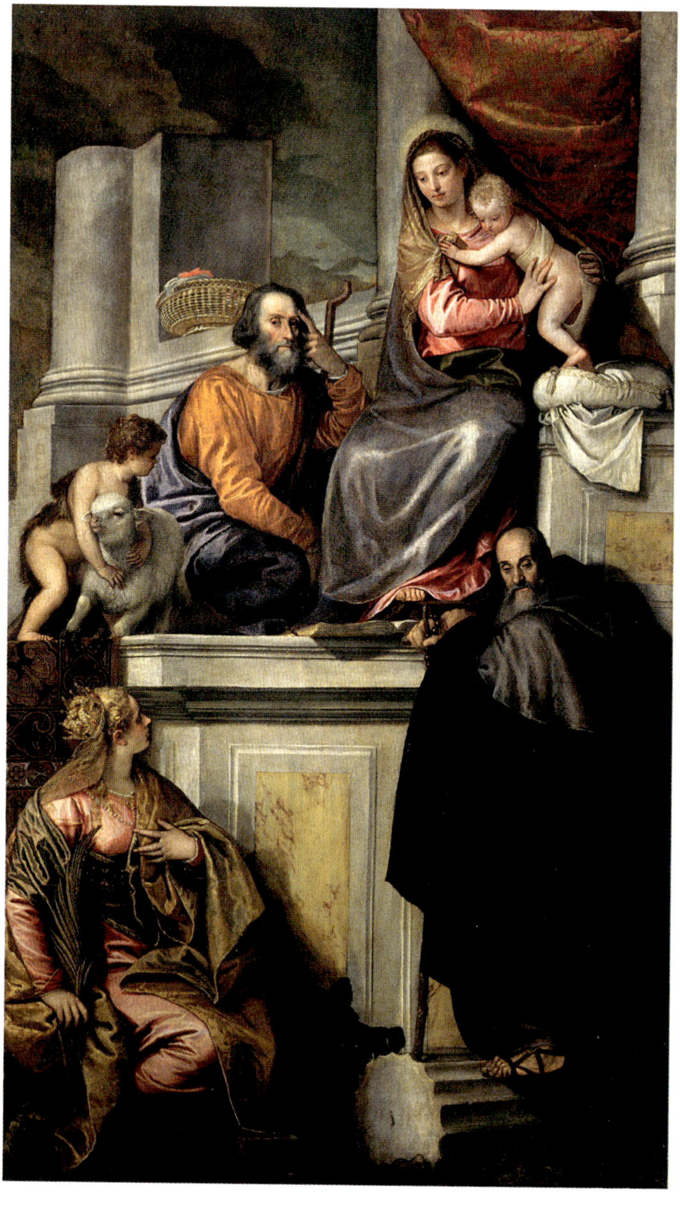

8 Veronese, *Virgin and Child with Sts Joseph, John the Baptist, Catherine, and Anthony Abbot* (the Pala Giustinian), *c.* 1550–51, oil on canvas.

relation to Sansovino's actual building, and is essentially arbitrary and non-naturalistic, while the perspective is to some degree self-contradictory.[21] If Anthony's downward glance and Catherine's upward one, like the shadowed rims of the architectural edges, indicate that the prime viewing position is from below, then Joseph's penetrating outward stare directly across at us from higher up in the picture countermands this suggestion, indicating that the spectator is parallel with his elevated level. Once this is noted, it becomes hard to understand the space of the picture as a consistent entity that can be fully understood in rational or optical terms.

NON-VENETIAN SOURCES

Despite Veronese's engagement with Titian so evident in these works, he also responded to a wide range of other artistic examples in his early period, often by masters from beyond the territory of the Venetian Republic. The impact of the widely disseminated and influential style of Raphael (1483–1520) on Veronese was of particular and lasting significance, as is evident enough from his propensity to generate rich colouristic effects and enlarged – but also softly rounded and proportionate – forms. Ridolfi reports that Veronese made a copy of Raphael's *Virgin and Child with Sts Anne and John the Baptist* ('La Perla'; *c.* 1518–20, Madrid, Museo del Prado), then on display in the Palazzo Canossa in Verona, where he had painted ceiling frescoes in his early career.[22] We cannot know quite what Veronese's 'La Perla' looked like, but it might have offered a visual *paragone* with a revered Renaissance prototype, just as his Pala Giustinian invited comparison with Titian's canonical work in the Frari. Rather than slavishly following his model, the ambitious young Veronese may have taken it on more purposefully. If he remained close to Raphael's complexly interlocking group, then perhaps in his version sharp sculptural contrasts between them were downplayed, the figures' overlapping surfaces intermeshing as they spread along the picture surface.[23]

Veronese's early engagement with Raphael's painting was in keeping with his interest in the progressive examples of art and architecture that he encountered on the mainland of northern Italy. In 1552 he was commissioned to make an altarpiece for the Duomo in Mantua: home of the Gonzaga court, where the energetic work of Raphael's one-time leading pupil, Giulio Romano, had made its mark since his arrival there as court painter in 1524 (illus. 9).[24] Veronese's painting stands as a counter-example to the idea I have been advancing so far: that his style was self-consistent and resistant to variable local conditions or patronal tastes. In this dramatic narrative altarpiece, Veronese clearly responded more directly to artistic predilections in Mantua, drawing on the exaggerated figural complexities and foreshortenings championed by younger generations of Raphaelesque painters, such as Rosso Fiorentino (1495–1540), Parmigianino and – most obviously – Giulio himself. He had probably already done so in a slightly earlier work featuring the self-sacrificing Roman hero Marcus Curtius (a painting which might also have been commissioned in Mantua), in which he had demonstrated willingness to take on the daring *trompe l'oeil* illusionism fashionable in the city-courts of northern mainland Italy (illus. 10).[25]

The spectators crowding in around the perimeters of this circular work – probably a ceiling painting – as Curtius plunges into the abyss to save his city, recall the similarly placed figures at the edges of Mantegna's oculus in the so-called Camera picta (Camera degli sposi) of the Mantuan Ducal Palace.[26] If the fallen St Anthony in the Duomo altarpiece quotes a figure in Giulio's fresco in the nearby Palazzo Te then the extravagantly rearing horse in the *Marcus Curtius*, seen in a steepling *di sotto in su* ('from below to above') perspective, brings to mind the equivalent animals in another Giulio painting in that location.[27] However, Veronese retreats from the exaggerated physicality and animal energy of Giulio's rearing horses. As the hero's anthropomorphized steed plunges into the void – playfully made identical with the real space of the viewer below – it appears to smile insouciantly, as if it were complicit with the viewer's delight at such an unlikely visual caprice. Veronese's partial emasculation of his rearing horse offered a telling departure from Giulio's more conventional manly stallions, undermining to some extent the usual martial meanings of such works. He subsequently returned to rearing horses seen from below in several other paintings, in which the animals are similarly prettified, sporting smiling mouths and doe eyes with long lashes, rather than inspiring powerful emotions of terror or awe, as such creatures usually do in equestrian imagery of the Renaissance (illus. 18, 36).[28] The concealment of the stallion's genitals in the *Marcus Curtius*, managed via a convenient play of shadows, further allows Veronese to substitute a feminized, or at least non-gendered, equivalent for masculine equinity. Something similar is in play when Veronese grants new prominence to a beautiful female saint in the foreground of the Pala Giustinian, or unexpectedly feminizes an armoured male portrait of this period against the conventional expectations.[29] In the *Marcus Curtius*, the distraction of the pretty horse means that the hero's contrasting resigned gesture and upward glance to heaven are not quite enough to secure the authority of the heroic narrative of patriotic male self-sacrifice against the temptations of playful pictorial artifice.

The physical reality of closely interacting bodies is more apparent in the Duomo altarpiece, in which the emphasis appears to be on violence and torment, as a muscular male devil – in the guise of a mythological satyr – strikes the saint with a severed hoof, potent symbol of Satan. Given Veronese's more general tendency to grant a positive role to attractive women in his

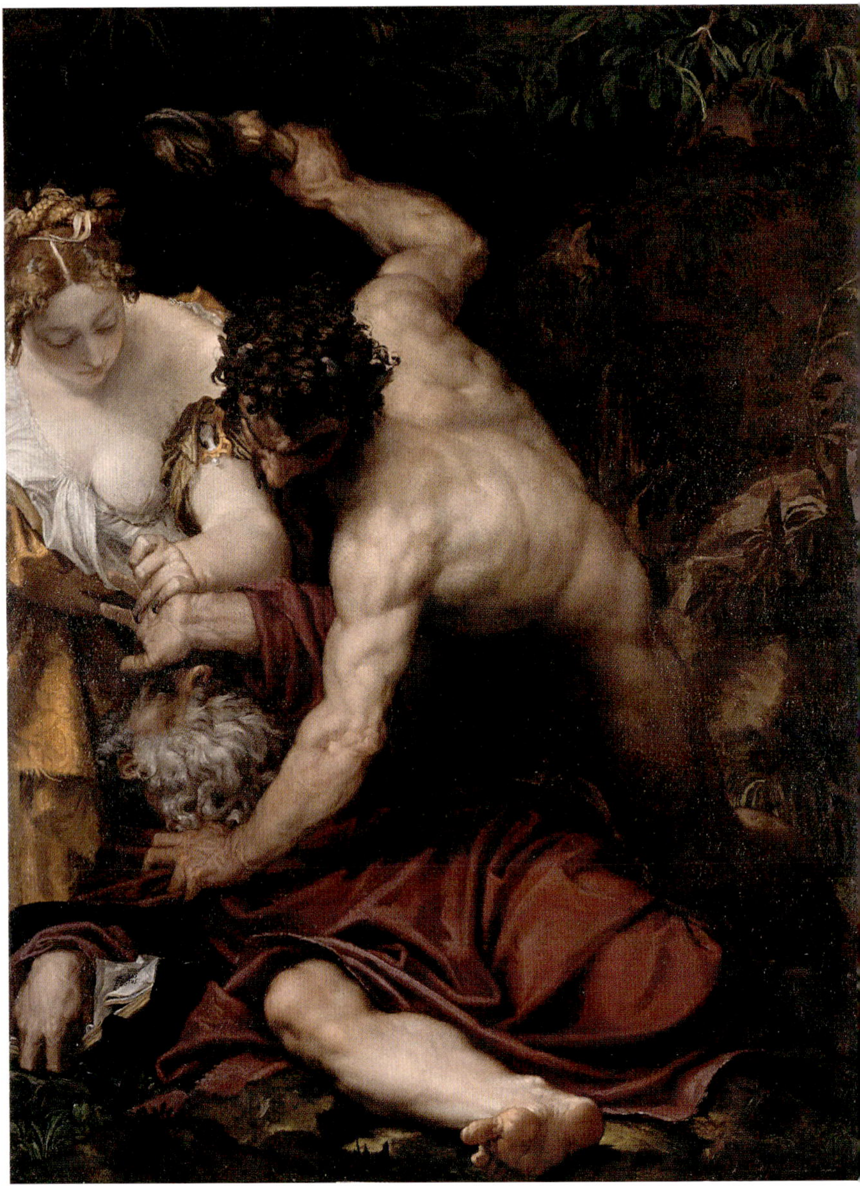

9 Veronese, *Temptation of St Anthony*, 1552, oil on wood, transferred to canvas.

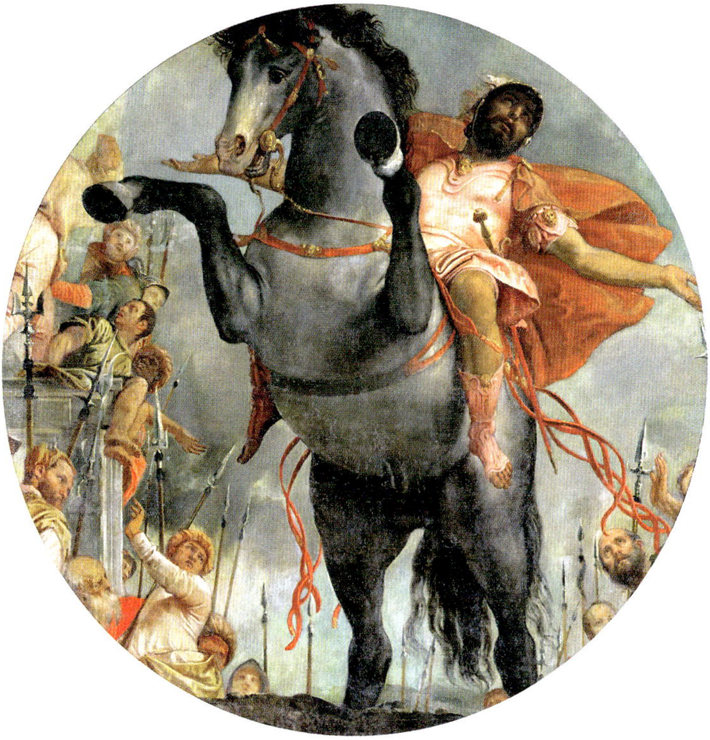

paintings, the she-devil included here is anomalous. Her clawed hand studiously bending back Anthony's fingers to increase his suffering is a rare example in his oeuvre of a negative image of a young blonde.[30] Her elaborate fashionable coiffure and expensive jewellery make her comparable with the kind of sensual *belle donne* (beautiful women) often featured in Venetian painting of the sixteenth century. In this example, Veronese appears to offer a critical commentary on Venetian sensuousness, in the brief period before he finally decided to settle in the lagoon city. But is the devil-woman's imagery so negative? The emphasis laid on her tumbling décolletage and pale exposed flesh remains tempting enough, even once the claws are noticed – and of course this

10 Veronese, *Marcus Curtius*, *c.* 1551–2, oil on canvas.

might have been Veronese's point. Yet it is also difficult to take the sufferings of the old St Anthony at the hands (or claws) of this young temptress as seriously as we might. Even in this apparently pious and profound work of bodily desecration, the expected sombre tone is partially compromised. An air of artificiality attends the studied foreshortenings and display of musculature, while the obvious quotation in the saint's figure from Giulio's fantastical *Fall of the Giants* fresco at the Palazzo Te further distances us from the reality of the scene. The supposedly 'tragic' presentation of the suffering saint is not typical of Veronese's work, at least before 1580, and it may be that he was uncomfortable with his final solution. He rarely returned to this intensifying dramatic manner, although the divergence towards Mantuan style that it reflects might have developed further had he not, shortly after, decided to move to Venice.

In a highly finished chiaroscuro drawing related to the altarpiece, the subject of St Anthony's temptation is handled in a manner closer to his usual approach (illus. 11).[31] The extent of the differences from the altarpiece suggests that the drawing was not a preparatory sketch, but rather a subsequent standalone finished work, perhaps made as a working example maintained in the studio as an exemplar for study; or as a design to be followed by a printmaker.[32] However this may be, Veronese radically rethinks the figures of all three protagonists. The two tormentors retreat to passive and secondary positions behind the saint, their proclivity to physical violence emphasized in the altarpiece now downplayed, so that the narrative becomes more difficult to follow. The saint's body, meanwhile, gains much greater prominence, even if we can no longer see his face. His figure is still angled into depth but nonetheless extends across much of the lower foreground. That this drawing was retained in the workshop rather than sent to a patron is suggested further by the fact that the sprawling figure, albeit with modifications, was subsequently reused by the master in several later works.[33] The drawing is sometimes seen as less successful than the related painting. But that judgement depends on the assumption that Veronese was – or should have been – fundamentally committed to conveying the narrative content of his work.[34] Whatever its original function, the drawing of *St Anthony* shows Veronese retreating from his overblown attempt at dramatization in his Giulioesque altarpiece for Mantua towards a pictorialized composition more in keeping with his deflecting aesthetic principles. The lowering

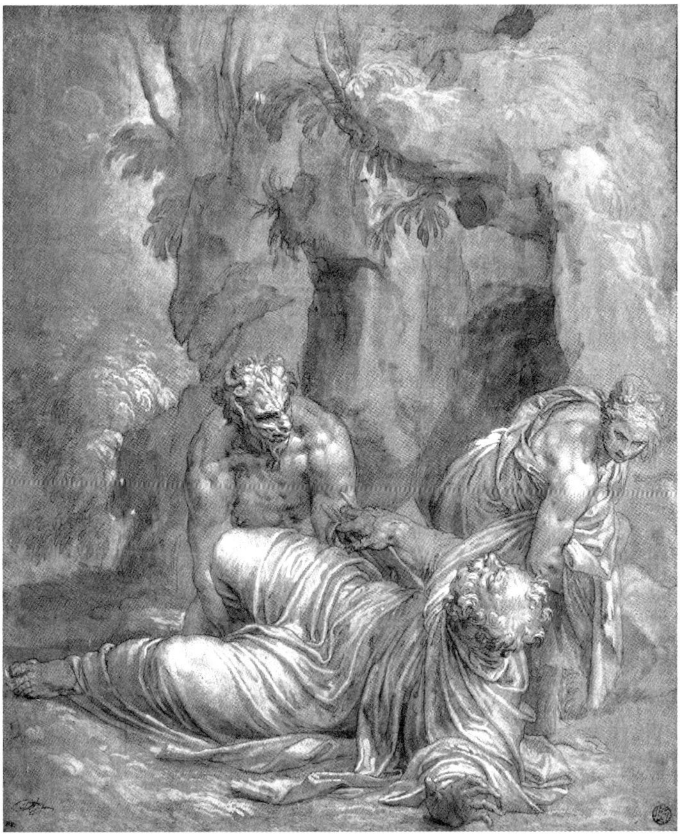

11 Veronese, *Temptation of St Anthony*, *c.* 1552–4, pen, ink and chalk on paper.

chiaroscuro in the painting is replaced by a pleasing pastoral landscape, generating an evenness of interest across the entire surface: a measured, all-over visual effect that downplays dramatic fury or narrative focus.

ROME AND ROMANISM

The impact of the Giulioesque variety of *maniera* painting practised in Mantua on Veronese's work of the early 1550s can still be felt in his paintings of the mid- and later 1550s, and is typically more apparent than any close or direct dependence on the art and architecture of Rome. Ridolfi reports that Veronese travelled to the Eternal City at some unspecified point in his earlier career in the entourage of the leading Venetian patrician Girolamo Grimani, who had been appointed orator to the pope. As part of Grimani's courtly entourage, Veronese, we hear, was 'witness to the magnificence of the buildings', and enthralled by 'the precious relics of Roman grandeur'.[35] It is difficult, though, to find any hard and fast evidence in Veronese's paintings themselves for a Roman visit.[36] There are relatively few direct quotations from then-existing buildings in Rome in his work, while references to those of 'locals' such as Sanmicheli and Palladio are more frequent. Borrowings from sculptures or paintings that he could only have seen in Rome are equally rare, at least by comparison with those from antique works then held in collections in Verona and Venice, or known from widely circulated reproductive prints.[37] Given this kind of counter-evidence, it may be that Ridolfi's story of a Roman visit early in Veronese's career is no more than a convenient literary invention that allowed him to contest Vasari's claim in his *Lives* that the Venetian masters were insufficiently classical and lacking in 'disegno'.[38]

Veronese's broad interest in the sculpture of Roman antiquity is evident enough, however, although it appears to have been focused primarily on reliefs, in which the figures only partially emerge from a shallow ground that delimits movement into depth and encourages overlapping and horizontalized compositional arrangements.[39] The spatial compression evident in many antique reliefs makes the space beyond the figures appear too narrow to fully contain them, and the given narrative action can consequently be difficult to follow. Veronese might have broadly modelled his approach to painting on such friezes, even if this kind of influence was typically generic in kind, rather than closely based on specific models or examples.[40] In studies of Veronese's early work, the crowding effect and consequent narrative obscurity is sometimes noted as if it were a problem or mistake that the still-juvenile artist would later rectify. But this aspect of his style might be better considered as a matter of pictorial choice that only intensified in his work as time went on. It was also a factor in Veronese's prioritization of the picture over the exposition of his given subject. Ridolfi's account of Veronese's sojourn with Grimani does, however, usefully indicate the painter's close association in the early 1550s with the circle of patrician families since dubbed *papalisti* because of their extensive connections with the papal court in Rome and their taste for all things Roman in art and culture.[41] Members of this circle had closely supported Doge Andrea Gritti (dogate 1523–38), who had backed the previously Rome-based architect and sculptor Jacopo Sansovino to remodel the medieval centre of Venice along *all'antica* lines in the 1530s and '40s. The group of families around Gritti may even have imagined Venice as a 'new Rome' in the decades following the devastating Sack of the Eternal City in 1527, an idea that meant turning away from older appropriations of Byzantine culture. However that may be, the emergent courtly elements of Veronese's artistic identity probably owed a significant debt to his patronage in the earlier 1550s by the *papalisti* circle: families who were especially concerned to promote their aristocratic

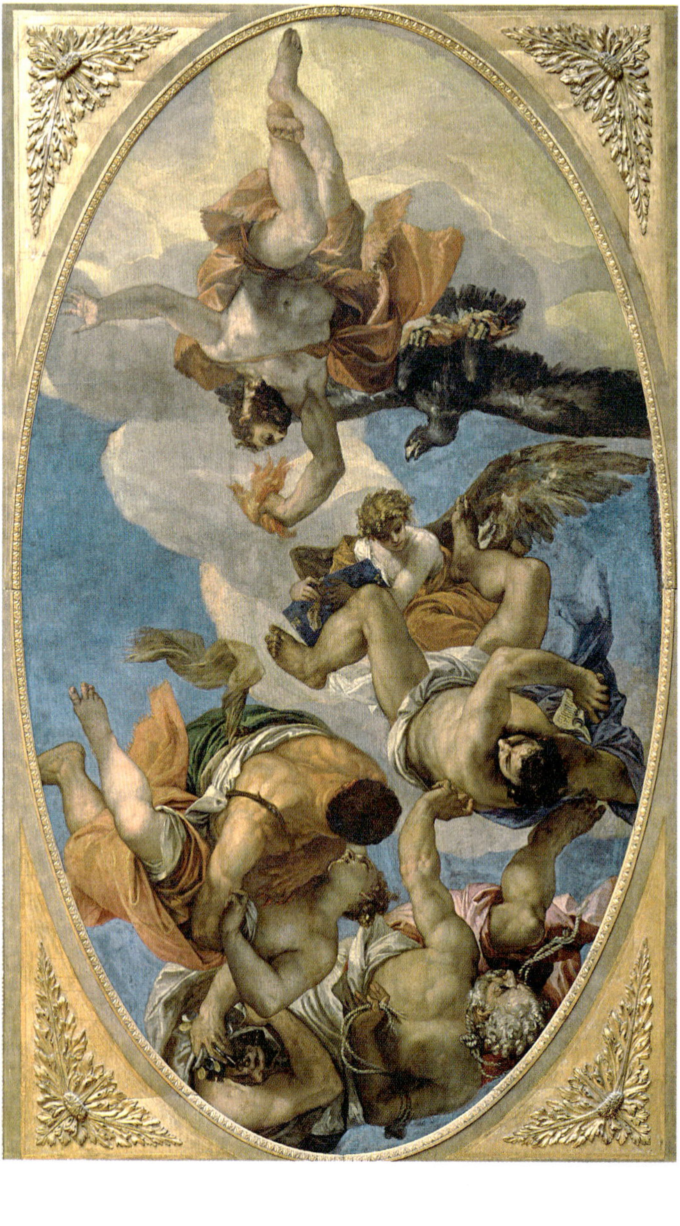

12 Veronese, *Jove Expels the Vices*, 1554–5, oil on canvas.

credentials beyond Venice via association with the prestigious Roman court.

This circle had effectively overseen the building and decoration of San Francesco della Vigna, site of Veronese's first major work in the city, the altarpiece commissioned by the Giustiniani.[42] Support from the brothers Marc'Antonio and Daniele Barbaro, related through marriage to the Giustiniani, probably gave the young painter his first commission for the Venetian state in the rooms of the Council of Ten at the Ducal Palace in 1554.[43] The wider impact of *papalisti* cultural values can certainly be felt in Veronese's ceiling paintings, which feature monumentalized Roman-looking figures in complex postures. In the central panel, the semi-nude and predominantly masculine forms dominating the picture space are closer to Michelangelo (1475–1564) than in any previous (or subsequent) work by Veronese (illus. 12). The tumbling figures in the lower foreground recall those featured in Michelangelo's *Last Judgement* in the Sistine Chapel, a work that Veronese would have known through several recent reproductive prints. However, no single figure in the painting is closely dependent on Michelangelo's great fresco. The swooping Jove at the top of the painting has more in common with Tintoretto's airborne St Mark in his *Miracle of the Slave* (1547–8, Venice, Gallerie dell'Accademia), even if the latter artist had derived his saint's flying, downward-angled body from a print after another Michelangelo fresco in the Vatican.[44] Veronese's Michelangelism in the rooms of the Council of Ten was to this extent second-hand rather than based on direct engagement with the given fresco in Rome, mediated through the examples of the local Venetian master with whom he now competed.

Veronese's own penchant for performative visual display is in any case evident enough in the complexly foreshortened nudes that engage the eye beyond the strict demands of the subject. The overlap between forms makes them difficult to distinguish or read as separate entities. Especially towards the bottom left it becomes difficult to disentangle – and therefore to logically reconstruct in the mind's eye – the exact positions of the entwined and knotted cluster of bodies. Who owns the inverted lower left leg exposed to view? If it is the woman whose torso and head appear to the right, then how does it articulate with her upper body? The writhing of these three tumbling Vices, like the implied break-up of their bodies as they fall, certainly engages the moral and patriotic theme of the painting (evil driven out by the Jupiter-like power and justice of the Venetian state). But they also provide an opportunity for Veronese to introduce visual puzzles. The internally consistent anatomies and sharp figural definitions typical of Michelangelo give way to a pictorialized conception that defies rational understanding and collapses the impression of a coherent perspectival or gravity-dominated space. If the patronal circumstances of this commission indicate that Veronese is at his most 'Romanist' in such works, then the ambiguities he introduces also show that he generates visual solutions that take him beyond the scope of a central Italian, *disegno*-orientated, aesthetic.

ANOINTING OF DAVID

In a large religious narrative painting by Veronese from the mid-1550s, a multitude of figures are crushed together in a narrow spatial plane, making the given narrative difficult to establish (illus. 13). As many as nineteen figures, some concealed by others, are packed in to the middle area, bounded by a mysterious awning-like structure behind, and by a landscape sliver to each side. The dark backdrop serves to fix the viewer's attention on this brightly lit knot of figures, establishing a shallow frieze-like space. The alignment of the figures' heads, all at the same height, further aids the effect of visual compression. Within this dense figural strip, bodily contours become less distinct as highly mobile forms overlap and interlock to create a complex play of arbitrary pictorial shapes. Among this crowd only the kneeling figure of David, who is about to be anointed by Samuel, and the two monumental walking figures to either side of him, reveal themselves in full length. These latter two – like St John in the *Jaïrus* sketch – step into the picture, hinting at the existence of another forward spatial plane. Their inward movement does not, though, create additional depth, merely serving to further compress the central group, and to separate it off from the landscapes at either side.

Veronese's visual approach does not mean that he is uninterested in the historical and typological dimensions of the narrative. At the left of the group are two figures from the social margins: massive but infirm elderly men who are presented in this Old Testament work as the ancient forerunners of the deserving lame and sick who will, in later centuries, become the objects of Christian alms. And the key Christian virtue of Charity is mirrored to the right, prophetically personified in the woman with two children. Veronese's figures bring intimations of the harsh reality of age, poverty and suffering, about which the innocent young David, shown as partially nude and with the tight curls of a pagan classical putto, knows nothing yet. The men use sticks to support their halting bodies as they limp forwards to witness the anointing of the ancestor of Christ that foretells their future hope of succour and redemption. The way in which they turn their backs on the ruins pictured at the background left has a further temporal and symbolic resonance. A piece of classical architrave has fallen to the ground there, establishing that David's anointment signals the end of the old pagan dispensation.

This ruined fragment is, however, so carefully and respectfully depicted that it seems in danger of escaping its symbolic meaning. And Veronese's aged sufferers are absorbed into the crowd so that their more specific social and iconographic identity is easily missed. The most daring formal clustering that Veronese had yet attempted

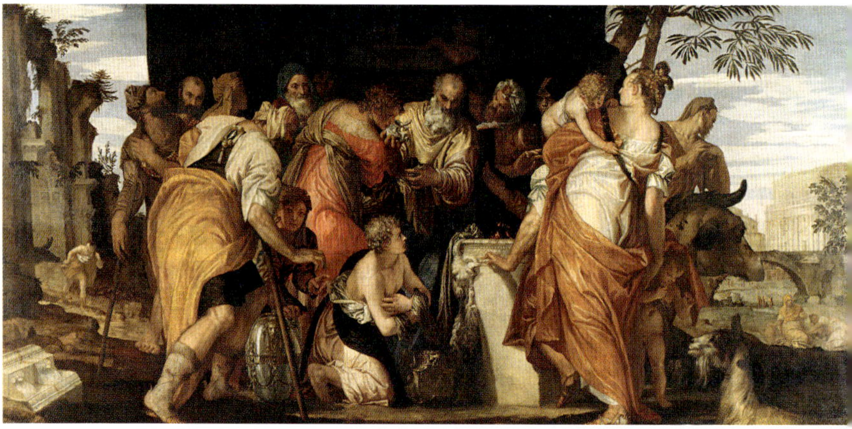

appears on the right side of the group (illus. 14). In this passage, body parts float free of their precise owners, with the heads and limbs of some completely hidden, or appearing like illogical prosthetic extensions of the concealing bodies in front of them. The 'Charity' figure presents a striking visual conundrum. Her tall and upright figure completely hides from view a man whose left leg and forearm appear as substitutes for her own hidden limbs. The continuity of his drapery folds and colouration – his muted pink red is close to her orange – makes it difficult to see two different persons. Even once the man's existence in the picture is noticed, the visual effect remains unsettling and generates questions. Is there really room for him at all as he reaches forward to touch the altar? What does his presence add to the narrative? The interplay of their arms and feet is particularly complex: the manly left forearm contrasts with her more delicate and pale-skinned right one, but it also faces downwards and might be mistaken as hers. His sandalled foot might equally be taken for hers but is only a second left limb glimpsed near to her own, even if its appearance makes the position – or the existence – of her right one impossible to determine.

13 Veronese, *Anointing of David*, c. 1555–8, oil on canvas.

Formal intersection or elision is apparent again just beyond these conjoined figures, where an enormous bull's head peers out towards the right landscape view, its horned silhouette linked to that of the shepherd above. Reading leftwards from this striking bovine form – a reference (like the foreground 'donor' goat) to David's previous role as a shepherd – it is impossible to imagine a space to contain his equally voluminous body. There is simply no room for the animal's enormous bulk between the woman and children, the sectionalized man behind her and the altar.[45] And so he remains a creature who only makes sense in non-naturalistic terms: his function is pictorial, given that he defines an edge to the wider formal amalgam of which he is a constituent part. It is the irregularity of his outline that counts most in Veronese's visual thinking, and the way that it comments on the wider complexities

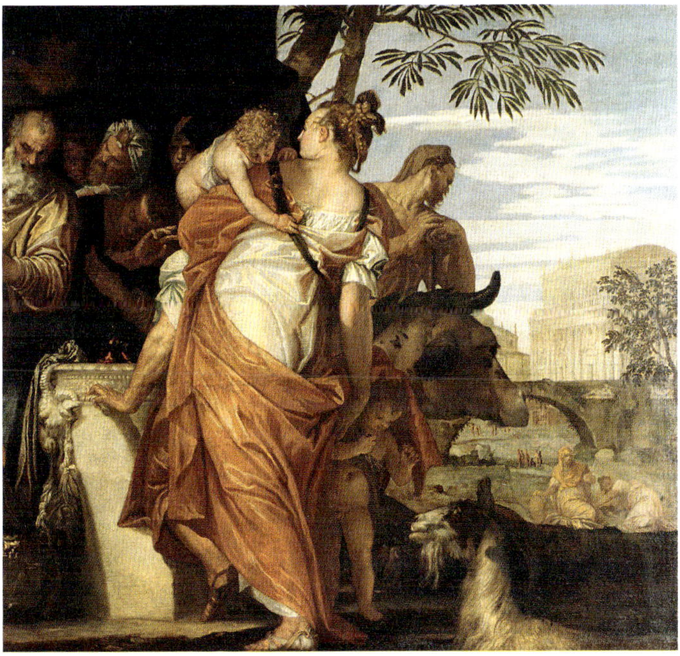

14 Veronese, *Anointing of David*, detail.

and ambiguities of the formal group from which it emerges. The generation of striking silhouettes also determines the visually rhyming figure of the second disabled person at the leftmost extension of the central group, whose bodily contours sustain and re-enforce the vertical division of the backcloth behind him, separating the central group off from all beyond itself.

The *Anointing of David* is a characteristic example of Veronese's demandingness as a painter in visual terms. His attention to such formal aspects does not mean that he disengaged with the given biblical subject (it is not a matter of *either* subject *or* form). The complex arrangement of the figures nonetheless provides the main effort that Veronese requires his viewer to make in his painting. Veronese's unlikely figural amalgams defamiliarize otherwise ordinary forms, making them tantalizing and elusive. Within the main figural group, the usual hierarchies of significance or meaning are disrupted. Although David is placed at the centre and framed by the enlarged figures to either side, the viewer's eye is tempted away from him, caught up in the intricacies of the formal arrangements to the left and right. Within individual bodies a certain visual democracy also comes into play, with the 'lesser' parts – elbows, noses, hands, feet and so on – granted sudden prominence, while heads have a habit of disappearing, or of detaching themselves from torsos.

Veronese's propensity to visual digression or wit has occasionally been discussed but has proved difficult to accommodate in those accounts seeking to justify Veronese as a master of narrative clarity and transparent meaning. The semantically occluding or excessive aspects of his approach are typically understood as secondary, or as providing diverting momentary asides that do not ultimately distract from the cogent expression of the all-important subject-matter.[46] But visual play may have been more significant and central to his picture-making than this would allow. His penchant for figural doubling, severing, splitting or dismembering insists on our attention to the mechanics or language of representation itself, even if it does not openly attack or undermine the more usual concerns in a subject work. The precise relationship between form and subject in a Veronese painting is difficult enough to understand in a critical analysis, and in many works seems to have remained fluid and open-ended. In the *Anointing* the ludic aspects of the presentation do not undermine the comprehensibility of the subject-matter, but they nonetheless appear as more than just a passing distraction, readily engaging and absorbing the viewer's attention beyond the stricter dictates or promptings of the biblical story itself.

A SHEET OF SKETCHES AND VERONESE'S WORKING METHOD

Veronese's preparation for the *Anointing* is in part revealed by a sheet of pen-and-ink studies, which includes many brief indications of ideas for the figures and animals in the painting (illus. 15).[47] The sheet includes as many as four brief studies of a bull's head, while the long-eared donkey that eventually found a minor role at the extreme background left in the painting is present at the upper right. In a series of rapid sketches at the lower foreground and centre, Veronese repeatedly brainstormed ideas for figures, paying particular attention to the old beggar with his back turned and to the boy David kneeling before the altar. Other standing figures in this lower area of the drawing relate to those nearby in the final painting, including Samuel pouring the libation. Elsewhere in this sheet the link to the *Anointing* is more difficult to establish. Only the sketch of the bull's head to the lower left is close to the lost profile position adopted in the painting. Those above it indicate instead his first thoughts for a Rape of Europa, although his surviving paintings of this subject date to the later 1560s and '70s (illus. 48).[48] The connection of this sheet with

Veronese's frescoes at the Villa Barbaro has been doubted. Yet several of the figures *do* find close echoes in his imagery at the Villa.[49] One of these, shown twice to the left, shows a sprawling figure, with back turned, raised upper body, legs akimbo and one knee elevated. This figure recalls that of the fallen saint in the chiaroscuro drawing illustrated above, as it does a fresco of Venus in the Sala dell'Olimpo at the Villa. At the upper right of the sheet, Veronese briefly indicates his awareness of the architecture included in a print of 1551 by Hieronymus Cock (*c.* 1517/18–1570) that he went on to use in one of the landscapes there.[50]

A sizeable number of sheets like this are known, typically filled with partially repeated figures delineated using vibrating, febrile outlines in pen and ink. It may be that the current example is among the earliest drawings of this kind that now survives.[51] It seems likely that such sheets were made early on in Veronese's thinking about his paintings, to define initial ideas for figures and groups. They would later have been followed by more carefully worked studies of details, often in black or red chalk on blue paper, which brought the imagery closer to the appearances of reality (illus. 38).[52] These pen-and-ink studies typically cover the entire sheet, as if to make the most economical possible use of it. In their overall appearance they are not so different to the paintings they relate to, clustering densely packed forms across the surface. Many of the figures reflect first thoughts rather than anything closely attached to a given painting, commission or subject-matter, and to this extent they are generic or transferable in kind. In the current example, as in a few others, Veronese had in mind at least three or four paintings, with widely different subjects and in different media, even if the sheet relates most closely to the *Anointing*. This drawing may indicate that the Vienna painting and the Villa Barbaro frescoes were painted within a few years of one another. However, it was clearly not strictly 'preparatory' in nature, insofar as it contains overlapping ideas for a number

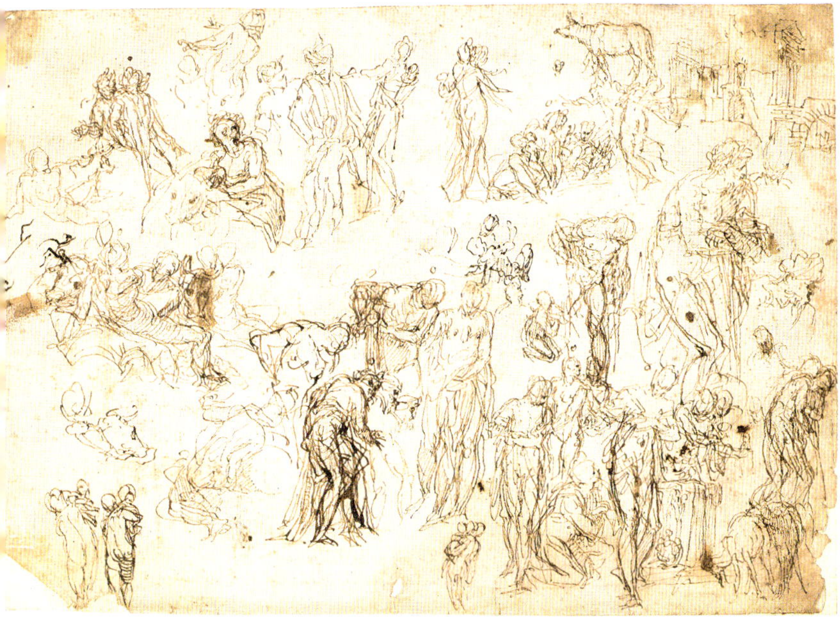

of paintings and subjects at once.[53] As the sprawling figure noted above tells us, a single formal idea, albeit it with variations, could serve widely different pictorial projects, suggesting too that this relatively non-specific initial concept had priority over its final use in a given iconography. It may be that Veronese's simultaneous thoughts for more than one work were time-limited insofar as the envisaged paintings were subsequently executed within a few years of one another.[54] But the present drawing stretches the temporal span further, recalling at least one figure already deployed in a finished graphic work of the early 1550s, while also indicating *primi pensieri* for another – the *Rape of Europa* – not realized in painted form much before 1570.

Such rapidly executed pen-and-ink sketches suggest that Veronese's pictorial thinking was, at least at an early point in the process, fluid and independent in nature. In these initial sketches,

15 Veronese, *Sheet of Studies*, c. 1555–8, pen, ink and wash.

his figures and compositions were not closely based on natural appearances, owing more to his inward or mental ideas, some of which revisited his own earlier works. These conceptions were essentially self-reflexive and transferable between the given themes that the artist was asked to depict by his patrons. Veronese's pictorial thinking in such drawings was at least partially independent of external prompts or agencies. It may be better understood as reflecting an organic internal process that was intellectual rather than pragmatic in kind.[55] Veronese's preparatory work was more extensive and elaborate than that of contemporary painters in Venice and this helps to explain the more settled and finished appearance of his paintings as also the relative lack of *pentimenti* on his painted surfaces.[56] Defining and then honing visual ideas through a varying range of material media and supports, Veronese made ready to paint in a relatively systematic fashion. However, his graphic approach also generated a certain visual freedom from the external demands of patrons, picture-types or iconographies, providing the foundational point or source of his artistic control. The origin of Veronese's pictorial thinking in his own mental conceptions is powerfully revealed in his pen-and-ink sketches. And these initial promptings were never wholly countermanded by the subsequent process of realization in the completed work.

TWO

San Sebastiano, Portraits, Villa Barbaro

Around the time of his permanent transfer to Venice, Veronese secured a plumb commission in the small church of San Sebastiano in the Dorsoduro area of the city run by the Jeronymite order of monks. Initially he worked on ceiling paintings in the sacristy (1554–5) before moving on to complete cycles of ceiling and wall paintings in the nave (1556–8); the shutters and supporting imagery for the church organ (1560); the High altarpiece and side paintings for the presbytery (1562–5); and a lavish feast scene for the monk's refectory (1567–70).[1] Over the course of some fifteen years, Veronese completed more than sixty paintings of differing types, working in oil, tempera and fresco on surfaces of canvas, wood and plaster, thereby covering the vast majority of the visible surfaces of the church with his imagery. Although Veronese was helped by his younger painter-brother Benedetto and his early assistant Giovanni Antonio Fasolo (1530–1572), he remained the leading figure at San Sebastiano, achieving an individual monopoly over an extensive multi-painting commission that was almost unprecedented in a Venetian public building.[2] The level of personal control that Veronese enjoyed in the church, which eventually extended to the design of the church organ and of new windows for the presbytery, contrasts markedly with the shared or 'communal' commissions typical of his early career in private villas and palazzi, or in Mantua Cathedral and the Venetian

Ducal Palace.[3] Veronese's dominance at San Sebastiano tellingly coincides with his newly self-assertive identification as 'Paolo Caliaro Veronese', and stands as a marker of his arrival in Venice as an ambitious and individualistic young master practising a self-consistent, independent and unique new style of painting. From 1554 onwards Veronese transfigured the interior surfaces of the church in accordance with his own expansive visual ideas, eventually making the entire interior over to the semi-independent, heightened world of his pictures.

SAN SEBASTIANO: THE CEILINGS

Veronese won the commission through the help of certain of his compatriots active at San Sebastiano. The prior of the monastery, Fra Bernardo Torlioni, was from Verona, as was the painter Bonifacio de' Pitati (1487–1553), whom Torlioni initially employed to decorate the sacristy walls of the newly completed church around 1550.[4] It is likely that the successful, but now elderly and declining, Bonifacio encouraged the prior to employ Veronese to paint the sacristy ceiling. He might also have suggested to the young painter that further commissions in the church would follow with a wider opportunity to dominate a multi-picture commission, as he himself had in previous decades at the Treasurer's Palace (Palazzo dei Camerlenghi).[5] Perhaps just because of this support from a non-local network, Veronese was, at first, careful to suggest the continuity of his style with leading Venetian models, as he had been, a little earlier, at San Francesco della Vigna. In the central ceiling painting showing the *Coronation of the Virgin* (illus. 16), Veronese allied his composition to another canonical Titian in the Frari, this time recalling the upper part of the older master's *Assumption of the Virgin* of 1516–18. Veronese's softly painted protagonists are bathed in a warm liquid mix of red and gold Titianesque pigmentation, even as his model is adapted to serve the idea of the Virgin's

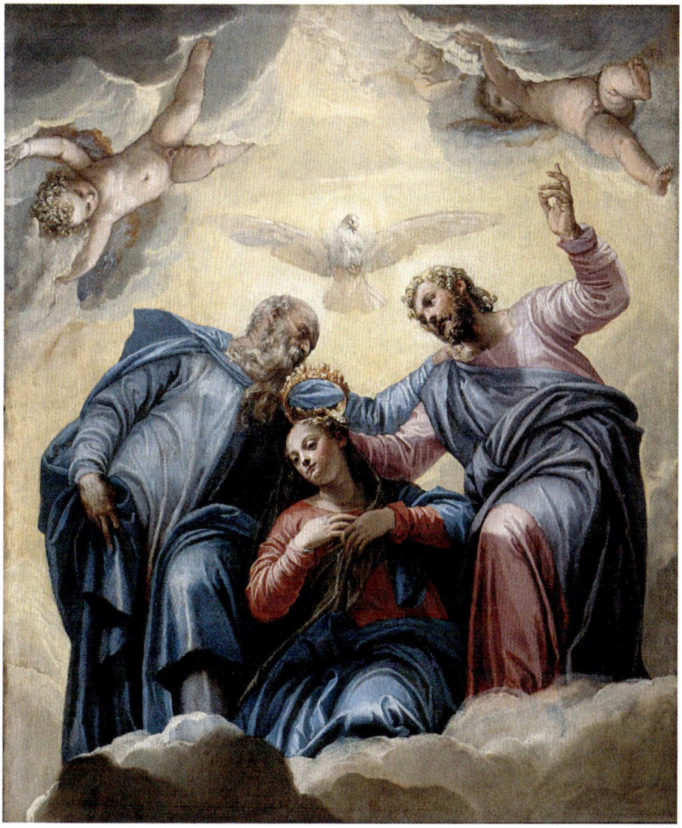

alliance with the Holy Trinity, perhaps with reference to a well-known Dürer print, the woodcut of the *Coronation of the Virgin* (1510). Accordingly, Veronese included the dove of the Holy Spirit as also the figure of Christ, who takes over the open-armed 'orant' posture of Titian's Virgin, while she kneels, her arms closed across her chest, in a gesture of humility. Her glance downwards towards the viewer indicates her compassionate, intercessory role, while her heavenly origins are emphasized by the fact that God the Father and Christ are clothed in her traditional colours.

16 Veronese, *Coronation of the Virgin*, 1554–5, oil on canvas.

Veronese effortlessly generates a view from below in accordance with the spectator's position, looking upwards, but his figures are nonetheless moved forward in the picture space, their enlarged and overlapping forms conjoined in a narrow and forward spatial plane. As in many of his other earlier paintings, the composition is relief-like insofar as it does not extend far into depth, holding the eye near to the richly articulated surface. The repeated blue–red colour combination in the draperies supports this spatially flattening effect, even as it also makes an iconographical point. The golden background recalls the time-honoured tradition of Veneto-Byzantine icon painting, an ultra-traditional or archaic style still practised in the city by Greek painters and sometimes referred to in works by Titian and Tintoretto. But the self-conscious *venezianità* that these aspects indicate was not to be sustained in the cycles of paintings for the nave and presbytery of the church that followed, which draw instead on the painter's recent experience of art on the mainland at Mantua.[6] The primarily non-Venetian sources underpinning Veronese's imagery in the main body of the church indicate that he meant his work to appear, in stylistic terms, as a non-local import.

Perhaps in accordance with these non-Venetian visual sources, the appearance of the heroine Esther in the three large nave ceiling paintings is strikingly courtly, suggestive of pageantry and opulence. The original, intensely coloured smalt blue skies in the main paintings, which could not be recovered from their present faded pale grey during the restoration of 2009–11, would have further enhanced this richness of effect.[7] In the central square panel showing the *Coronation of Esther* (illus. 17), the scene is an especially regal one. The decision to depict the Persian king Ahasuerus crowning Esther as his queen, rather than the more obvious narrative episode in which she intercedes with him in order to save the Jewish people, was probably encouraged by the need to establish a close typological concordance with the *Coronation of the Virgin* in the sacristy. Esther could then appear as an Old Testament prototype of the Queen of Heaven herself. But it also allowed the painter to generate a simplified visual schema or motif that he would redeploy in a number of later paintings with different iconographies, both religious and secular. A beautiful young heroine bows down before an enthroned authority figure on some grand steps leading up to a lavish palace portal, watched by an admiring caste of handsome, armour-clad soldiers and elegantly dressed women. There is little to indicate the deeper theological significance of the action beyond the above-noted concordance with the Virgin's coronation.

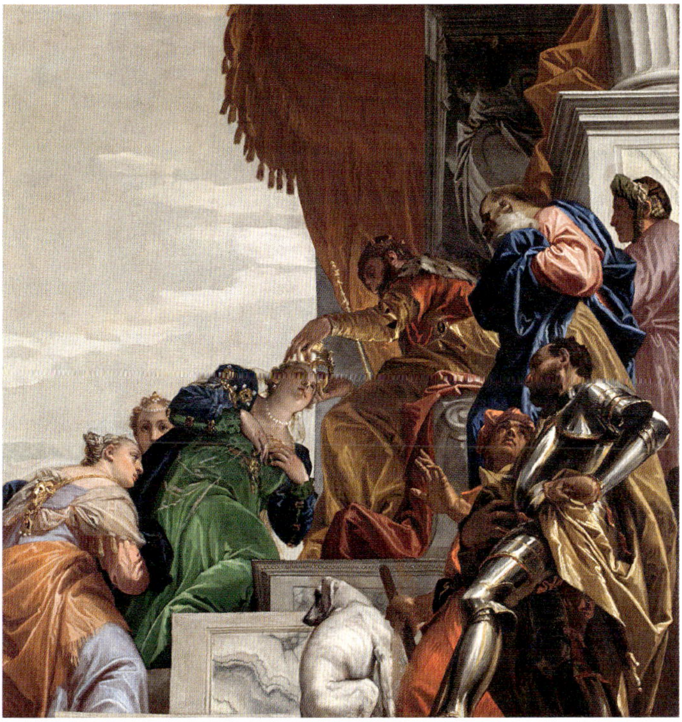

17 Veronese, *Coronation of Esther*, 1555–6, oil on canvas.

Nothing much happens in these narrative works on the nave ceiling, which share a generic quality rather than being closely specified by the given biblical text that is illustrated. Energetic dramatic action, especially violence, conflict or strife, is downplayed or avoided. A king crowns a young woman; some soldiers and their rearing horses march; and a woman quietly leaves a palace. In taking this attenuating approach to the story, Veronese may have relied on his viewers' prior knowledge of the text to fill in the gaps. But it is nonetheless no accident that there has been some confusion over the precise subject-matter of one of the oval paintings. It probably shows the Banishment of Vashti, King Ahasuerus's disgraced former queen, although some (now in the minority) believe that it features 'Esther Brought to the Palace': the moment when the heroine agrees to her uncle Mordecai's plan to save the Jewish people.[8] The confusion is understandable enough, given that Veronese's composition in this work so closely mirrors that in the central canvas. Not for the first or last time, the precise subject-matter illustrated in a Veronese painting becomes a matter of doubt. Veronese's settings in the main ceiling paintings are heavily cropped or sectionalized: glimpsed fragments that do little to establish a precise place or time for the scene illustrated. The appearance of the figures is likewise not consistently (or even predominantly) historized given that the actors sport sixteenth-century costumes that would have been familiar enough to the contemporary viewer, even if they appear more spectacularly lavish than those observable in reality. If these figures are not portrait-like, they nonetheless conform to the painter's own, half-fantasized, vision of leading aristocratic mores or behaviours in the current day.

In the *Triumph of Mordecai* (illus. 18) the precise narrative moment depicted is equally hard to pin down. The biblical account tells us that Mordecai had asked his niece to intervene with the king against the antisemitic decree of his first minister, Haman, who was subsequently sentenced to hanging on the gallows he had prepared for Mordecai. Given that unsolicited disturbance of the king was punishable by death, this was a high-risk undertaking, even more so given that the king did not know that Esther was Jewish. In Veronese's painting few elements drawn directly from this highly charged narrative are apparent. The scene is presented instead as a martial triumph in the Roman style, in keeping with the *all'antica* Winged Victories that surround it on the ceiling inspired by those often featured on imperial triumphal arches. Veronese does seem to draw attention to the given hero of the story by placing Mordecai at the dead centre of the oval. As in the other main ceiling paintings, the main protagonist's importance is indicated again by the vertical angling of the architectural cornice down towards him. But if the evil Haman is shown as the armoured man on the dark horse to the left, then his part in the tale is not strongly demarcated in any other way. Thinking of rearing horses seen from below, Veronese revisited his own earlier ceiling painting, possibly made for a Mantuan patron (illus. 10). As in *Marcus Curtius*, the entire triumphal figural group, combining partial views of handsome noble knights with their rearing steeds and followers, are watched by waving and cheering crowds on the palace balconies above, as if these spectators are enjoying a magnificent courtly joust.

The dispersal of towering, silhouetted forms near to the foreground lower lip of the picture space in each of the main ceiling panels counteracts, to some extent, the sharp or deep *di sotto in su* recession into depth that had become something of a pictorial convention in works of this type. Instead, Veronese's arrangement pushes the given scene down towards the viewer in the nave below, maximizing the material splendour of the visual effect. As in many of his other paintings, forms cluster together to stress surface values, countering the depth – creating suggestions of the figural foreshortenings. In the *Mordecai*, this crowding and

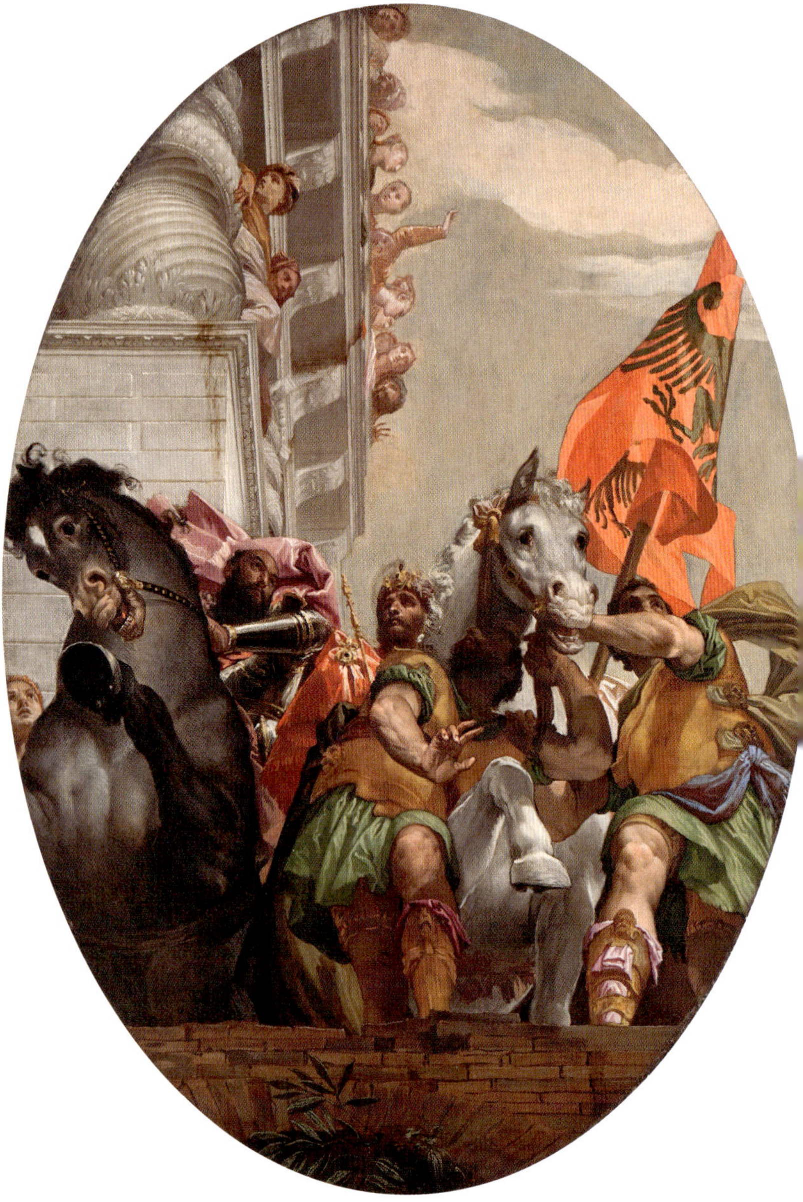

18 Veronese, *Triumph of Mordecai*, 1556, oil on canvas.

overlapping of forms means that we are permitted to glimpse only the hero's face while being led into mistaking his body for that of the servant leading his horse, whose own head disappears into the shadow it casts. Visual substitution or ellipsis of this kind does not directly challenge the primacy of the given theme, but it complicates it in visual terms. It is the playful precarity, verging on logical impossibility, of the toppling, closely intertwined figures as they perform on the narrow ledge of Veronese's pictorial stage which constitutes the main visual interest. All three paintings are intensely coloured, agglomerating a wealth of moulded stone, marble and stucco surfaces in support of the impeccably dressed figures, who display equally expensive fabrics, or sport finely polished and chased armour, in addition to (half-imaginary) displays of jewellery. That worn by the heroine in the central canvas particularly draws attention, the sharp, cool light catching the sumptuous surfaces of her earrings, necklace and enlarged arm brooch.

Our effort of looking up into this world of enhanced material richness inaugurates an immediate sense of difference or otherness – an apprehension that this pictorial domain will not operate as a naturalistic extension of the everyday reality beyond it. But Veronese's arrangements also seek to maintain connectivity with the spectator. If we view an ideal domain of existence, then this is not dependent on intellectual or formal abstraction, or limitation of bodily contact. If the Veronesian world is high in relation to us then it is not too high. As John Ruskin pointed out, Veronese's pictorial actors always possess physical weight, presence and energy. The surfaces of dazzling and finely worked materials support a wider impression of the 'stout, self-commanding, magnificent animality' of his performers.[9] Any sense of being patronized by the pomp that we might have is quickly countered by the recognition that 'looking up' involves an intensification of the sensuality of the world presented to us rather than an enervating retreat from it. These ceiling paintings, as has often been observed, were vastly influential on later painters from Rubens (1577–1640) to the Venetian rococo masters of the eighteenth century. But their impact was based less on their expression of abstract theological ideas than on the power of their visual realization.

META-PAINTING AT SAN SEBASTIANO

The nave ceiling at San Sebastiano gave Veronese scope to rapidly expand his visual command in the church. In addition to the three main narrative scenes, it included more than twenty smaller works, all finished in little more than ten months, for a lowish fee of 150 ducats.[10] The completion of the ceiling in such a short space of time is the first – but not the last – instance of Veronese's readiness and ability to produce paintings quickly, cheaply and at high volume. This suggests a parallel with the practice of his rival, Tintoretto, rather than a sharp distinction in their approach to the business aspects of painting. Veronese's early experience as a fresco painter would anyway have encouraged promptness of execution. The landscapes he painted in this medium at Villa Barbaro were each completed in (at most) a day and a half.[11] But such promptness could also be transferred to oil painting when occasion demanded. Veronese finished three altarpieces in as many months for the Mantuan church of San Benedetto Po in 1562, again for a discounted overall price of 123 ducats (altarpieces by leading masters typically fetched fees of 100 ducats or more each). In each case, the result was a rapid expansion in the quantity of visual imagery covering the available spaces of public and private buildings. At San Sebastiano, the sheer scope of Veronese's visual ambition is often forgotten in favour of a reading that foregrounds the importance of the iconography. Regarding the ceilings, emphasis is usually laid on the typological link between Esther and the Virgin Mary. Given that the Virgin had come under attack by the Protestant reformers, the cycle at San Sebastiano has been understood as offering a Counter-Reformatory response and rebuff to the northern European 'heretics'.[12] These rebels had challenged the traditional sacred authority of both the Virgin and the saints, and had also attacked the traditions of popular devotion these figures had inspired. Following the completion of the nave ceiling, Veronese was commissioned to paint frescoes around the upper walls featuring scenes from the life of St Sebastian, drawing on Jacobus de Voragine's still-popular account in the *Legenda aurea* (compiled around 1260). The promotion of the saint's heroism again answers these theological questions. Veronese eventually depicted scenes of Sebastian's martyrdom – both the failed attempt with arrows and the successful one with clubs – as many as four times in this church, reiterating the special significance of his story as a model of moral behaviour, and his close emulation of Christ's own self-sacrifice.[13]

Despite this, there is no precise historical evidence that Veronese or his Hieronymite patrons were especially or directly concerned with answering the questions raised by the Protestant rebellion in parts of northern Europe. It is possible that Veronese used his patrons' growing awareness of the attack on traditional cultures of visual display in churches to encourage the further progress of his commission at San Sebastiano. But a sizeable number of his paintings were already in place before the Council of Trent finally formulated a concerted Catholic response to Protestant attacks on religious imagery in early December 1563. The proliferation of paintings in this church is just as likely to reflect the expansive visual ambitions of the artist himself. At the Scuola Grande di San Rocco, where Tintoretto later gained a similar kind of visual monopoly, it was the painter who drove things forwards, repeatedly cajoling his patrons into commissioning further cycles of paintings by making a series of donations and discounts on prices. Tintoretto may have followed Veronese's earlier proactive example at San Sebastiano in doing so. Veronese's

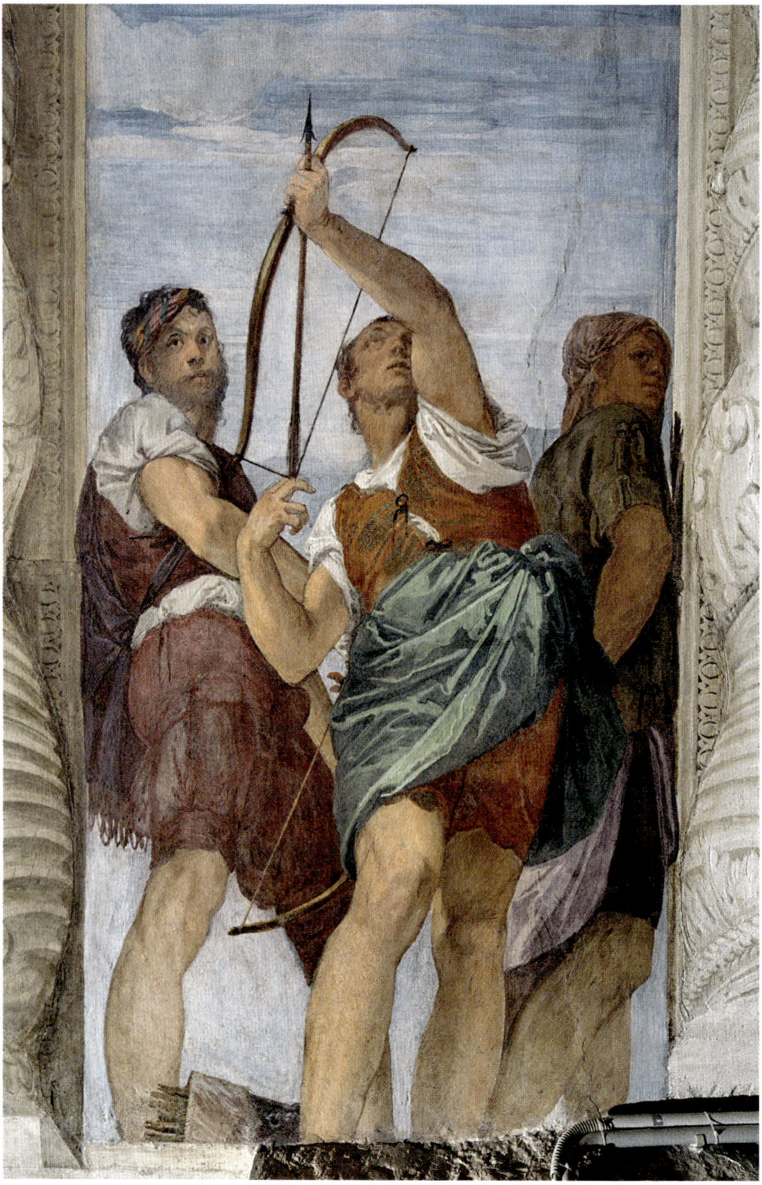

19 Veronese, *Three Archers*, 1558–9, fresco.

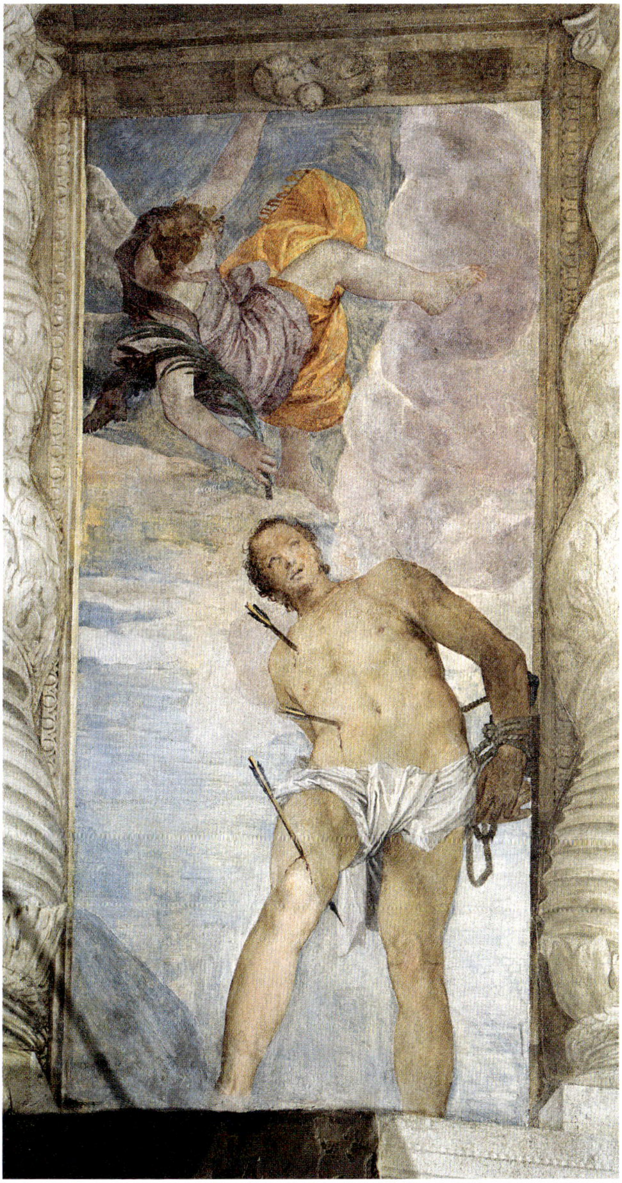

20 Veronese, *St Sebastian*, 1558–9, fresco.

'loss-leader' price for his nave ceiling suggests as much, as does his active role in the design of the church organ and of the presbytery windows to accommodate his paintings.[14]

Veronese's religious subject-matter remained important, of course, and I am not suggesting that the painter defied his patrons' wishes. But his paintings nonetheless transformed the real space of the church in ways that they might not have originally anticipated, challenging rather than merely accepting the spatial limits of its existing architecture. So much suggests that the dictates of the iconographic schema did not finally determine or circumscribe the appearance of the paintings. Rather, the illusionistic or *trompe l'oeil* effects that Veronese introduced actively impinged on or displaced the given physical structure, substituting it for his own image-world wherever possible. In accordance with this, his figures increasingly respond to one another across the actual space of the church. An example of this kind of internal image-to-image 'conversation' occurs in the two frescoes showing the attempted martyrdom of Sebastian with arrows painted on the upper nave wall (illus. 19, 20). In these works, Veronese sacrificed narrative clarity or iconographic comprehensibility for striking visual effect by cutting the scene in two, showing half the story on the left-hand wall of the church and the other on the opposite one. The figures in these narrow spaces rebel against their beaded frames, which are themselves overlapped by the giant Solomonic columns that establish the framework of the painted frieze. Veronese's playful illusionistic layering of his imagery alerts the viewer to the fictive status of the entire visual ensemble. The painter thus comments reflexively on the performative or artificial status of his work in a way that recalls the playfulness of *maniera* art on the mainland. The decision to switch from oil on canvas to fresco on plaster must reflect Veronese's already well-established reputation in the latter medium. The visual sophistication of his *trompe l'oeil* approach, soon to be developed further at the Villa Barbaro, was perhaps deemed suitable for the paintings on the upper part of the wall, intended primarily for the eyes of the monks themselves, rather than those of the wider church congregation gathered in the nave below.

Veronese's division of the attempted martyrdom of Sebastian by arrows served to further extend the painting cycle in that it necessitated another painting. It also had a peculiar effect on the appearance of the imagery concerned, sectionalizing and partially defamiliarizing the well-established iconography of this scene. The lack of any sacred or historical figures in the *Three Archers*, in particular, make the fresco appear as if it were drawn directly from nature, like a genre scene of everyday life in which the painter demonstrates his mastery over varying perspectival views of the male figure seen in action from below.[15] It is only when the painting is reconnected across the actual space of the nave with the parallel one of Sebastian on the opposite wall that the traditional hagiographic meaning is re-established. This play between subject and non-subject seems to suggest the ultimate priority of the paintings themselves, introducing a meta effect that unifies the visual ensemble by making it appear self-contained and self-generating. In this context, Veronese's picture-making itself presides, as he supplies or withholds meanings at will.

In a small fresco placed just below the frieze on a section of the upper wall only visible to the monks, Veronese dipped down again into the realm of contemporary life, moving beyond Sebastian's heroic story to depict monks conversing across two suggested apertures: a moulded stone doorway and, at a lower level, a round-topped arch (illus. 21).[16] This little scene, placed below the other images in the frieze like an afterthought or humorous aside, was probably included for the pleasure of the monks occupying this part of the church, who would have enjoyed its playful reference to their everyday presence there. The easy transition from seriousness to triviality, past to present, narrative to description, that this little image suggests also tells us something important about Veronese's pictorial approach more widely. Although it is in a damaged state, the *Two Monks* is also oddly evocative and alluring. The casual ambiguity of the foreground figure's pointing gesture, like the sudden attentiveness of the smaller figure or boy beyond him, sometimes identified as a person of colour, speaks of a more immediate and ordinary level of reality that also comments in a knowing and humorous manner

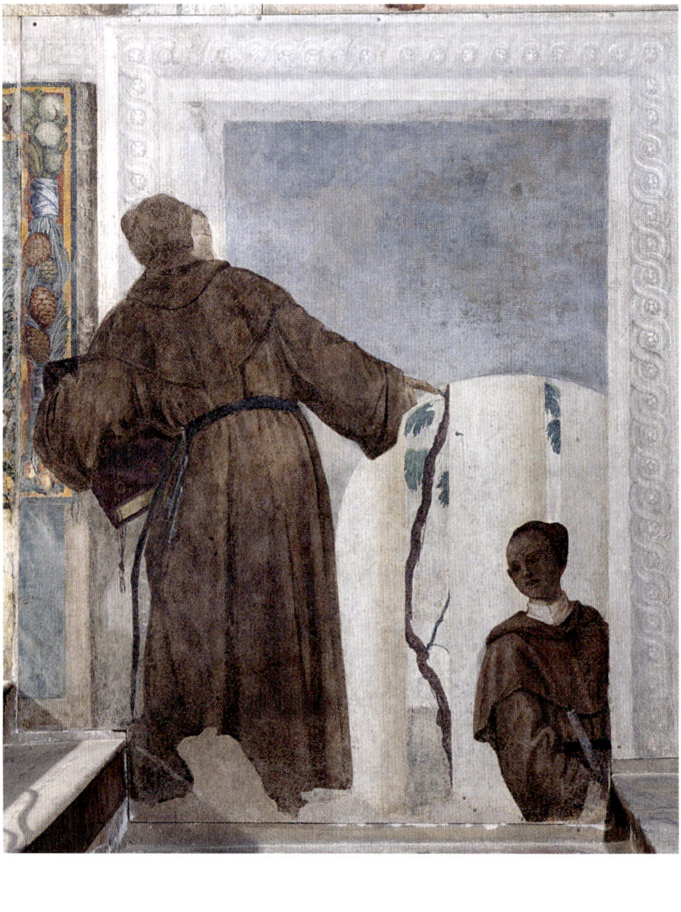

21 Veronese, *Two Monks*, 1558–9, fresco.

on Veronese's presentation of the higher actors in other paintings nearby.

The joke seems to be that the pious figure of the monk turns his back, obliviously, on the sacred dramas featured in the other frescoes, as also on the viewer, not knowing that he is seen. His insouciant absorption in conversation is matched by the close attention that the 'boy' beyond pays to him: both are unaware of the meaningful and tragic narrative of the eponymous saint of the church unfolding on the walls. But the monks' convivial communicativeness is made a matter of pleasure and delight rather than of moral castigation. Everyday life and its more commonplace distractions must and will go on, however important the foundational heroic stories might be. Veronese's willingness to visualize the realm of the quotidian and ordinary is not, in fact, so unusual in his oeuvre. His propensity to 'wander at will' is already hinted at in the *Three Archers* nearby and recurs at the Villa Barbaro as too in his refectory paintings showing biblical feasts. In many instances, the adventurous visual byways Veronese takes beyond the well-worn paths of the given story lead him towards the less exalted or notable, towards the multifarious appearances and unexceptional doings of servants, entertainers and casual passers-by.

Veronese's gendering of the iconography at San Sebastiano is also worthy of note: feminine elements are interlaced with the masculine heroic narrative of a Christianized Roman soldier. As we have seen, Esther dominates the imagery on the nave ceiling as a type of the Virgin, who is exalted as she joins the Holy Trinity in heaven on the Sacristy ceiling. The Virgin reappears on the inner doors of the organ, in an image of the *Annunciation* painted on the spandrels of the entrance arch to the presbytery, and once again in a now-lost fresco of the *Assumption* initially painted on one of its walls. She is dominant, too, in the High altarpiece of 1562, where she triumphantly appears seated with the Christ child in the upper part of the painting, above Sebastian and a gathering of saints,

Overleaf: 22 Veronese, *Sts Marcus and Marcellinus Led to Martyrdom*, 1562–5, oil on canvas.

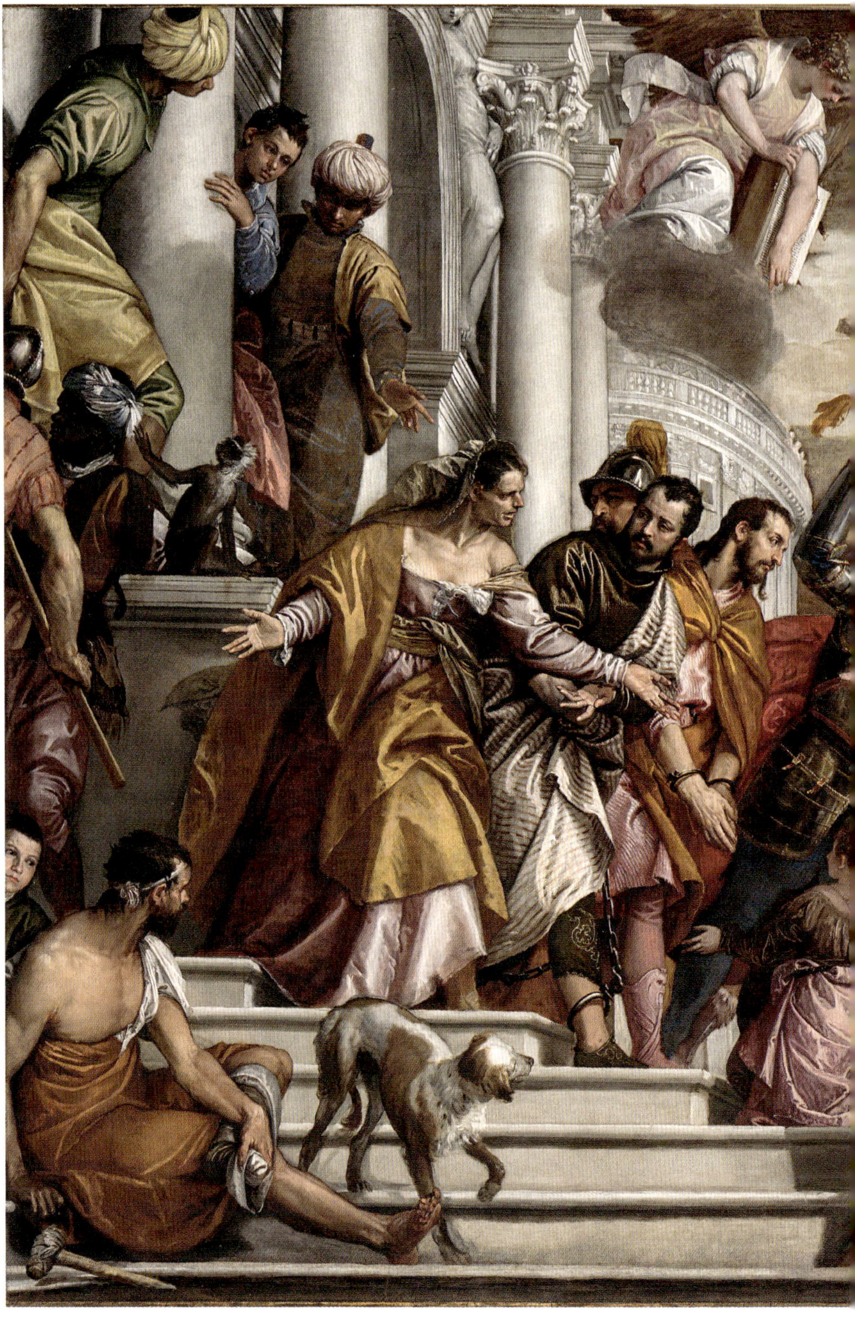

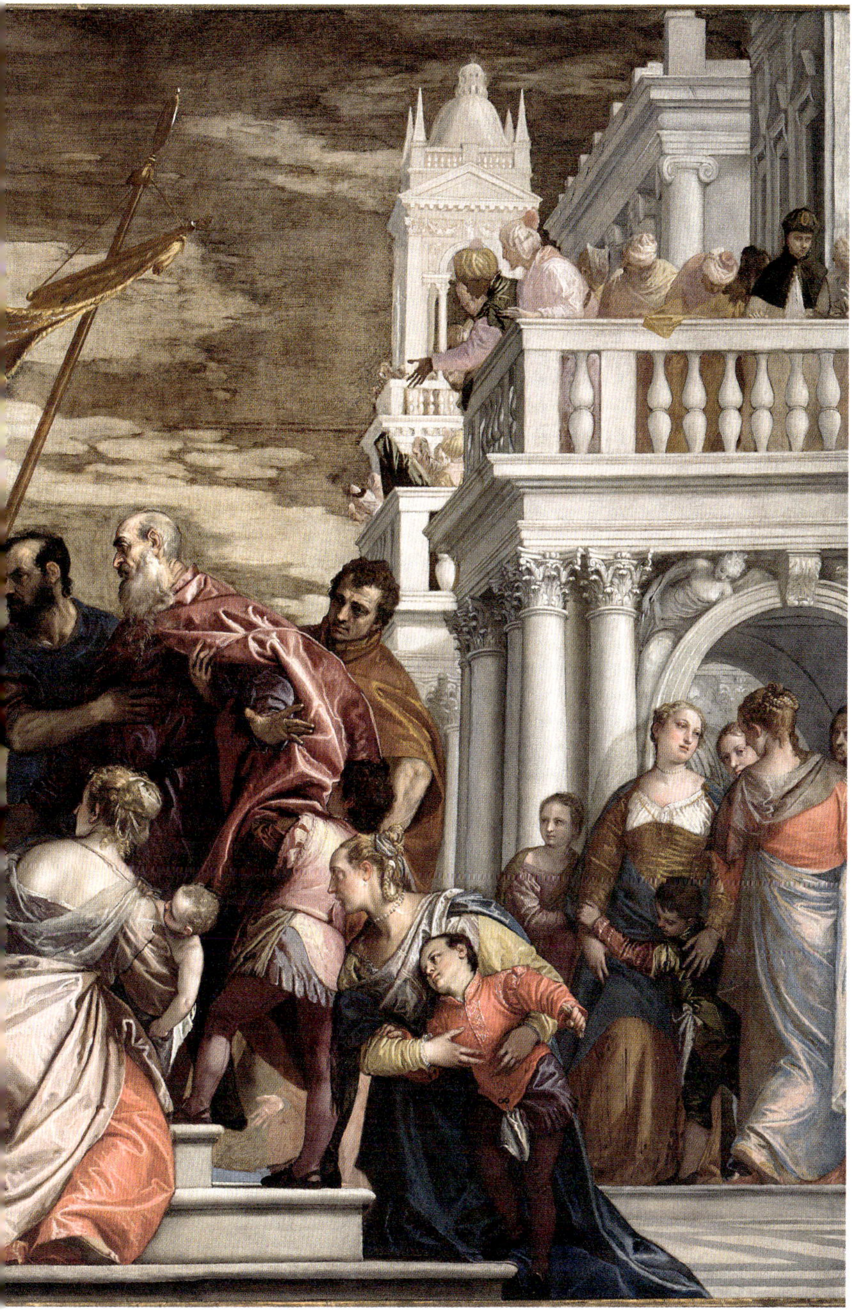

who are cast into shadow below her. In two so-called 'laterali' – horizontally shaped narrative paintings to either side of the main altar – that Veronese subsequently painted, crowded narrative scenes from the life of St Sebastian return attention to the primary story of heroic martyrdom. But in the *Sts Marcus and Marcellinus Led to Martyrdom* on the left-hand wall, the flow of the narrative across the painting surface from left to right is at least partially disrupted or compromised by the desperate appeal of one of their mothers. The woman throws her arms wide with palms upturned, as the two would-be victims are led down the steps of the family palace by Sebastian towards their death (illus. 22). The armoured saint's contrasting pointing gesture towards his own image of martyrdom featured in the recently completed High altarpiece across the real space of the presbytery to the right indicates that the call of Christian duty must win out against the ageing woman's objections, and that Sebastian's followers will ultimately fulfil their glorious destinies. But Veronese is just as interested in the conflicted family dynamics: the current moment of hesitation that is generated by the mother's powerfully felt plea. Her son turns back towards her, perhaps half-persuaded by the justice of her appeal, and a father figure and two other younger men seem equally to fall under the sway of her strong maternal emotion. As he had in the *Anointing of David* (illus. 13), Veronese includes imagery that can be taken as a prophetic reference to the future Christian world: young mothers and children are multiplied to the right, reminding the viewer of *caritas* figures, a forward-looking association that is strengthened again by the presence of the beggar on the steps. But the two kneeling wives with their young children, like the others further to the right, also press back against the underlying left–right, past–future flow of the narrative. If they do not quite block the way of the would-be martyrs, they at least remind them of what they are about to lose. The feminine principle – family-based, domestic and to some extent anti-narrative – is not wholly overridden in this balanced scene of competing sacred and secular values, set (as was Veronese's wont) in the more open-ended and non-teleological moments before the bloody resolution of a Christian climax.

VERONESE AND THE COURTLY PORTRAIT

In the portraits that Veronese regularly (but not frequently) painted throughout his career he developed a 'regal' pictorial language that was non-Venetian insofar that it promised his sitters a newly heightened aristocratic profile, more in keeping with that of the foreign courts and the established *terraferma* nobilities. Often reprising mainland cultural ideas and related visual formats, these works granted those who sat for him an extended sense of private or individual identity that suggested their connection with the old nobilities of Italy and Europe.[17] Veronese undoubtedly drew on his own background as a painter from Verona in his prescient development of this aspirational portraiture. Prior to his move to Venice, he occasionally made likenesses of leading mainland families who were perhaps less anxious to prove their aristocratic credentials than their Venetian counterparts. In pendants showing the da Porto family from Vicenza from 1552, Veronese produced two of his most direct and unaffected portraits: works characterized by qualities of immediacy and informality rather than courtly hauteur (illus. 23, 24).[18] It is hard not to feel intimately connected with the four people shown in these paintings, whose vivacious appearances make them seem more like close friends, relatives or social equals than reserved and superior aristocratic beings. Veronese's presentation avoids the immortalizing or heroizing qualities given to sitters in many commissioned portraits of the Renaissance, offering a frank visual presentation that allows of sudden and unanticipated movements, momentary expressions and close physical connections. This shading-off

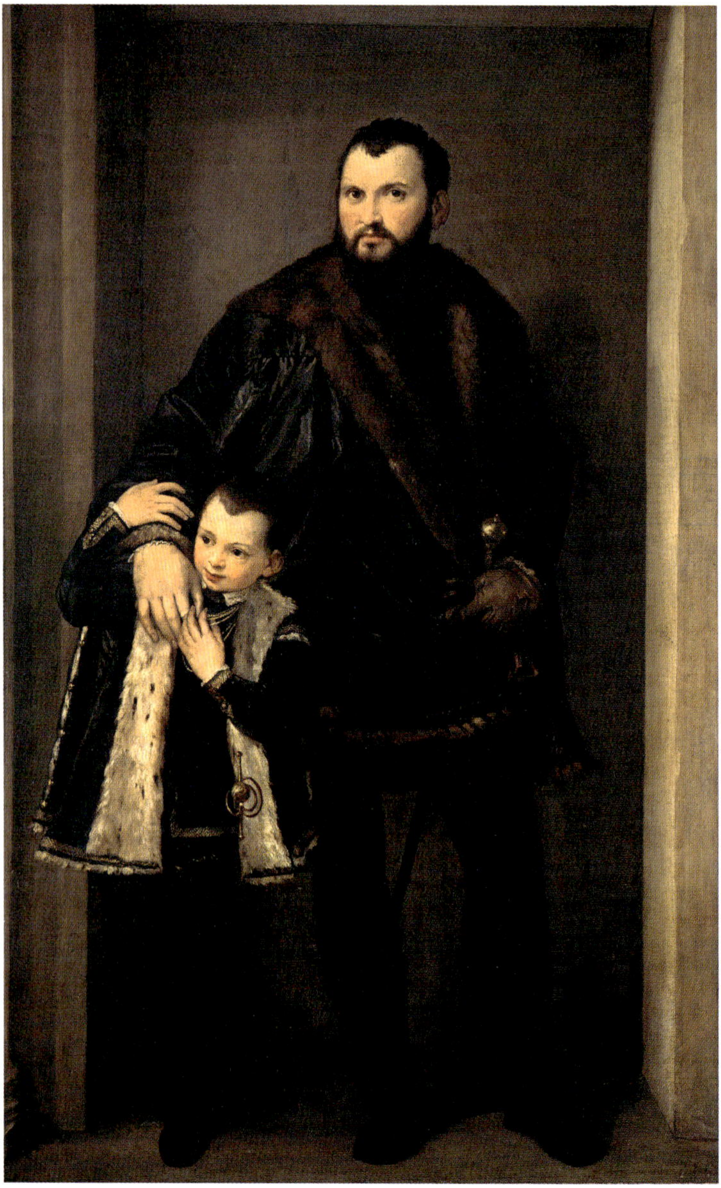

23 Veronese, *Iseppo and Leonida da Porto*, 1552, oil on canvas.

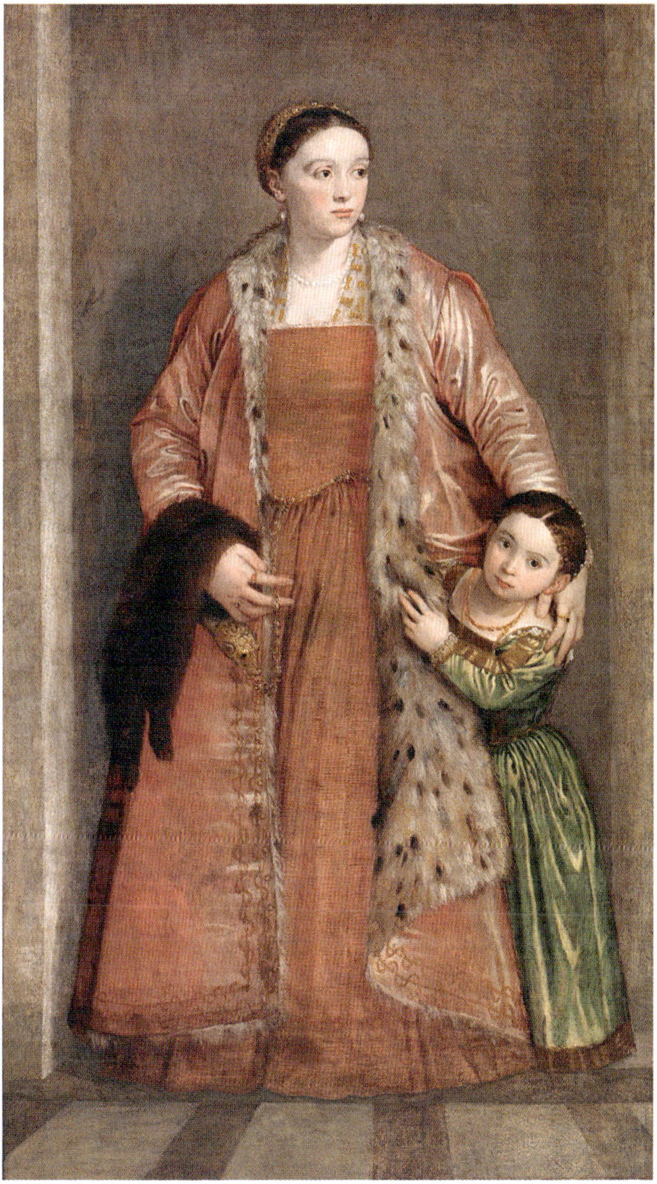

24 Veronese, *Livia and Deidamia da Porto*, 1552, oil on canvas.

into a less formal and more digressive realm of everyday appearances and happenings is something we have already noted in certain of Veronese's paintings for San Sebastiano; it emerges once more at the Villa Barbaro, as discussed below.

In the male pendant, the son, Leonida, looks across to his mother in the work originally hung to the left, while his father, Iseppo, confidently and steadily catches and holds our attention, expressing the certainty and confidence of the head of the household.[19] On the female side, the arrangement is reversed, with the daughter, Deidamia, peering out towards us. Livia, her mother, turns her head away, her expression tinged with pensiveness. Her translucently pale flesh suggests her vulnerability, as if she doubted the fabled ability of the decorative, gold-headed marten draped across her right arm to protect the unborn child she carries. Veronese might depict Livia in the role of the ideal wife, as it had been defined in influential books such as Francesco Barbaro's *De re uxoria* (Venice, 1415).[20] She and Deidamia are depicted in a separate painting to her husband and son, as if to re-enforce a standard gender division between male and female within the family, and her expression is less assertive or openly communicative than that of her husband.[21] But the conventional ideas do not quite explain the nervousness or apprehension of this mother and mother-to-be: emotions that suggest something other than settled resignation in the face of the potential dangers of the upcoming birth of another child. Livia's doubts and apprehensions are made especially poignant by the contrasting eagerness of her innocent and unknowing daughter, for whom a similar difficult fate might be in store.

In these works, Veronese appears especially alive to emergent or updated ideas about 'nobility' that suggested that this quality was based more on relaxed and human behaviours than on the naked display of high social position. The 'naturalness' of the presentation indicates his sophisticated awareness of such progressive ideas as found in works such as Castiglione's *Book of the Courtier*, mentioned in the Introduction. In this book, the author had promoted elegant wit, informality and – above all – nonchalance (*sprezzatura*) as the true signals of nobility, arguing that gentle social manners and conviviality were preferable to the cold and arrogant assertion of authority, wealth or power. Veronese's Count Iseppo da Porto keeps his mouth closed in accordance with a long-accepted decorum in upper-class portraiture, but he is nonetheless ready to speak in the next moment, as if to converse with some much-loved familiar. His open sociability is in line with Castiglione's equation of true nobility with the equality of friendship: one that had already been given shape in painting by Raphael's famous portrait of the author (1514–15, Paris, Musèe du Louvre). It is not that Veronese cancels all signs of high social status in these portraits – note the way Deidamia casually strokes the fur lining of her mother's gown, or the parallel sword hilts sported by father and son – but these are reduced to the details, so to speak, rather than made obvious or explicit.

In several portraits of leading members of the Barbarigo, Barbaro, Contarini and Soranzo families, Veronese refashioned the Venetian patriciate as a courtly leisured class, offering them a visual release from any taint of trade.[22] In a work such as the *Portrait of a Man* (illus. 25), it is tellingly difficult to determine whether his sitter is a Venetian patrician or a member of the *terraferma* nobility. As in the da Porto pendants, Veronese adopted the grand full-length format familiar in mainland aristocratic portraiture, but unlike in those works we must now 'look up' to this elegant man. Despite the horizontality of his gaze out towards us, we are placed at a lower level than he is: an angle of view that exacerbates further our sense of his high aristocratic standing. It is no accident that Veronese based the gentleman's pose quite closely on a portrait by Titian for the Spanish court of the young king Philip II (*c.* 1550, Madrid, Museo del Prado).[23] But equally notable is the way in

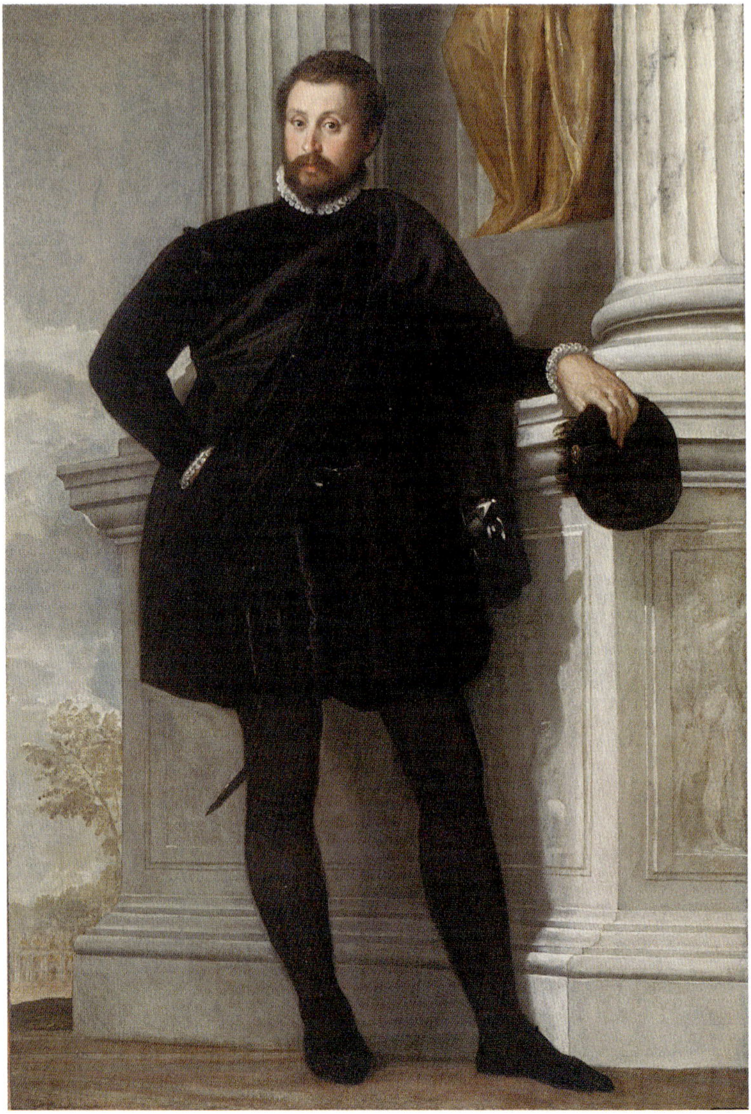

25 Veronese, *Portrait of a Man*, *c.* 1560, oil on canvas.

which Veronese adapts his royal model to a more local question of social identity.

It may be that Veronese suggested to his sitter that he should wear a Spanish-style ink-black costume rather than his traditional Venetian toga. Black was especially recommended for the ideal courtier by Castiglione, given that it allowed him to avoid a vulgar display of his wealth or position.[24] In Veronese's portrait, the man's costume makes a striking tonal contrast with the fine-veined pale marble of the building, recalling the favoured 'black on white' colour scheme of Giovanni Battista Moroni (*c.* 1520/24–1578) in his portraits of the *terraferma* aristocracies in Bergamo and Trento.[25] As he rests his weight on his right leg, the man's body takes on an elegant but nonchalant *contrapposto* position that perhaps recalls a classicizing sculpture: an effect re-emphasized by the *all'antica* architecture that he leans against. The angled view towards two giant columns seen from the right that extend upwards out of the top of the picture recalls Titian's Pesaro altarpiece, via Veronese's own earlier adaptations of this in his early works of this type. This derivation indicates that Veronese sought to monumentalize his portrait by referring to large-scale altarpiece design, while (once again) making his new work appear compatible with a revered example of local painting. In addition to barely discernible relief work in marble on the lower part of the facade, a raised plinth supporting a bronze sculpture appears between the columns.[26] The draped legs of this fictive artwork echo (albeit in reverse) the arrangement of the living sitter's own lower body, suggesting his close or defining attachment to this classicizing edifice and the noble values it embodies. If he was not its architect, then perhaps he was its owner.

Veronese's monumental building is tellingly closer to the pale, temple-like classicizing architecture championed by Sanmicheli and Palladio on the mainland than to the age-old Veneto-Gothic style that dominated the built environment of the lagoon city itself. The prime example of this traditional Byzantine-orientated architecture is quoted in the view of St Mark's at the far background left. But its potentially defining authority is reduced by its minuscule scale and sketchy handling, its insubstantiality made to contrast with the massive solidity of the ultra-modern foreground structure. This difference between the background and foreground buildings initiates an architectural *paragone* within the painting that may re-enforce the wider recalibration of cultural and artistic values suggested in this contemporizing portrait. The inclusion of the view of St Mark's seems to indicate that the sitter is indeed a Venetian patrician, and a continuing servant of the state in some capacity. But the placement of the city's Mother Church so far away, in a dissolving distance, also suggests the man's cultural distance from the traditional values of his birthplace. Conversely, his proximity to the grandeur of the fashionable Palladian building he so nonchalantly leans against suggests his reshaped identity as a mainland-orientated young aristocrat of the emergent courtly mould.

PICTORIALIZING PORTRAITS: PORTRAIT OF A LADY / *'LA BELLA NANI'*

Veronese painted relatively few portraits by comparison with Titian and Tintoretto: perhaps no more than forty or so across the four decades of his career, and thus not more than one each year.[27] The towering example of Titian in this picture type, and the readiness of Tintoretto to satisfy the demands of the local market, undoubtedly had a role to play in generating Veronese's comparative reticence with works of this kind. He was less comfortable with this picture format than with large-scaled and multi-figured works based more definitely on his own artistic projections. His hesitancy might reflect the added measure of control that patrons could expect to exert over a portrait that they had commissioned. Works of this type necessitated a more passive or inductive relation to outward reality than was the case with subject pictures that gave freer rein to the painter's *fantasía*. Portraits did not offer so many opportunities for visual play of the kind that Veronese particularly enjoyed. In the portraits that he did make, it is no surprise to find that he often pressed against the existing outwardly determined or indexical conventions of the picture type, spreading the forms of his sitters across the picture surface, or taking liberties with their physiognomies, clothing and jewellery, so that the work, in part at least, reflected his own pictorial ideas.

In the *Portrait of a Lady*, known as *'La Bella Nani'*, it becomes difficult to determine whether Veronese depicts a living individual or a more generic type of the beautiful woman (illus. 26).[28] These possibilities are not, after all, so mutually exclusive. The lavish presentation might seem to make her the female counterpart of the *Portrait of a Man* discussed above insofar as she too conveys a cultural ideal of aristocratic magnificence, elegance and sophistication. Her hand-on-heart gesture suggests loyalty to a husband rather than sexual availability. But even if she is a patrician wife, perhaps depicted in the short time between her marriage and the commencement of her child-bearing duties, she still carries vestiges of the *belle donne* picture type that had become popular with Venetian painters and patrons in the first half of the sixteenth century: genre-like works featuring sensualized depictions of unspecified, unmarried and sexually available young women, presented in a portrait-like format. Veronese's *'La Bella'* is, after all, shown as beautiful and blonde while his picture draws attention to itself as a consummately composed work of art.[29] This, too, was an expectation of the *belle donne* pictures, in which the beauty of the anonymous sitter is made a figure or metaphor for the surpassing beauty of the painting itself. Attention to such formal needs also encouraged painters to defy immediate appearances, to push against the empirical controls that underpinned naturalistic representation in a commissioned portrait. Veronese's '*La Bella*' wears three pieces of golden jewellery at her shoulders and around her waist that are larger than their counterparts in reality, and that she might not typically have worn in everyday life. These elaborately moulded, pearl-studded objects seem about to break free of their inanimate status. The lower, girdle-like piece is particularly intricate and extended, featuring a mask-like face surrounded by vegetal forms and wing-like scrolls above what may be a family coat of arms below, offset by dangling rubies to either side. Placed over the young woman's lower abdomen, seat of her future fertility, it may have an emblematic significance. In visual terms, the ornate object links up with the two epaulettes above, as too with the woman's similarly coloured – but organic – braided hair, which is also jewel-spangled. Natural and man-made entities align and overlap under the generative illusionistic power of Veronese's brush.

Veronese's portraits often knowingly misrepresent the actualities of the ongoing commercial and business-orientated lives of the Venetian merchants they depict, showing his sitters as a sophisticated and leisured class apart. Perhaps, too, his sitters are 'mispresented' in sartorial terms, given that their bodies are enfolded in the lavish silks and furs that were prohibited by the Venetian sumptuary laws.[30] The authorities would surely have questioned *La Bella*'s exaggerated display of jewellery, if she had ever worn it in reality. But in the protectively fictive world of Veronese's paintings, she was exempt from such legal strictures on decorativeness. It may be that in completing this work, Veronese painted the woman and her resplendent dress on separate occasions. If he took her portrait quickly, perhaps in a single sitting, then it may be that her dress was borrowed by the painter and placed on a dummy so that the subtle reflections and variations playing across its richly reflective surface could be studied more

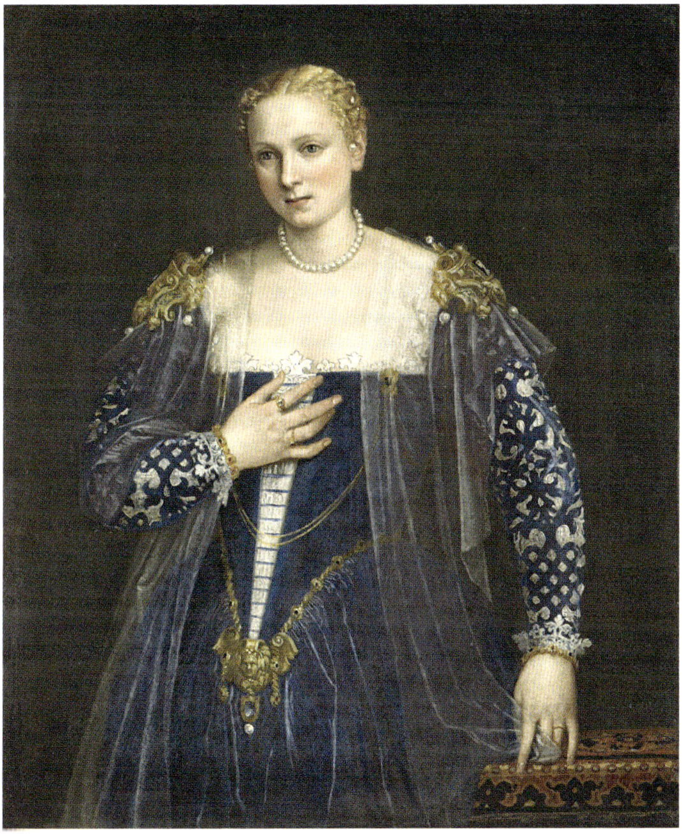

closely and at length. This proceeding might also explain the way in which the dress becomes, to some extent, the true subject of the painting, dominating over the sitter's relatively small (and visually retreating) head.

The shimmering garment, perhaps decided on by the artist, offered itself as the true field for Veronese's pictorial play and extension. Here we might recall Leon Battista Alberti's recommendation to painters in 1435 not to use gold leaf, but rather to paint an illusion of real gold using cheaper gold-coloured pigment.[31]

26 Veronese, *Portrait of a Lady ('La Bella Nani')*, c. 1560, oil on canvas.

This was to extend the imitative opportunity for the painter beyond his materials, even as it saved his patron money, given that paints were so much cheaper than gold itself. In *'La Bella'*, the predominating ultramarine blue was expensive by comparison with the other pigments deployed, but it was nonetheless of much lesser value than the dress itself; the same can be assumed for the painted gold jewellery that she wears. By depicting such valuable items in the much less costly medium of oil paint, but also providing brilliantly illusionistic representations of them, Veronese offered his patrons inexpensive painted surrogates for their own treasured material possessions. Moreover, these items could also be exaggerated in the painting to heighten still further the effect of lavishness and *richezza*. From the artist's point of view, the depiction of such objects offered a further field for the display of illusionistic skill and invention. In *'La Bella'*, Veronese delicately transposed the fall of light on subtly variegated surface textures generating virtuoso visual effects, such as the matting of the shiny velvet fabric of the dress seen through the diaphanous lace veil, and the contrast of both these surfaces with the harder pearly sheen of the silk sleeves.

It is nonetheless possible to exaggerate the significance of *La Bella*'s dress. Veronese's almost obsessive attention to it does not, after all, cancel his interest in the young woman herself. The move towards a less corporate or communally defined social identity for the Venetian patriciate that his paintings reflect extended rather than suppressed the idea of the free individual and of her or his personal identity. Although he painted fewer portraits than his main rivals in Venice, a higher proportion of these were of women, suggesting his special sensitivity to female subjects, already noted in his mainland portraits of Livia and Deidamia da Porto.[32] In *'La Bella'*, Veronese offers an easily missed suggestion of the more independent aspects of her personality that lurk behind the lavish opulence of ornate surface appearances, even if this is not quite imagined in alternative or contrasting terms, as modest and simple.[33] Mistaking it for that, we might be inclined again to read her tentative expression in terms of Francesco Barbaro's ideas about the subservient self-suppression of the perfect wife. But the sitter's physical gaucheness, shaded with melancholy, suggests something more than easy conformity to the conventional social role she must play. It even registers a fleeting moment of resistance to the patriarchal display culture that already so completely encloses her.

ALLEGORY, PORTRAITURE AND ILLUSIONISM AT THE VILLA BARBARO

Veronese's early connection with the *papalisti* circle in Venice soon bore further fruits when he was commissioned by Marc'Antonio and Daniele Barbaro to decorate their new villa at Maser, near Asolo on the *terraferma*, built on a design by Palladio around 1556.[34] Veronese probably completed his frescoes between 1558 and 1562. The commission offered the painter a newly close working alliance with Palladio, whose temple-like pale stone buildings featuring simplified but enlarged classical features were more certainly based on his first-hand experience of Rome. Veronese's painted architecture at the Villa certainly harmonized with the appearance of Palladio's aggrandizing exterior, further developing its effect of visual expansiveness or amplification. The painter was especially responsive to Palladio's aspirational implication that the building should be understood as a dignified villa of the ancient Roman *campagnia* – as described by Pliny the Elder, Vitruvius and other much-read classical authors – rather than a contemporary working farmhouse. But he also introduced certain elements into his painted architecture that do not derive from Palladio, such as the twisting Solomonic columns already featured at San Sebastiano, based on Giulio Romano's paintings in Mantua. On the lower walls, where

Veronese was less closely tied to his patrons' iconographic programme, he gave freer rein to his visual imagination, introducing a plethora of *trompe l'oeil* combinations that reflect the independent energies of his pictorial *fantasia*.

At the crossing area (the Sala a Crociera), painted figures and landscapes are set within a richly complex architectural framework, including fluted columns with Corinthian capitals and carved entablatures, pedimented doorways, richly decorated arched windows, balustrades, sculptural niches and inset cameos (illus. 27). This lavish language of pictorial illusionism was not closely anticipated in Palladio's restrained and monumentalizing use of classical forms in his architecture. Little is known about the relationship between architect and painter, but it may be significant that Palladio makes no mention of Veronese's paintings in his discussion of the building in his book on architecture, *I quattro libri dell' architettura*, published in 1570.[35] Veronese more certainly had to reflect the various concerns and interests of his illustrious patrons, and did so with great skill and sensitivity. But the painter himself may also have played an active role in suggesting just how their ideals of agrarian productivity underpinned by notions of cosmic harmony, primarily articulated through allegorized figures of the pagan gods and goddesses of ancient Greece and Rome, might best be expressed in painted form. If the ceilings and upper sections of the pictorial decoration follow an iconographic programme that reflected the intellectual interests of Daniele, then those of the more worldly and family-based Marc'Antonio – statesman, diplomat and husband – come into play further down the villa walls.[36] The extent of the brothers' input is nonetheless difficult to determine, while the precise subject and meaning of certain key figures in the frescoes remains equally hard to pin down. This might indicate again the extent of Veronese's own input, given that his approach to iconography was often oblique, non-explicit and open-ended. The meaning of the woman in white on a dragon

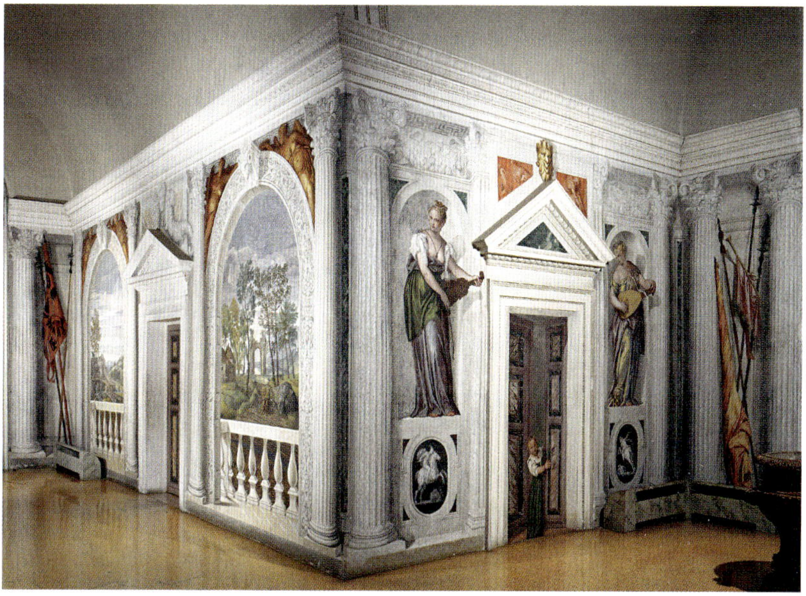

depicted at the centre of the Sala dell'Olimpo ceiling has become something of a cause célèbre of iconographic detection in art history (illus. 28). Does she represent 'Universal Harmony' or 'Divine Love', as has been suggested? Or is she – according to a recent theory – Latona, the mother of Apollo and Diana, depicted to either side of her, with reference to their sacred birthplace at Delos in Greece?[37] The latter reading is the most convincing to date, given that it can be linked to Daniele's very learned interest in Greek scholarship. But the lack of a clear visual precedent for a Latona riding a dragon, and the woman's more obvious connection with the Christian imagery of St Margaret, often shown with this attribute, must give us pause.

St Margaret was patron saint of childbirth and it may be that the dragon-riding woman provides an important link to the imagery on the upper part of the wall below, where Marc'Antonio's wife, Giustiniana, is pictured on a fictive balcony (illus. 29).

27 Veronese, *View of the Sala a Crociera*, 1558–62, frescoes.

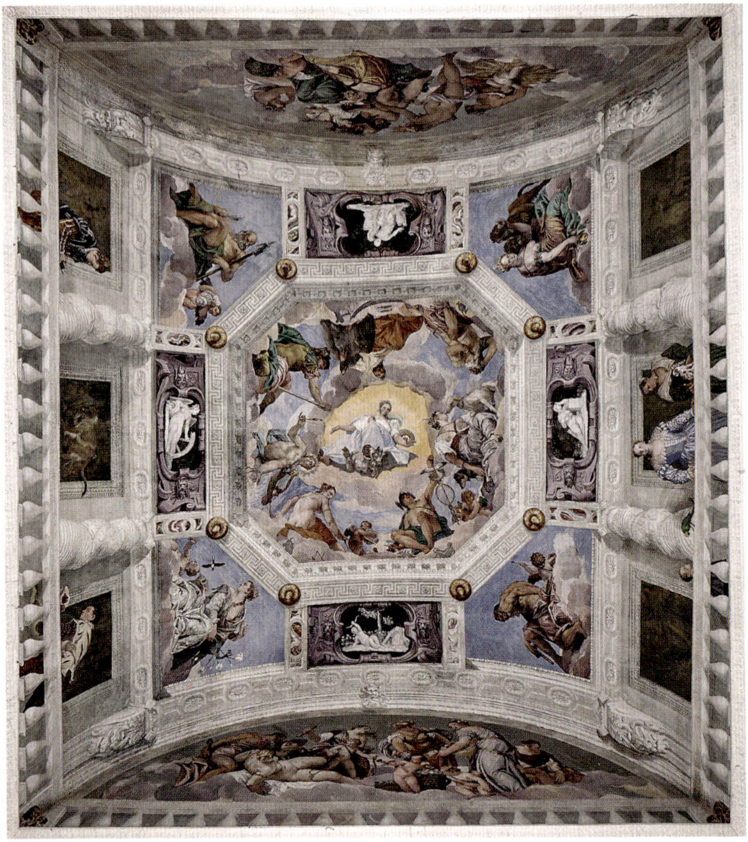

Giustiniana appears with her youngest son, Alvise, while her two older boys, Almorò and Daniele, appear on the opposite side of the vault. Giustiniana's portrait is strategically placed directly below a double representation of Artemis/Diana, who appears first as a many-breasted reclining figure in a fictive cameo just above, and then again as a huntress with her hounds, closer – if the recent interpretation is followed – to her mother Latona at the centre of the ceiling (illus. 30, 31). This vertical alignment would make Giustiniana appear as the living representative or

28 Veronese, *View of the Sala dell'Olimpo Ceiling*, 1558–62, frescoes.

descendant of these successive generations of all-powerful women, suggesting her direct link to the revered goddesses of Greek antiquity. Her special relationship with Artemis/Diana reveals her as the living embodiment of both fertility and chastity, and thus as the very model of the ideal wife, as outlined in *De re uxoria*: the still influential treatise on the family by the brothers' fifteenth-century ancestor Francesco.[38] Veronese's penchant for iconographic slippage is once more in play, given that she also recalls Venus, the goddess of Love, as she grasps two red roses in her right hand, and the Virgin herself, via the symbolism of the parrot. Her velvet and silk blue dress, set off with golden jewellery at her waist, upper arms and chest, with pearls at her ears and around her neck, evokes more than just a memory of the '*La Bella Nani*' portrait, even suggesting that we see the same woman. However that may be, Giustiniana is no longer shown like the tentative '*La Bella*', appearing instead as an authority figure within her domestic domain at the Villa Barbaro, as she leans commandingly over the balcony to meet the eye of the viewer below, probably imagined as that of her husband Marc'Antonio, perhaps recently returned home from business. Seen in her commanding raised position, high above his on the ground level, and with her all-powerful mythical forebears arrayed above her, she is depicted by Veronese as something more than the kind of passive, subservient and dutiful wife often imagined in contemporary writings.[39]

The family portraits at Villa Barbaro are not clearly separated in spatial or other ways from those of their servants or pets.[40] Giustiniana and her son are pointedly joined by an impressive elderly servant, a small dog and the above-mentioned parrot, while opposite, the older boys share a space with a larger dog and a chained monkey.[41] This was not untypical of Veronese's portraiture, which often has an open-ended and connective relationship with immediate reality, such that it is sometimes difficult to know whether we see portraits at all. Lower down the walls, family

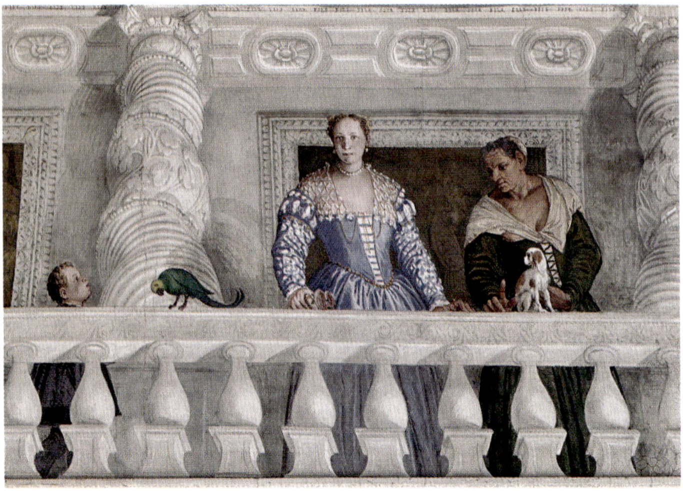

portraiture readily shades off into genre-like scenes of the everyday life in the Villa. Images of contemporary-looking men, women and children may be further portraits of now-unknown family members. But some, at least, are portrait-like depictions of family retainers and servants. The floor-to-ceiling wall paintings of the Crociera include a little girl dressed in contemporary dress entering through a fictive door, who might be either another Barbaro child or – more likely – a serving girl (illus. 27). The full-length depiction of a young man arriving through another fictive portal is similarly ambiguous (illus. 32). His image is compromised as a portrait proper by the multiplication of actual and fictive door and picture frames through which his already liminal image is seen along the enfilade of the northern wing of the Villa (illus. 33).[42]

Veronese's densely layered and multi-media *trompe l'oeil*, replete with knowing cross-reference to pre-existing works of art as well as other artistic media, piles up in front of the foremost doorway. A grisaille oil painting featuring a charging horseman with an elaborately carved wooden frame is seen behind an impressively three-dimensional *sopraporte* featuring 'marble' nudes that recall

29 Veronese, *View of the Upper Wall with Family Portraits*, 1558–62, frescoes.

certain of Michelangelo's seated *ignudi* on the Sistine Chapel ceiling. To either side fluted columns with Corinthian capitals frame illusionistic landscapes based on pre-existent *all'antica* prints rather than on actual views of the countryside from the Villa windows. Given this welter of knowing visual effects and allusions, it seems likely that Veronese fully intended to make his 'portrait' of the returning hunter with his dogs ambiguous. The young man has sometimes been seen as a self-portrait of Veronese but looks little

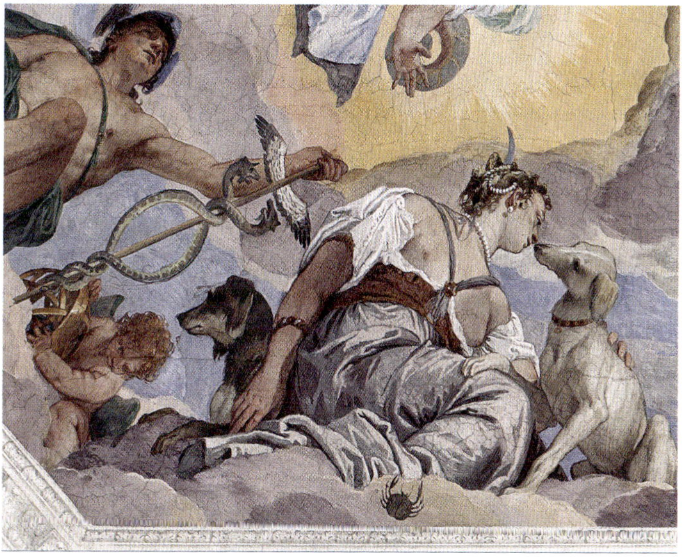

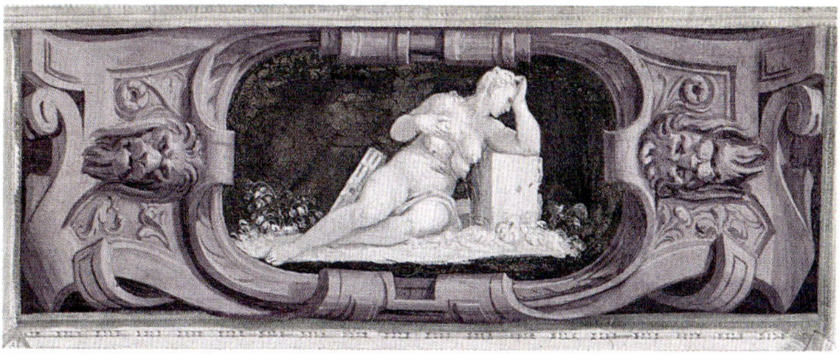

30, 31 Veronese, *Depictions of Artemis/Diana*, 1558–62, frescoes.

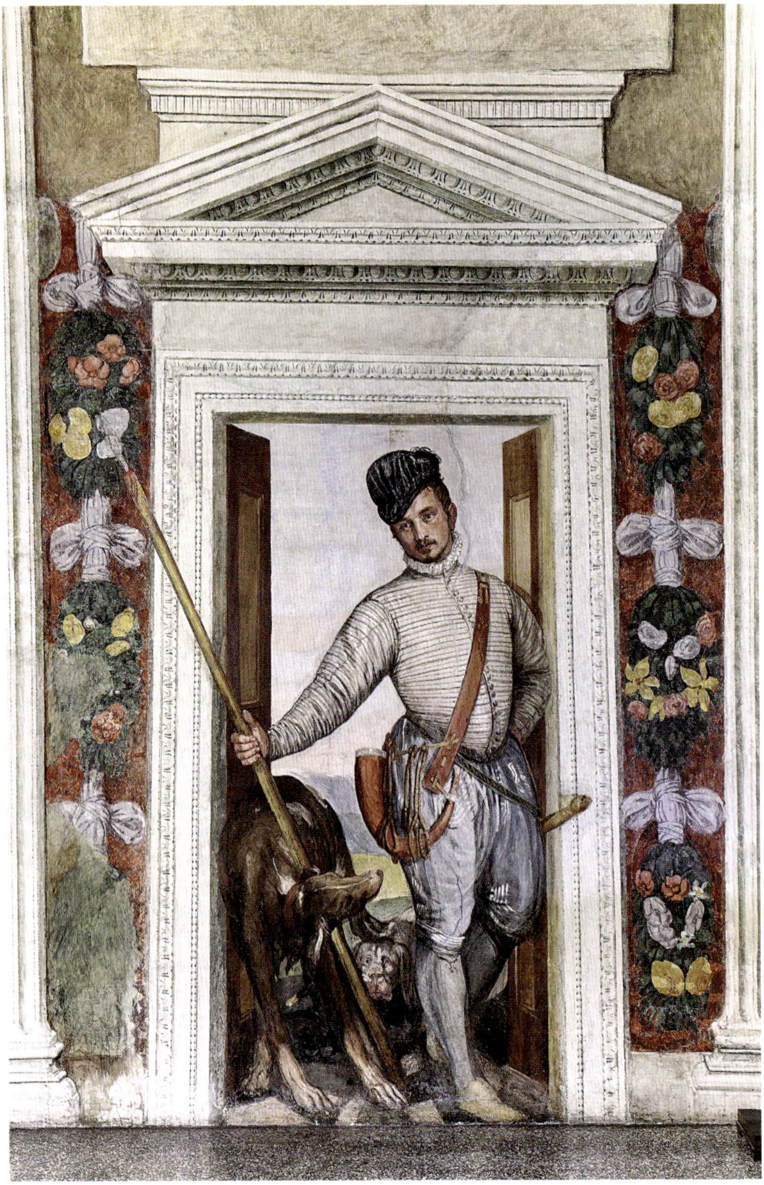

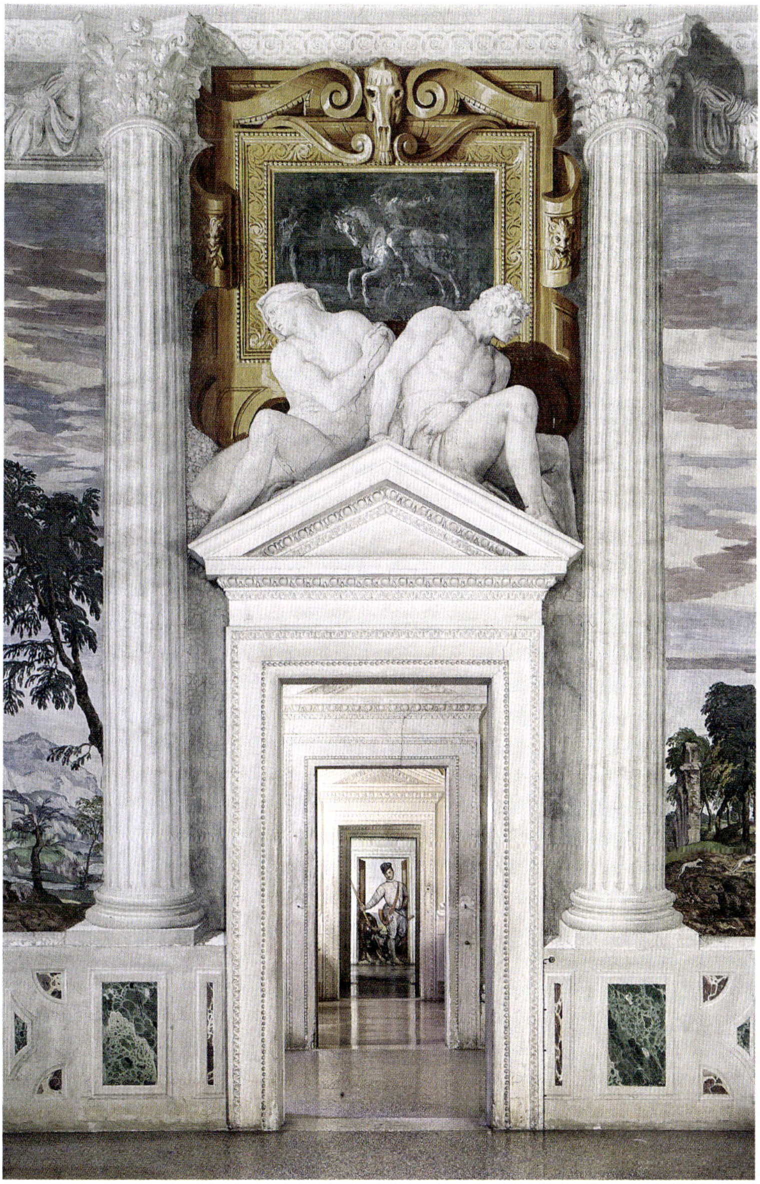

32, 33 Veronese, *View of the Gentleman/Hunter*, 1558–62, frescoes.

like the musician in the *Cana* (illus. 3). Perhaps he is Marc'Antonio Barbaro, dressed up or disguised as a rustic huntsman, bringing 'high' and 'low' together in a single playful image? But given that underlings were often granted a prominent visual profile in these frescoes, he is just as likely to be a much-loved family retainer, returning from a hunt in the immediate outdoors.

Further up the walls at the Villa Barbaro, portraiture and elevated allegory are closely allied, but nearer to the ground the former morphs more readily into the iterative, genre-like everyday world, with figures presented casually, often in a semi-ludic fashion, their postures and appearances released from the formal constraints operative in the imagery above. Something of this visual playfulness or nonchalance is already apparent in Veronese's depictions of the da Porto family, shown stepping out from their shallow niches to generate a *trompe l'oeil* effect. But this connection with Veronese's commissioned portraiture might not be so telling as the one with the multifarious supporting or serving cast that populates many of his narrative paintings. In any case, these playfully depicted persons remain excessive or surplus to the stricter dictates or requirements of the prescribed iconographic scheme. And as such they serve more properly as vehicles for the free play of the painter's artistic licence. It is in these ambiguous figures that Veronese's *trompe l'oeil* is at its most inventive and intense, his fictionalizing most playfully insistent. Set towards the outer edges of the visual ensemble in physical and semantic terms, they operate in a broadly similar fashion to those seen at the pictorial outskirts or margins in Veronese's other works. Their informality is part of the conceit, as is their relative triviality. Different ages and social conditions coalesce together with rank becoming less stable, fixed or settled. If they support the authority of the meaningful imagery further up the walls, lending everyday or material substance or reality to its ideal and fixing narratives of heavenly inspired order, then they are nonetheless not wholly determined by its narrower allegorical or ideological demands. Rather than disappearing, as has recently been claimed, the family servants are insistently present in Veronese's decorations at Maser, playing a pivotal role in a pictorial world that inclines towards social inclusivity rather than exclusion.[43]

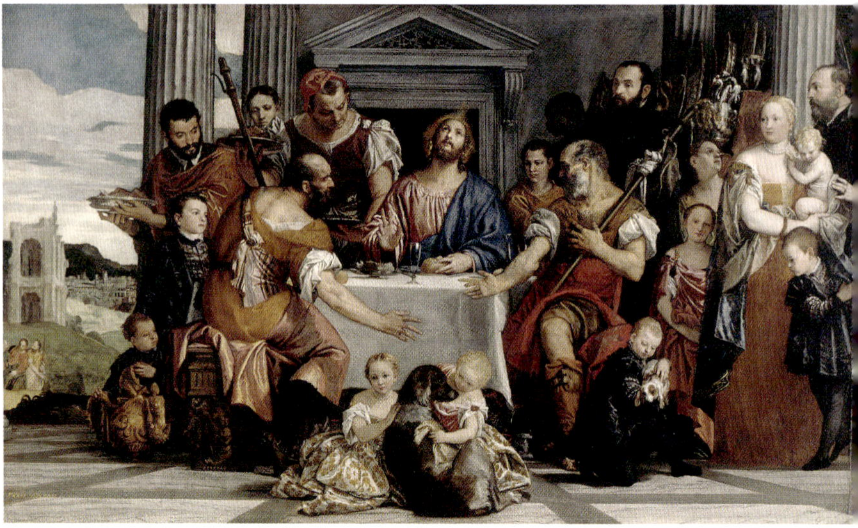

THREE

Religious Paintings of the 1560s and '70s

Veronese's groundbreaking introduction of portraits and portrait-like imagery in his frescoes for the Villa Barbaro was paralleled in certain of his religious works in oils, in which the donors are granted an unusually extended visual role. In several such paintings for private residences, Veronese incorporated prominent images of contemporary families, making it difficult to know whether they are sacred works or secular group portraits. In the *Supper at Emmaus* (illus. 34), a group of at least fourteen family members (ten of whom are children) crowd around the three 'core' sacred figures demanded by the biblical text: Christ and his two disciples, Cleopas and (probably) Luke.[1] The admission of this populous contemporary family into the conventionally hallowed or reserved space of a sacred history painting was found problematic by French academicians in the following century who were keen to separate out the pictorial genres in a hierarchical fashion (with history painting at the top and portraiture nearer to the bottom).[2] Much later, in the 1840s, Ruskin ultimately celebrated Veronese's daringly close combination of sacred figures and portraits in the painting, but still noted its capacity 'at first to shock, with its seeming irreverence, a spectator accustomed to the formalities and abstractions of the so-called sacred schools'.[3]

Veronese did attempt to maintain visual decorum by limiting the interaction of the family members with one another and

34 Veronese, *Supper at Emmaus*, 1555–60, oil on canvas.

turning their gazes away from Christ and his apostles, who are, in accordance with Renaissance compositional norms, placed at the picture centre, in a stronger light. The family are not quite allowed to occupy the same spatial or temporal zone as the Holy protagonists, even if they – or at least the adults and older children – seem to contemplate the sacred meaning of the event in their minds. These aspects indicate Veronese's close awareness of the visual conventions delimiting the depiction of donors in sacred paintings. But he nonetheless pushes against these accepted decorums in details such as the young man to the left, certainly a donor portrait, who is permitted to participate in the historical scene as a second servant at the table where Christ sits. The nobleman mimics the plate-offering action of the lowly woman to his left, who is placed in still closer proximity to Christ. She too might just be a disguised portrait of one of the family's retainers: her posture, with humble downward glance, bears analogy with that of the old servant depicted by Giustiniana's side at the Villa Barbaro (illus. 29). Like her noble master who emulates her serving at table in a demonstration of humility defined through class inversion, she is a liminal figure who traverses the gap between past and present, sacred and secular, non-portrait and portrait.[4]

It is possible that the family depicted are *terraferma* aristocrats, but it is just as likely that they are Venetian patricians, given that Veronese was busy aligning the identities of these nobilities.[5] As in his individual portraits of leading patricians, Veronese carefully acknowledges the social aspirations of his patrons, although here the emphasis falls on their closeness to God, rather than their courtly credentials. The underlying suggestion is that the place where Christ and his two disciples have stopped for the night is the family's own grand palazzo, rather than the humble country inn indicated in Luke's gospel. The *all'antica* facade is generic in kind but might still suggest their home, its massive, fluted columns echoing and monumentalizing their figures. Such an extended self-display is justified, in the terms of the image, by Christ's visit to them, indicating both their hospitality and their piety. But insofar as the painting is seen as a religious narrative then the inclusion of the family was novel enough.[6] Their prominent presence was almost certainly dependent on the original display of the painting in the secular and private context of the family's home – probably in the *portego* or main living space of the palace – rather than in a church.[7]

If the *Supper at Emmaus* does indeed feature a Venetian noble family, then it offered them an extended visibility in the field of religious painting that paid little heed to the traditionally more self-effacing values of the patriciate. Veronese's willingness to elevate or flatter his sitters was not, though, narrowly confined to this particular social caste. In a later work, certainly made as a *quadro da portego* for a private palace in Venice, he depicted a family of Bergamese wool merchants who had only arrived in Venice in the 1540s and were particularly intent on integrating themselves into the city's ruling social elites (illus. 35).[8] The immigrant Cuccina family had achieved naturalized 'citizen' (*cittadino*) status in Venice, but Veronese's depiction of them gathered before the Virgin and Child owed more to patrician prototypes, especially to the long tradition of votive portraits in a horizontal format, typically showing doges and their wives, the earliest of which dates to the mid-fourteenth century.[9] Although Veronese's painting is deliberately archaic in its processional presentation, its imagery is more informal, personalized and domesticated than many of its precursors. The Cuccina are shown visiting their altar in the sacristy of the fashionable church of San Francesco della Vigna, where Veronese had already completed an altarpiece for them. Their new palace on the Grand Canal, Ca' Cuccina, appears at the background right.[10]

As in the *Supper at Emmaus*, certain conventional distinctions are maintained, with the Cuccina shown as divided from the

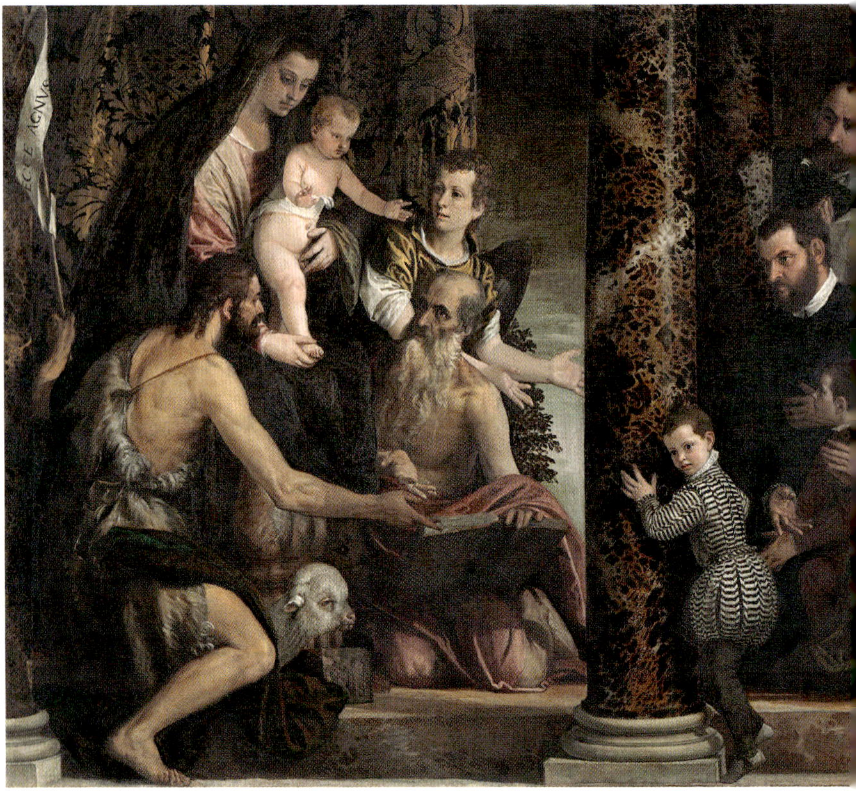

sacred figures – the Virgin and Child with St John the Baptist, St Jerome and an angel – to the left by two polychrome columns. But this seems like a mere nod in the direction of a now outmoded moral scrupulousness about the separateness of the sacred and secular worlds. The sumptuous marble columns speak not only of the sacredness of those to the left, but of the material *richezza* of the adoring family. The three theological Virtues, Faith (in white), Hope (in green) and Charity (in red), are visitors from the unseen spiritual world, but they move freely among the Cuccina and could easily be mistaken for family retainers. The

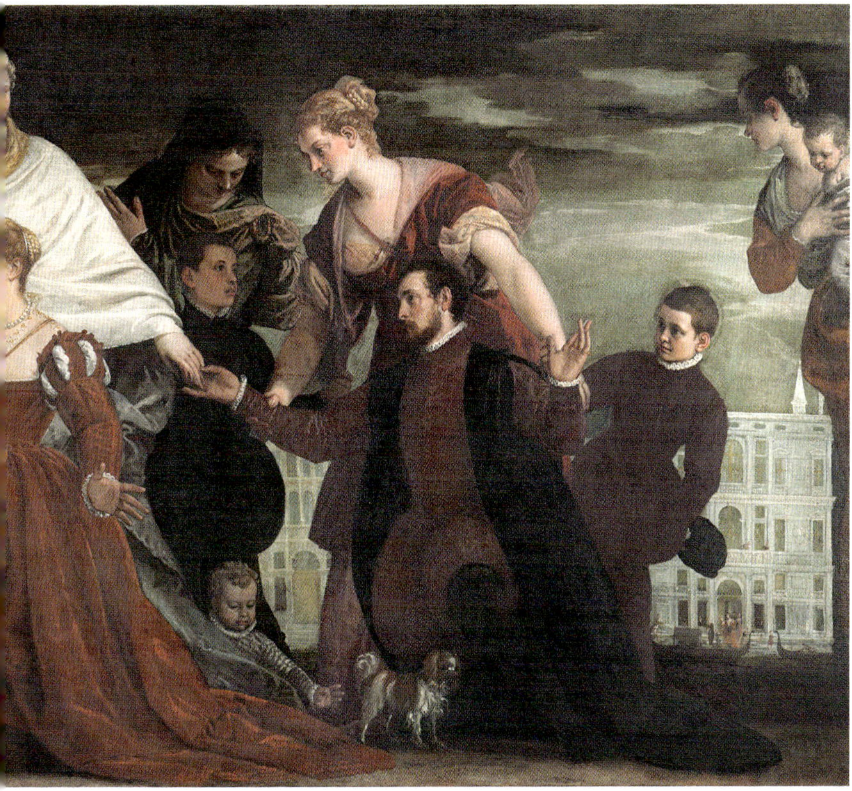

Holy figures themselves are crowded into a narrow space to the left, taking up no more than a third of the picture space, and are less likely to catch the viewer's eye than those who worship them. In this way, Veronese mitigates the more hierarchical and ritualistic arrangement of the patrician votive painting, introducing his trademark figural overlaps, sudden movements and distracting visual asides. His usual equality of treatment between adults and children, already so apparent in the *Supper at Emmaus*, is evident once more. The younger scions are again shown as innocently oblivious of the seriousness of the devotions they partake in, but

35 Veronese, *The Cuccina Family Presented to the Virgin and Child with St John the Baptist and St Jerome*, c. 1571, oil on canvas.

are also carefully individualized, their spontaneous movements and distractions further humanizing the scene. Spotting them also becomes part of the visual game, and it is easy enough to miss one son or another. There are seven boys depicted in all, including Giambattista, the baby held by the serving woman at the extreme right, who might also be a second personification of the presiding virtue of Charity, in its more active guise as *amor proximi*.[11]

Veronese lays particular emphasis on the family matriarch, Zuanna di Mutti, who takes centre stage, the dominance of her resplendent figure recalling that of Giustiniana Barbaro at Maser.[12] Placed at the picture centre, Zuanna wears an expensive red satin dress with silk sleeves, fashionably slashed at the shoulder, her blonde head set off against the pale robe of the figure of 'Faith' just behind her. By comparison, her husband, Alvise Cuccina, is partially hidden by the press of children, while one of her brothers-in-law, Zuan'Antonio, is reduced to peering out from behind a column. The other, Antonio, is consigned to the rear of the group, where his pious gesture is controlled by another dominant woman (Charity, probably in the form of *amor Dei*).[13] This arrangement reflects the underlying control of the Virgin herself, with the female figures (including Zuanna) appearing like mirroring emanations of her virtuous influence. But the displacement of the usual male authority figures within the painting is striking enough, offering a sharp contrast to the usual dominance of men in more recent patrician votive paintings, such as Titian's *Vendramin Family* (1540–60, London, National Gallery) in which the women of the family are excluded altogether.[14]

This might be a reflection of the non-noble status of the immigrant family depicted, whose social values may have been less closely dictated by stringent patrician patriarchalism. But women and children already outnumber their adult male counterparts in Veronese's *Supper at Emmaus*, which probably features a Venetian patrician family. At the Villa Barbaro, female figures are, as we have seen, similarly dominant, even if the patrons were two powerful men.[15] Perhaps the determining factor was Veronese's special readiness to develop 'feminine' aspects within his pictorializing style, above and beyond close considerations of iconography or social class: a tendency to which we will soon have cause to return. The discussion above in any case indicates that Veronese played a leading role in the spread of painting beyond the established sphere of public art in churches and other institutions into the more personalized, family – and feminine – domain of private palazzi and villas. Veronese's pictorial innovations in the works discussed above were encouraged by the original home-based context of the commissions, even if these large-scale, multi-figured and spectacularly pictorial productions also contributed to the publicly orientated display culture of Venice.[16] Veronese's approach only superficially privatizes the traditional reserved domain of the sacred image, given that it makes visible in painting an inner domestic world that had traditionally been excluded from the wider cultural purview.

TWO ALTARPIECES FROM THE MID-1560S

In the mid-1560s Veronese returned to Verona, completing two important altarpieces for the church of San Giorgio in Braida. On the same visit, he re-established his earlier professional and personal bonds with his hometown, marrying the 24-year-old Elena Badile, daughter of his recently deceased one-time master, Antonio. In 1566 Veronese moved to a larger rented house on the Salizada San Samuele in Venice, to accommodate his bride and with their future offspring in mind. The couple went on to have five children over the next thirteen years, two of whom – Gabriele (1568–1630) and Carlo, known as Carletto (1570–1596) – were subsequently trained as painters in their father's workshop at San Samuele. Paolo's marriage to Elena rather than a Venetian woman tells us that he had not lost contact or rejected the more artisanal world of his pre-Venetian past in his maturity, and that he sought to maintain continuity and consistency between the Veronese and Venetian sides of his personal and professional identity.

In the *Martyrdom of St George* (illus. 36) for the High altar of San Giorgio, Veronese – not for the first time – drew on Tintoretto's *Miracle of the Slave*. As in that work, the earthbound pagan figures lack any awareness of the airborne sacred ones above them. A passive, pious and pale semi-naked Christian body is contrasted with the mobile, swarthy forms of those around it, with the presiding ruler placed high to the right.[17] Like Tintoretto's similarly unclothed slave, Veronese's saint is uninjured, but in his work the executioners' aggressive attempts to violate it are downplayed. One merely holds up an emblematic sword, another is busy with George's armour, while a third moves up close to his body in an oddly intimate embrace as he begins to remove the martyr's underclothes. Veronese relocates the scene to an earlier moment, just before the martyrdom itself. This was in keeping with his typical deflection or avoidance of the climax to the story: his preference for visual intimation, or the mere suggestion of a key event that remains unrepresented. Veronese instinctively turned away from bodily desecration or from showing writhing flesh being hacked or limbs being broken, with their inevitable appearances of physical ugliness or distortion.

This entailed a departure from Titian's two great altarpieces featuring saintly martyrdom for the Venetian churches of Santi Giovanni e Paolo and the Crociferi.[18] Both these works feature the very moment of the violent murder of the given saint, whose body is shown fallen and supine as the executioners complete their grisly job. Veronese, on the contrary, stilled the action, maintaining an underlying sense of the picture as a self-sustained visual spectacle. Current suffering is deferred in favour of future

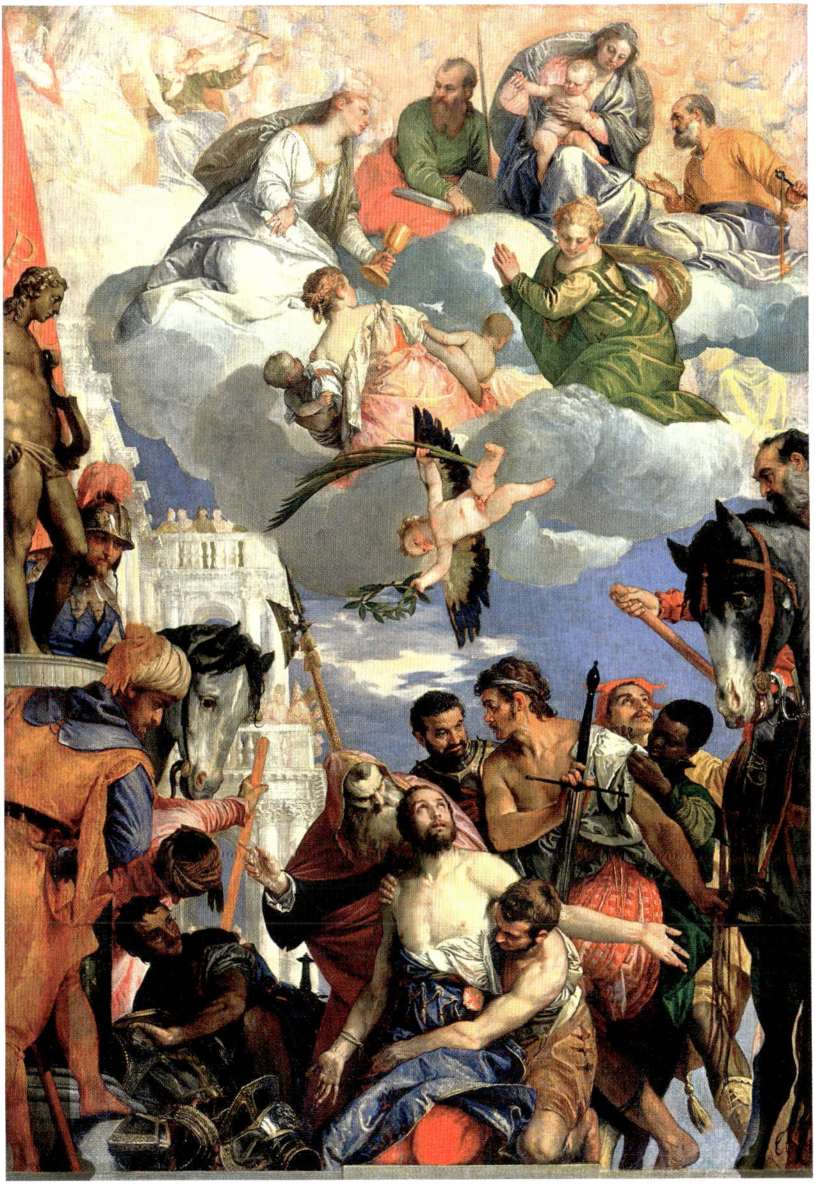

36 Veronese, *Martyrdom of St George*, *c.* 1565, oil on canvas.

triumph through the promise of the saint's everlasting life in heaven, quite explicitly depicted in the upper part of the picture where the Virgin and Child, Sts Peter and Paul and the three Theological Virtues disport themselves. Henry James described Veronese's works as essentially 'joyous' and as underwritten by a sense of life 'as a kind of breezy festival'.[19] And this is the case in the *St George*, which manages to present a positive effect even as the saint's torture and death is imminent. Veronese might be understood as substituting Titian's tragic mode in his later works for one closer to the comedic, at least insofar as there will be a happy outcome, as the greatly extended heavenly caste above indicates, while an angel swoops down to award a laurel crown and martyr's palm.[20] The spilling of the saint's blood soon to come may be indicated by the scarlet of his pantaloons, and more obviously by the enormous sword, but in the moment actually depicted all remains suspended, the immediate dark future of mutilation and death made a matter of mere suggestion.

This approach is common enough in many of Veronese's narrative paintings in which the picture is presented as if it were a pleasing or improved alternative or substitute for a more troubling story. Veronese's habit of narrative deflection also heightens the theatrical effect of his paintings, generating possibilities for meaningful hints, implications and suggestions.[21] It allows him to present his painting as an achieved or finished composition in its own right, rather than as a *non-finito* momentary snapshot, driven by sudden and unanticipated violent action, as in Tintoretto's *Miracle of the Slave* or Titian's *St Peter Martyr*.[22] Veronese was discomforted by 'the event', preferring relatively static scenes that take on an out-of-time quality, removed from all that is temporally adventitious or contingent. Sudden or unexpected happenings are downplayed within a restabilized visual *mise en scène*. In the current example, we have no doubt about the given subject-matter depicted. But as we have already seen, this approach could lead to difficulties in establishing what story is shown, or the precise moment within it that we witness.[23]

It is not that the subject is forgotten or overridden, exactly, and the iconographers are right to note Veronese's oblique but persistent references to his given theme. The saint's turn away from the pagan image of Apollo to the upper left in the *St George*, despite the priest's attempt to make him worship it, is significant enough; his open-armed, self-abnegating posture makes a sharp contrast with the sensuous, self-contained *contrapposto* of the statue. The bodies of Apollo and the saint set in train a series of thematic contrasts between hard metal and soft flesh, art and nature, pride and humility, pagan and Christian. George's gesture is rhetorically anti-classical, its cruciform a reflection of Christ's posture on the cross, and thus quite deliberate in a theological sense.[24] The 'joyous' or triumphal tone of the picture might easily be seen as apposite to the theme, with its promise of salvation through Christ-like self-sacrifice. It is nonetheless visuality rather than iconography that sustains Veronese's mode. The painter's emphasis on his supporting cast is also significant in this regard. His stock extras – armoured soldiers and henchmen, a Muslim man, a black page and even a court jester – are in close attendance. The last, dressed in a fool's garb, glances upwards, and is thus the only earthbound figure other than the saint who has any idea of the presence of the Christian heaven above, even if his troubled face suggests that he cannot understand what he sees.

The main figures, such as the pagan priest and the exotic horseman-ruler, play their parts to perfection, such that it becomes hard simply to condemn them for their paganism. This may encourage a response that is not just or even primarily based on deep religious emotion, or respectful conformity to the external ritual function of the work within the Eucharistic mass. The pictorial presentation admits another register of aesthetic response, allowing for or even promoting the viewer's continued formal interest in the diverting details that organize the picture beyond its ideological message. The stage-set horses, featuring those Veronesian doe eyes and friendly, communicative expressions, are knowingly fictive creatures, elegantly doffing their thoroughbred heads to maintain an air of playfulness and jubilation. The way in which the multifarious torsos and heads of George's would-be tormentors explode outwards from the saint's own is a visual conceit that recalls Veronese's ludic approach to overlapping forms in works such as the *Anointing of David* (illus. 13, 14). Even the saturated intensity of the pigments in the lower foreground area seem about to trump the given theme, offering as they do a colouristic feast for the eye. Such visual exuberance might even seem to border on the inappropriate, from a strictly pious point of view.

In a second altarpiece for the church, showing the *Miracle of St Barnabas*, Veronese modulated his pictorially enriched style in the High altarpiece towards a less colourful, triumphal or secular mode, drawing again on Tintoretto, but this time paying careful attention to his rival's moralizing and heroizing depictions of the poor (illus. 37). This more muted tone reflects the secondary position of the painting in the church: it hung on the left wall, under the organ, and its relatively sombre imagery must also reflect the role of the commissioning Secular Canons in the administration of a hospital dedicated to St Barnabas.[25] Veronese had already turned to Tintoretto when he needed to depict *poveri* in works such as the *Feast in the House of Simon* of 1556 (illus. 41) and the *Pool of Bethesda* of 1560 on the organ shutters (open position) at San Sebastiano. At the background right of the *Barnabas*, he drew on a foreshortened figure of a lame man carried by a helper, with bent knees raised and together, that he had seen in a Tintoretto altarpiece in Vicenza.[26] The influence of Veronese's immediate rival in Venetian painting is, however, offset by the studied Romanism of this new work, despite the fact that the miracle shown occurred

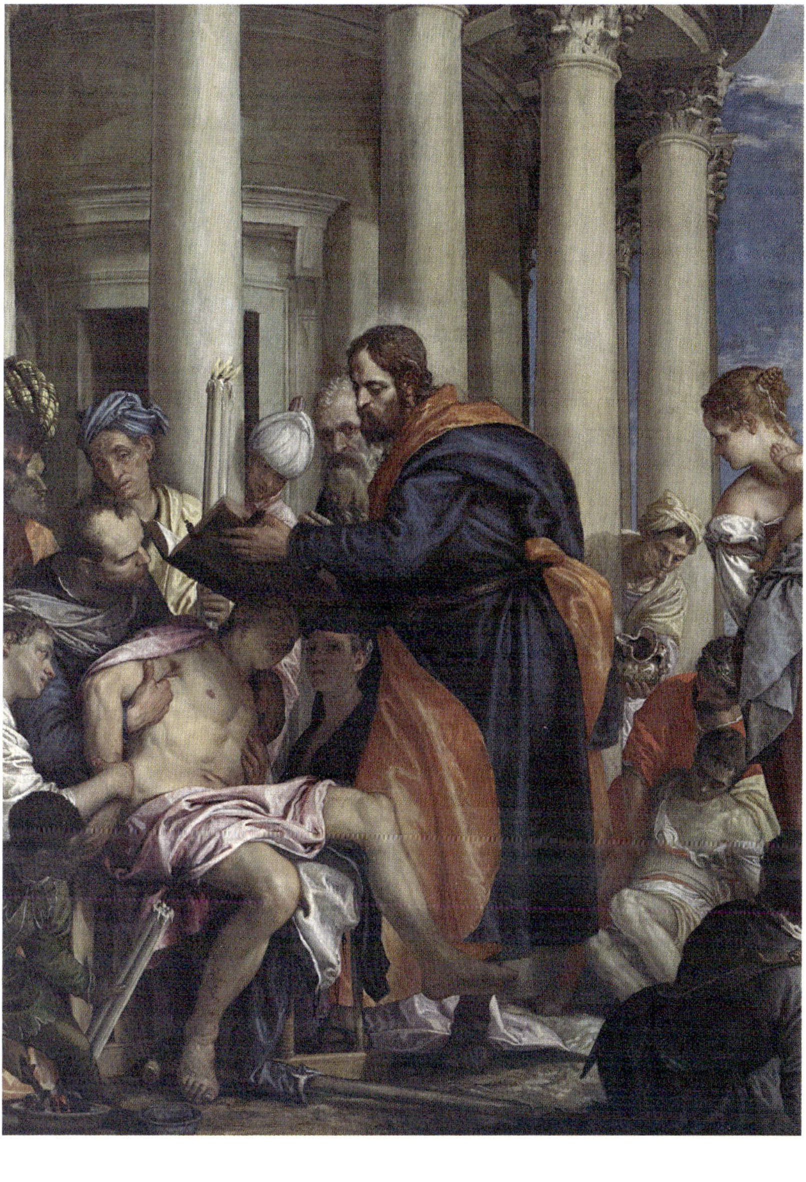

37 Veronese, *Miracle of St Barnabas*, c. 1565–6, oil on canvas.

in Cyprus. The circular building might recall Bramante's Tempietto in Rome but (as usual) draws more closely on architectural models that the painter had seen closer to home.[27]

The figures of the saint and the man he cures in the foreground are also intensely Raphaelesque, reprising the painter's tapestry cartoon of the *Healing of the Lame Man* (*c.* 1515–16, London, Victoria and Albert Museum), probably known to Veronese through a Parmigianino print after it of circa 1530. But the body of the sick man, healed by the mere touch of the saint's Bible, is carefully improved or beautified away from this model, taking on the characteristics of an ideal *all'antica* nude. Veronese decorously separated this fallen figure from the saint by way of the huge Bible that casts the former's head into shadow. Yet he also paid close visual attention to the sick man's body, carefully modelling his flesh, while saving his modesty by the addition of softly painted and classicized drapery. A surviving black chalk drawing provides further evidence of the painter's equalizing interest in this *povero*, perhaps even beyond his concern with the figure of Barnabas himself.[28] But rather than a life study, the drawing reveals Veronese's dependence on another classical Roman source: the late antique sculpture of the *Falling Gaul*, then on display in Venice in the Grimani Collection.[29]

The beautification of this foreground figure contradicts the otherwise sombre or muted tone of the altarpiece, focused as it is on Christian Good Works and the moral necessity of charitable succour to the poor. Drawing attention to itself as a virtuoso passage of painting, the elaborate treatment of the *povero* reasserts Veronese's own artistic mastery and control, demonstrating his abilities in the emulation of revered antique models. It also indicates his unexpected interest in figures from the social margins: one to which we will soon have cause to return. Lower still in the picture space than the sick man, a Black boy appears holding a candle which he is about to light from some hot coals.[30] Like many other of the sick and their selfless helpers depicted in this work, the boy's body is intersected by the frame, so that he appears to be half in and half out of the painting. His visual marginality in this way echoes his position in society itself. But a second surviving drawing demonstrates again Veronese's particular visual concern with even the least important figures in his composition (illus. 38).[31] Using black chalk with enlivening touches of red at the cheek, lips, ears and neck, and heightened with white lead, this drawing focuses solely on the boy's head, intensifying his expression, while also humanizing and individualizing him in a manner not granted to any other figure in the painting. It may be that the figure was included to provide a visual foil, his dark skin offsetting the pale flesh of the lame man nearby. But he was nonetheless the only one in the painting drawn directly from life.[32]

His depiction alerts us to the special importance of the accessory or secondary figures in Veronese's paintings. The painter probably saw the boy in Venice, where many enslaved or recently freed sub-Saharan Africans worked for noble families.[33] Seen in the context of the Christian miracle featured in Veronese's altarpiece we may take it that he has been, or is about to be, converted, like the others in the painting. In any case, he features as one of the charitable helpers of the sick, and thus is on the side of the worthy, the caring and the spiritually receptive. As the drawing in particular reveals, Veronese does not stereotype or distance the boy in racial terms. The latter is very unlikely to have given his permission to be drawn, and we seem to look down on him from a higher, superior, viewpoint. But then again, he also possesses an energic presence, suggesting his independent inner life. Veronese carries this approach across from his depiction of the children of the nobility in his portraiture, who are allowed a similarly vitalizing freedom from the more socially constrained domain of their parents. In any case, Veronese's equalizing of

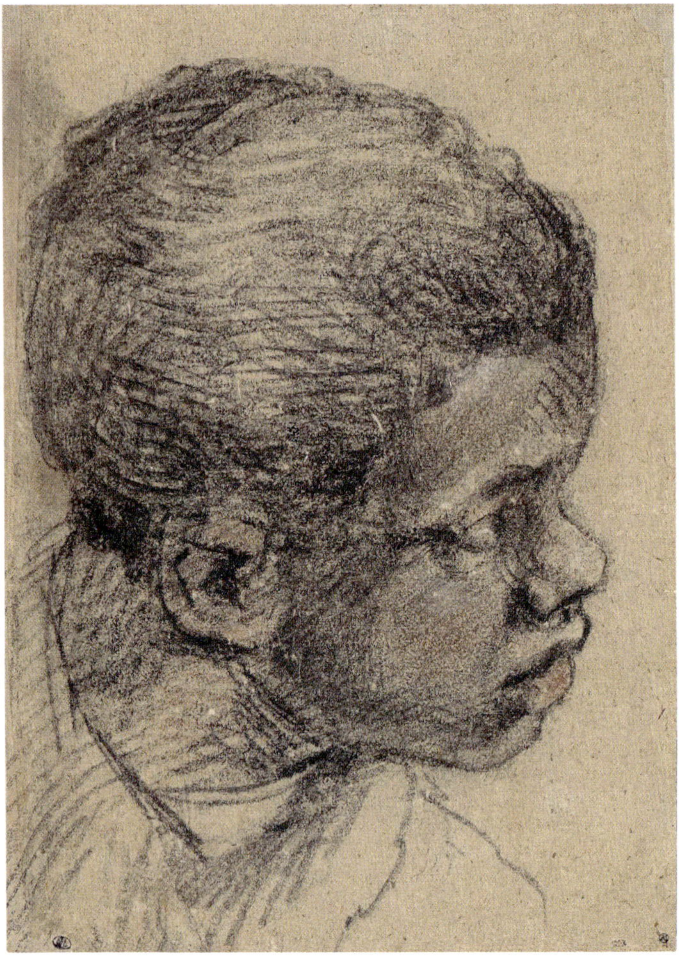

attention to his pictorial actors suggested the need to move beyond the established judgements and distinctions commonly made in the non-pictorial world. His approach makes the visual redemption of socially marginal subjects, where they are included, something of a working necessity.

38 Veronese, *Head of a Black Boy*, *c.* 1565–6, red chalk and charcoal with white highlights on paper.

MYSTIC MARRIAGE OF ST CATHERINE

In a further altarpiece from the later 1560s for the Venetian church of Santa Caterina, the impact of Titian's Pesaro altarpiece can still be felt, even if it is now made secondary to Veronese's penchant for compositional planarity and visual opulence (illus. 39). Two enormous fluted columns rise to the left of the painting, while the Virgin and Child sit on some steps leading up to them. Closely overlapping figures are now pressed into a narrow foreground space, their forms conjoined by a lavish spread of richly coloured patterned fabrics disposed across the picture surface. Veronese's horizontalizing and processional arrangement, featuring a chosen heroine ascending some steps towards an enthroned and ruling authority figure beneath a grand entrance to be crowned or blessed, had already featured at San Sebastiano (illus. 17), and he subsequently returned to this visual schema (albeit with variations) in several important pictures of the 1570s and '80s (illus. 56, 58, 68). In the *Mystic Marriage*, Veronese amalgamates different visual sources, *all'antica* and Christian, secular and sacred, to generate his characteristic effect of lush materiality. Certain of the angels' heads, with mask-like expressions, Roman noses and tightly curled hair, are clearly modelled on antique sculptures, while the risers of the steps are carved with an acanthus scroll design based closely on the painter's study of surviving classical reliefs in Verona.[34] The fluting of the columns and the intricately carved Corinthian capital glimpsed above one of them further classicizes the scene. Yet the position of the seated figure of the Virgin at the entrance to the building suggests her authority over it. She should be understood as the *Sedes Sapientiae* (Seat of Wisdom) and as the foundation of the Mother Church, identified as the building before which she sits.[35] Perhaps, too, the inclusion of the two massive columns serves to recall her Immaculate Conception, as they more certainly did in Titian's Pesaro altarpiece.

In this work, the appearances of the actors are made pointedly similar, making it hard to detect differences between the heavenly or sacred figures to the left and the earthly or secular ones to the right. This effect is most evident in the key figures of the Virgin and Catherine. Although their gazes are not allowed to meet, suggesting a decorous difference between divine and mortal, they appear as mirror images, their shared physical beauty and unfocused, impassive expressions making them appear as close reflections of one another. The act of crowning the saint was, after all, typologically linked to the crowning of the Virgin herself as the Queen of Heaven (see illus. 16). According to the theological scheme, the arrival of Catherine's heavenly crown means that her earthly one will become superfluous. The putti also bring her a palm of martyrdom, intimating the end of her life on Earth. But Veronese, as was his want, depicted the moment just *before* the landing of her new attributes, so that Catherine currently remains as the royal princess of Alexandria, wearing her original crown with her secular authority and worldly dignity still in place. Veronese is keen to draw the two contrasting domains of heavenly and earthly life, shown to left and right, into an intimate alliance, so that they become almost indistinguishable in visual terms. The scintillating handling of the fashionable draperies worn by the princess makes her appear as a finely dressed Venetian patrician woman of the present day. But the contrast with the timeless and unearthly figure of the Virgin that this might have generated is compromised. Although the latter wears her conventional and historical colours, the surface of her lower drapery takes on something of the silken sheen of Catherine's own, its royal blue flecked with fashionable gold to make it appear as a contemporary manufactured fabric. The overlap is restated in the two singing angels at the lower left who, although part of the Virgin's heavenly court rather than the earthly one of the princess, spill over onto the steps below. The expensively finished drapery of the foremost one is enriched with gold threads over silver silks, forging a close visual correspondence with the saint's dress displayed to view nearby.[36]

It might be that in establishing these overlaps Veronese responded to a Counter-Reformatory concern to re-establish an intimate relationship between outward visual or material richness and inward spiritual values that had been attacked by the Protestants.[37] But they also flattered his patrons: women from high-ranking patrician families who would have been happy enough to equate their wealth with heavenly values. The closeness of aristocratic life to heaven is anyway a favoured Veronesian theme, reflecting sensitivity to his patrons' notion that the social order that they ruled over was a close reflection of the divine one beyond. We must also acknowledge the possibility that Veronese's pictures accordingly reduce the world to an iterative set of 'noble actions', whether between high-ranking aristocrats themselves or between mortal and divine figures, as one elegant person bows down before another, more exalted than themselves, and by so doing is accepted into their still higher realm. Within the circular and self-enclosed semantic terms of these ennobling interchanges the usual boundaries between secular and sacred meanings become especially porous. In the *Mystic Marriage*, however, powerful women are once again allowed to dominate proceedings. Admittedly, it is the tiny figure of the infant Christ who has most narrative agency in the picture: he has already slipped a ring onto Catherine's finger, and with his raised arm gestures upwards towards the winged putti bringing her new heavenly gifts. But other than the sandalled page at the extreme right, he is the only male presence in the entire painting.

Veronese's feminization of the conventionally male-dominated space of an altarpiece in the *Mystic Marriage* must, in the first place, reflect his patronage by the Augustinian nuns of Santa Caterina.[38] But in Veronese's previous versions of this subject men play a similarly reduced role, perhaps suggesting that this owed more

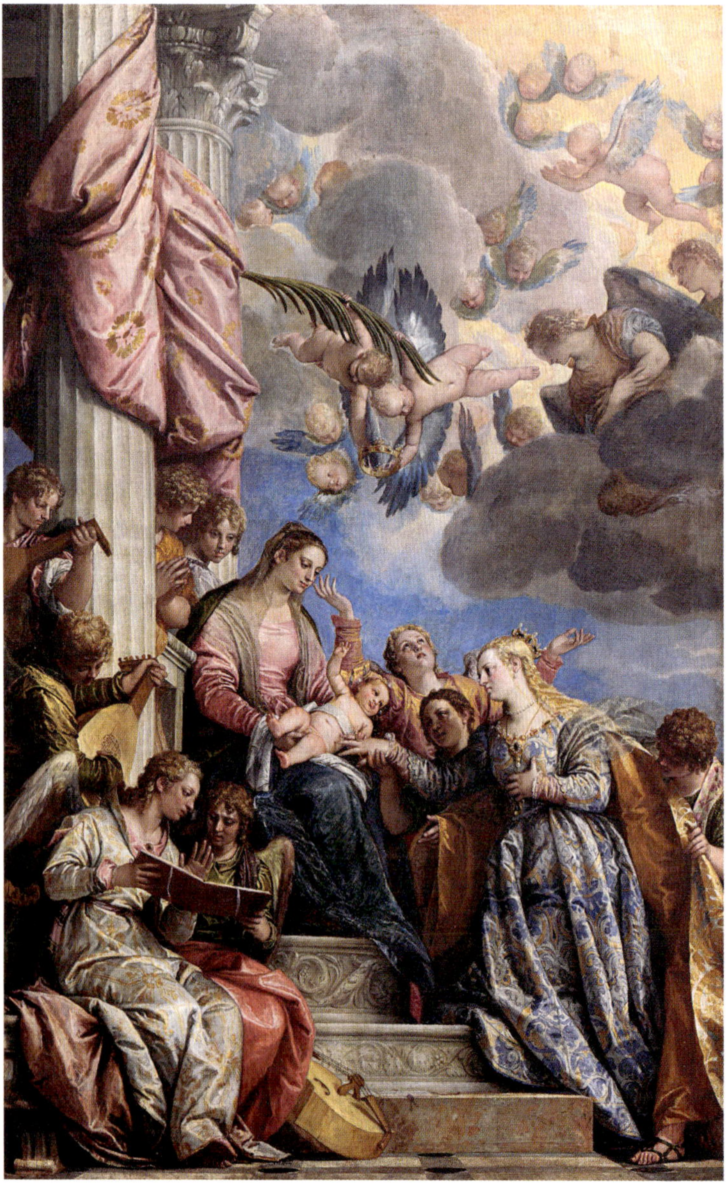

39 Veronese, *Mystic Marriage of St Catherine*, 1565–70, oil on canvas.

to the painter's own predilections than to the gender of his patrons.[39] In the altarpiece, Veronese offers an all-over effect of visual sumptuousness, but this does not distract the viewer's attention from Catherine's dominating figure: she has complexly and fashionably braided hair, and wears fine jewellery, while the flowing golden train of her dress is held out by her page to maximize our view of the garment as it spreads out across the picture surface. It does not seem necessary for her to give up her previous worldliness just yet, as she commits herself to Christ. Ridolfi had another (now lost) work in mind when he criticized the failure of one order of Venetian nuns to appreciate Veronese's fluid handling in a painting of Paradise that they had commissioned.[40] These women, we hear, had Veronese's work replaced by a more meticulously or minutely finished one by a visiting Flemish painter. But this misogynist tale, highlighting the female patrons' charlatan dislike of Veronese's style, arrived at second hand, recycled as it was from a passage in a mid-sixteenth-century book reporting Michelangelo's equation of closely imitative Flemish art with ignorant women.[41] Ridolfi placed his anecdote just after his account of the Santa Caterina altarpiece, perhaps indicating his discomfiture about the imagery in that work, in which two high-ranking queenly women dominate. However that might be, there is no evidence to suggest that Veronese's patrons were unhappy with their altarpiece: a work which so carefully symbolized their own values and aspirations as the chosen brides of Christ. Veronese's socially elite patrons would have especially appreciated Veronese's revisitation of the worldly lavishness they had given up after taking their vows. But while there might thus have been a compensatory aspect to his imagery, its very *richezza* of effect would equally have spoken to them of the new kingdom of heaven that they now embraced.

FINDING OF MOSES: A CONVERSATION PIECE

In an intimately scaled and conceived religious painting, dating from a decade or so after the *Mystic Marriage*, Veronese brilliantly demonstrated his ability to modulate or transpose his monumental, flamboyant and expansive visual style into a different key (illus. 40). His informal and pastoral approach in this sacred work is closer to the one he developed in his mythologies (discussed in Chapter Five). As in many of these secular productions, Veronese abandoned his massive stage-set architecture, setting the scene instead on a woody riverbank, to generate a relaxed poetic effect. The painting is more fluidly handled than in his large-scale religious works, with some extraordinarily virtuosic passages, whether one considers the briefly sketched city-view of (probably) Verona and the Adige at the background left, or the masterly depiction of the fall of light on the princess's silver and yellow satin dress. In this work, a cast of hired underlings is granted a significant role in generating the narrative. It is the interplay between these lowly and secondary figures within the princess's royal train that creates the key effect of courtly casualness or *sprezzatura*.[42]

When working on a reduced scale, Veronese becomes especially attentive to nuances of facial expression and bodily posture. In this work, the attendants are shown to be on particularly intimate and immediate terms with their mistress. A Black servant appears in a similar position to the *St Barnabas* boy at the lower left, although he now carries a picnic hamper rather than a candle and has become a grown man. His sensitive face peers across at the initially hostile response of the court dwarf opposite to the new-found baby. The man's dark profile head, answering that of the dwarf, is especially responsive, individualized and portrait-like, suggesting engagement and understanding. His response to the finding of the baby is not clear but may contrast with that of the dwarf. But even if this latter figure is childishly disturbed by the appearance of the sacred baby, Veronese's integration of his person into the narrative also remains significant, granting him emotional and therefore psychological dimensions that go beyond the usually more clownish role allowed to such anomalous social types. Dwarves, like other physically different people, were often kept at court in Veronese's period to provide a contrast with the dominant and normative figures, and as such could be treated as distorted or monstrous 'others'. Even if not, they were often seen as child-like or 'childish', rather than as adults, and thus as suitable playmates for aristocratic children.[43] But in Veronese's painting we are asked to allow that the small man's surprised and suspicious response to the finding of the baby is human enough. If he is initially conflicted – he might be replaced in his mistress's affections – then it is likely that he will listen to and understand the solicitous words of the lady-in-waiting nearby, who gently touches his shoulder to assure him that all will be well.

This secondary chain of reactions leads into the main interchange a little beyond, as five women gather around the young princess to explain to her the wisdom of accepting a new role as an adoptive mother.[44] It is not clear who all these encircling women are. The one most intensely talking to the princess who gestures to the baby with her left hand might be Moses's sister, sometimes named Miriam, who offered to find a Hebrew woman as a wet nurse for the child. Compressing the narrative, Veronese might already show the older woman, who is about to swaddle the baby in a blanket, as Moses's mother. But the painter is in no hurry to make these identifications explicit or certain as the women come together around the baby in a unified protective wave of sympathy and concern. The servants know first and know best, sensing that something more than mere kindliness might be at stake. So much might also be implied by the way that the baby Moses levitates upside down for a moment while he is transferred from one woman to another, as if to defy gravity and reveal his divine origins. Due to Miriam's ruse, Moses will be initially brought up by his own

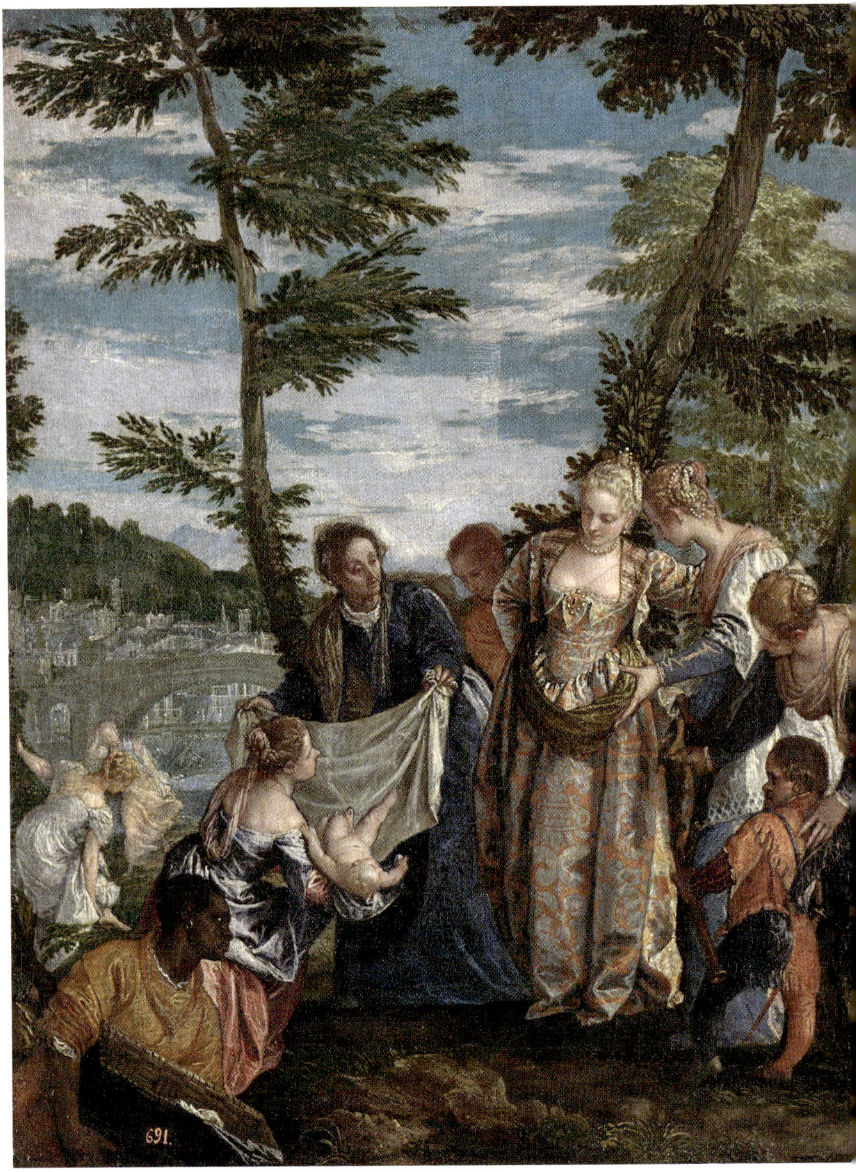

40 Veronese, *Finding of Moses*, 1575–80, oil on canvas.

Jewish mother. But he will eventually be passed on to the princess as her adoptive son. So much seems already to be apparent from her movement as she leans back with one hand on her hip in a matronly posture that expresses her readiness to take on a role that will mean laying aside certain of her royal privileges in the fulfilment of an onerous natural duty.[45]

There is little of the usual courtly pomp or etiquette depicted here. The bodily alterity of the Black servant and the dwarf is downplayed as they are integrated into the group, and thus into the story, while some, at least, of the retinue have laid aside their usual dignified restraint. The mysterious waif-like dancing girls enjoying the cool sensation of the water to the left, merely sketched in using free diaphanous brushwork, are no longer subject to outward show or the need to conform to the court behaviours. Some such departure from, or inversion of, expected roles and identities is central to the given biblical theme, as the daughter of a Pharoah is suddenly called on to set aside the cruel antisemitism of her father's decree, and to take on the duties of a surrogate mother. The possibility of a female-led escape from the oppressive hierarchy of patriarchally generated power, rank and decision-making is integral to Veronese's telling of the story.

FOUR

Biblical Feasts

Veronese's careful and respectful engagement with the sick poor and other socially marginal types in the *St Barnabas* altarpiece would seem to contradict his usual emphasis on joyous and carefree visual *richezza*. Yet in the earliest of his enormous paintings of biblical feasts for monastic refectories at least two lame *poveri* are present, even if their crumpled forms are confined within a narrow space to the left that appears to be separated off from the main scene (illus. 41).[1] As in the *St Barnabas*, Veronese's decision to include these marginal types was suggested by the given sacred subject-matter. The supper depicted – recorded in all four gospels – was held at the house of a man named by Luke as Simon the Pharisee, but by Matthew, Mark and John as Simon the Leper. This latter name might have encouraged Veronese's depiction of the sickly figures near the column. At this feast, Christ justified (against the objections of Judas) the Magdelene's use of expensive spikenard to anoint his feet, announcing that 'ye have the poor always with you, but me ye have not always.'[2] But in visual terms, Veronese's depiction of 'the poor' clustered beneath a darkened loggia follows a particular convention in Venetian painting initiated by Pordenone (*c.* 1483/4–1539) in a work from the plague-ravaged years of the late 1520s, when many desperate people congregated under the arcades in St Mark's Square.[3] Although Veronese delocalized his architectural setting in accordance with recent

Palladian models, the all-important foreground column is chipped and discoloured, bearing the polluting imprint of the unwashed marginal types who cluster around it (illus. 42).[4]

Despite the shadows, the marginal figures do not disappear readily from our view, their apparent visual seclusion contradicted by other aspects of the arrangement.[5] Their forms spill out beyond the loggia, the bandaged left foot of the semi-naked Lazarus-like beggar poking around the column towards the main scene, while (his?) dog has already moved beyond it and watches the unfolding drama intently.[6] Further back, the figure of a servant at the feast is cut in two by the column, his right hand and the basket he holds joining the space to its left, while his intently engaged head participates in the action to its right, as if he belonged half in one world and half in the other. The seated figure of Judas, dressed in pink, blue and yellow, turns towards the sprawling leper, pointing him

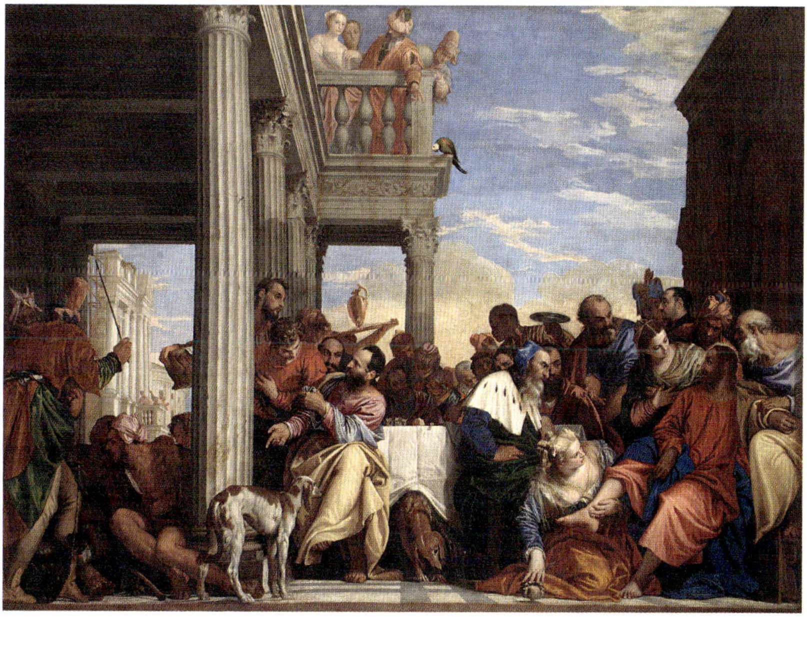

41 Veronese, *Feast in the House of Simon*, 1556, oil on canvas.

out to another servant, in response to the Magdalene's action. But not all of those under the loggia are desperate *poveri*. Ridolfi, writing in 1648, might have been right when identifying the two standing figures as 'mimes dressed in livery with monkeys, who come to entertain the guests'. In his view, these men thus become part of the 'pageantry and spectacle' of the painting.[7]

In contrast to the fallen semi-naked man nearby, these jaunty figures are physically fit: they sport performative particoloured fancy dress and eccentric headgear, responding jocularly to one another. The dark-skinned smiling figure further back holds a chained monkey, which has somehow found its way between the other man's legs, possibly with humorous or scurrilous connotations.[8] Monkeys, typically chained around the waist, as is the case here, are present in several other Veronese paintings: at the Villa Barbaro, one is depicted on the fictive balustrade in the Sala dell'Olimpo between portraits of the two elder Barbaro sons, directly opposite the creeping parrot depicted on their mother's side. The associations of monkeys and parrots with, respectively, lechery and virginity might seem only to make them contrast in symbolic terms. But these animals were similar insofar as they could both refer to imitative skills in art, and thus also serve as a self-reflexive comment on the painter's own mimetic performance. Kept as pets, such exotic creatures also formed part of the wider paraphernalia of courtly aristocratic life.[9] The same combination of monkey and parrot is already present in the *Feast* of 1556, where the bird perching high on the pediment above the main scene appears to have escaped its young female owner, as is angrily pointed out by her turbaned father, perhaps suggesting – via the parrot's association with the Virgin Mary – that her virginity has similarly flown away.[10]

The monkey at the bottom left might also indicate the unchaste qualities of its owners.[11] But if Ridolfi is correct, and these men are 'mimes', then their pet might just as easily serve as an attribute of their mimicking profession. The foreground man with his back turned raises a thin stick in his right hand, like a baton, as if he were beating time (rather than the leper below him, as is sometimes thought). His action implies that he is conducting music that no one else can hear. The suggestion is that these bizarre interactive entertainers will soon march further into the space beyond the column to amuse the guests with their playful silent mummery.[12] Their overlap with the main scene is indicated again by the presence of another Black servant, shown in striking silhouette, holding up a plate, towards the picture centre, where he attracts particular attention as one of the uppermost figures in the group. The mimes, on the other hand, are certainly placed close to the *poveri*, indicating their shared marginal position in social reality. But they also answer, in visual and symbolic terms, Christ's own position at the opposite corner of the picture. He, too, is shown as a shadowy figure towards the picture edges, as if to imply his identity with those beyond the column. The Magdalene, a former prostitute, whose left hand touches the flesh of Christ's lower leg so tenderly, is another of their representatives, as her kneeling posture, mirroring that of the fallen leper, seems to intimate. The viewer's eye switches constantly between the two domains, comparing the two opposing worlds of high and low, but understanding, in the process, their intimate linkage: the way that the one always seems to mimic the other. Veronese even goes as far as to revisit the colouration of Christ's red drapery, set against the nearby Martha's gauzy green, in the livery worn by the foremost figure at the far left, albeit that the latter's clothing is faded, tatty and threadbare by comparison. If the world of Veronese's grand feast scenes is always one of aristocratic wealth and privilege, then it is also dependent on the careful articulation of its opposite, so that the have-nots must be 'unfailingly there at the story's edge'.[13] Rather than providing a dingy foil to offset the *richezza* of the salubrious social world

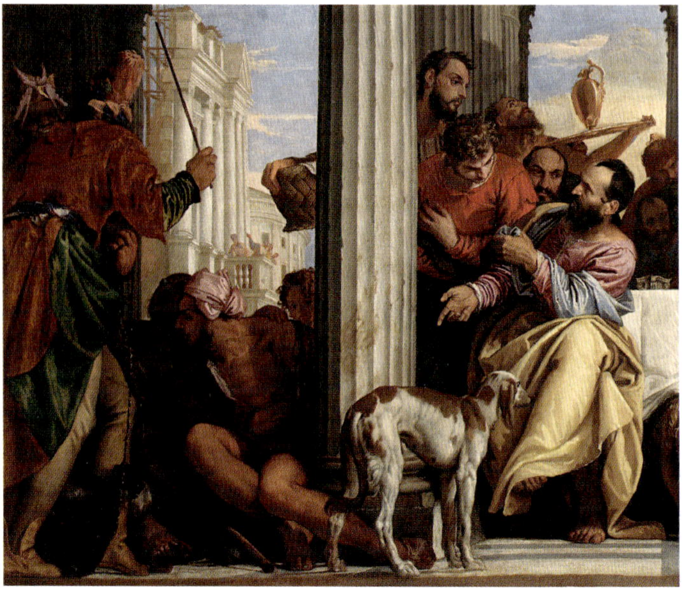

presented, they impinge more definitely upon it, becoming essential to its definition.

Veronese's banqueting world is anyway more populous than exclusive. As many as 24 people are crammed into the main area to the right of the column in the *Feast in the House of Simon*, squeezed into a characteristically compressed forward spatial plane. This was to continue his penchant for highly coloured and strongly lit relief-like compositions, in which multiple figures constantly interlink and overlap, generating difficult-to-read formal intersections and ellipses, with the presence of some indicated by the bare minimum of pictorial suggestion. Only six of these can be identified as text-derived biblical actors while almost half of the others are servants or attendants rather than guests. If Veronese was relatively constrained by his duties to the text in his depictions of 'the poor proper', drawing on earlier depictions of this worthy social type by Tintoretto, Pordenone and Bonifacio, he was more

42 Veronese, *Feast in the House of Simon*, detail.

himself when granted the freedom to imagine those, certainly low on the social spectrum, but not immediately in need of charity or succour. These types were more semantically fluid or ambiguous than the sick poor but were equally ubiquitous within the wider social world of the lower classes of Verona and Venice. As his great feast scenes amply demonstrate, Veronese was most at home when depicting those who serve, but not just with the aim of further displaying the wealth of their masters.[14]

THE SERVANTS KNEW: *MARRIAGE AT CANA*

According to John's gospel, the servants were the first to know about Christ's initial public miracle at a marriage feast at Cana, when he turned water into wine (John 2:9).[15] So much was perhaps inevitable, given that they had received direct instructions from him to fill six stone water-pots 'containing two or three firkins apiece' (John 2:5–8) and take them to the governor of the feast.[16] In Veronese's vast painting of this subject of 1562–3, painted to hang in the refectory of Palladio's new monastic church of San Giorgio Maggiore in Venice, servants – the non-guests, including a master of ceremonies, a sommelier, higher-ranking stewards, a clutch of musicians, several finely dressed Black page boys, a jester-dwarf with parrot, and a plethora of strong-armed labourers who take charge of the massive pots combine to dominate proceedings, and not just in numerical terms (illus. 43). It is true that Christ and the Virgin, dressed in their traditional historical robes, occupy the lower centre, having displaced the young married couple (shown as contemporary Venetian patricians) to the extreme left.[17] But it is nonetheless the typically highly mobile and visually attractive servants who generate the sense of ongoing and immediate life and energy at the feast. They predominate in the foreground front of the painting, as also in the raised area beyond the balustrade above, where their striking profiles are silhouetted against the billowing clouds in the sky.

Giorgio Vasari estimated in 1568 that Veronese had included more than 150 heads in this painting.[18] But fewer than thirty persons, including the Holy figures – Christ, his mother and several disciples – sit around the table as wedding guests proper.[19] Among these, some are certainly portraits, extending Veronese's habit of allowing contemporary figures to invade a scene from sacred history first developed in his recent *quadri da porteghi* (illus. 34).[20] By no means all of those shown as guests are Venetians and it may be that Veronese included depictions of the kind of 'exotic' foreigners who often visited the wealthy aristocratic monastery of San Giorgio. However this may be, beyond the Holy group few of the invitees are yet aware of what has happened. Many more of the 26 servants crowded into the immediate foreground area in front of the table – and thus closest to the viewer – are already aware of the transformation, if not of its deeper significance, given that they deal directly with the wine that has suddenly appeared in the huge containers. A posse of four of them, shown at the foreground left – the standing governor of the feast or major-domo resplendent in green silks; the equally lavishly attired dwarf with parrot; a Black page boy; and a lower servant manhandling one of the pots – indicate their awareness of the miracle from their urgent postures and looks of astonishment, as they present a glass of the new wine to the seated bridegroom. To the right, the silk-clad sommelier raises a glass to the light, like a priest raising the sacrament at the Eucharistic mass. If his upright and refined appearance as a connoisseur of good taste contrasts with that of the bending, bare-footed man pouring wine into a smaller vessel just to the right, then he (like the musicians nearby) remains part of the supportive retinue, extending upwards – in a social sense – our understanding of what it might mean to be a 'servant'. He perhaps already understands the deeper significance of what has just occurred.[21]

The academicians of the following centuries who complained about Veronese's visual excess must have had works like this one especially in mind, with its impression of almost limitless visual expansion, its myriad glittering manufactured surfaces, and its plethora of digressive vignettes and motifs. A random selection of these latter might include the bearded man, sometimes identified as the poet Pietro Aretino, doyen of Venetian literary and artistic culture, looking up at the two white roses thrown down to him by a young woman on a balcony at the upper right; a bored dinner guest picking her teeth towards the left; or a cat playfully attacking one of the all-important water-pots. But among those who have, in recent scholarship, become keen to save Veronese from the charge of superficiality, the *Cana* is quoted as a very model of pictorial decorum via the idea of 'ornament'.[22] Veronese's pictorial elaboration in this work, it is argued, should be understood as further elucidating and clarifying the given story, and thus as an ultimately 'decorous' response to the founding text itself. In an important article published in 1961, the Austrian émigré scholar Philipp Fehl explained that Veronese drew on Aretino's earlier literary expansion of John's sparse biblical account of the marriage in his popular *La Humanità di Cristo* (1535), even though this work had recently been put on the Venetian Index of Prohibited Books. Veronese, we hear, ornamented the subject in an analogous way to Aretino, and in a manner that was wholly 'in keeping with traditional exegesis'.[23]

Many passages in Veronese's *Cana*, however, have no basis in John's biblical account, or, for that matter, in Aretino's recent book. The painter's idea of pictorial *ornamento* was much closer to the notion of 'artistic licence': one derived from the pagan literary culture of Roman antiquity rather than the Christian tradition of biblical exegesis. In the *Cana*, Veronese's unrestrained pictorialism reaches a new level, his work presented as a totalizing image whose vast scale and scope reflects an epic effort of visualization

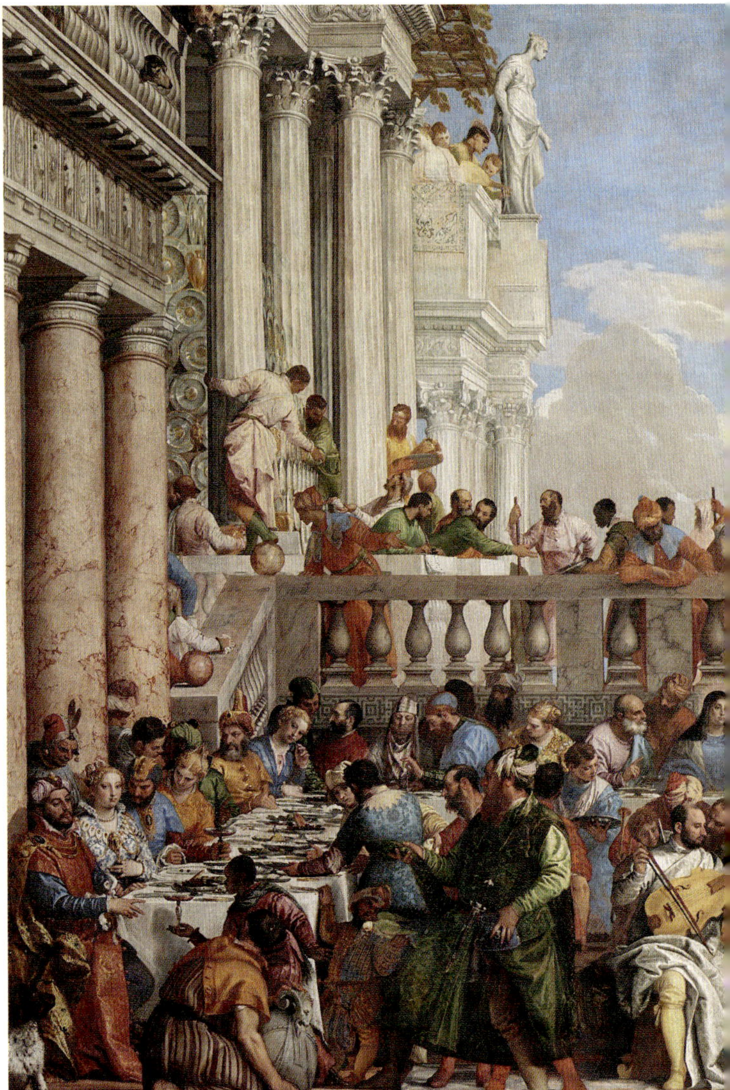

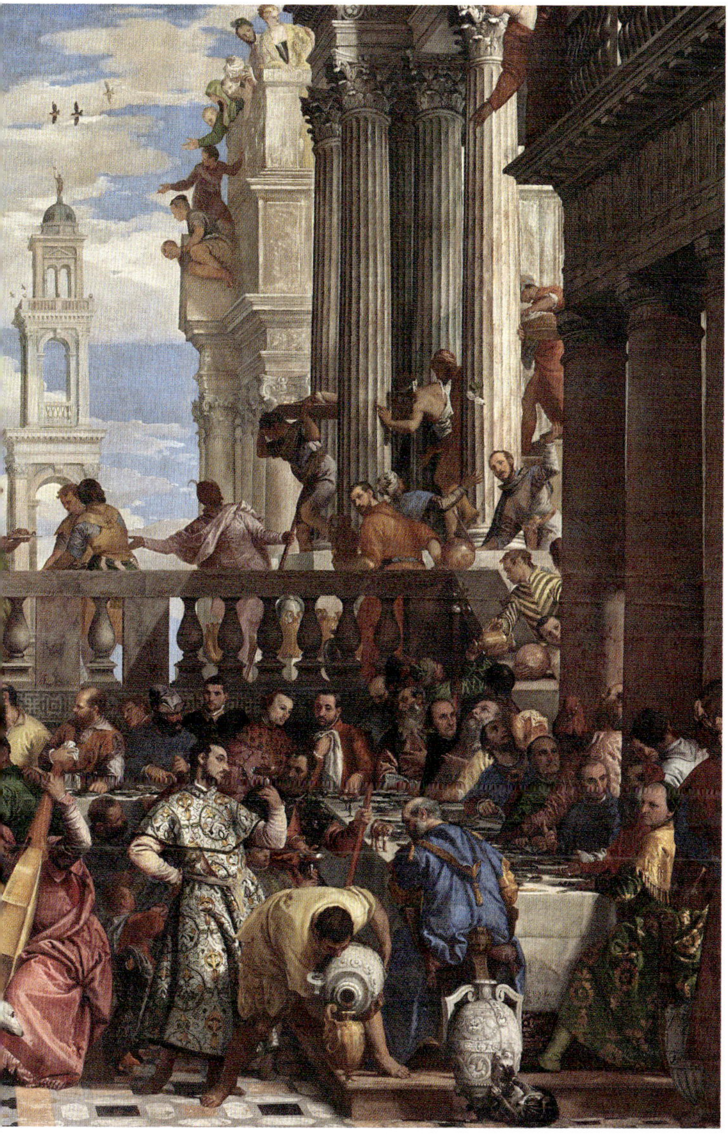

43 Veronese, *Marriage at Cana*, 1562–3, oil on canvas.

that makes it a convincing stand-in for the world itself. But just as this suggests the painter's essential independence from his textual sources, so too it indicates his move beyond strict adherence to the immediate physical realities beyond the frame. The *Cana* is a carefully fashioned and in certain ways self-sustaining work of art: a knowing visual fiction intended to serve as a pleasing substitute for real-world constraints, limitations or exclusions. Veronese's imagery may constantly suggest connection with what his viewer – in the first place imagined as a Benedictine monk, of aristocratic origin, sitting quietly at his meal in the refectory – already knows or has seen. But it just as insistently presents him with an expanded, more opulent and multi-sensual alternative reality.[24]

Veronese's approach to architecture in the painting is symptomatic of this effort of visual improvement, extension and substitution. It cannot be taken as an accurate reflection of the wider built environment of Venice, or even as making a close perspectival connection with the immediate space in Palladio's refectory. The painter was required by his Benedictine patrons to use the highest grade of ultramarine blue for the sky, which recalls the reflective luminosity of the waters of the lagoon. The pale dissolving light that softens the potential heaviness of the buildings might similarly remind us of atmospheric effects often to be observed in the city. But the appearance of this grandiose classical architecture would nonetheless have been experienced by many contemporaries as essentially non-Venetian or non-local. Most buildings in the city were constructed in the medieval Veneto-Gothic style, despite Jacopo Sansovino's recent updating of its central areas around St Mark's Square. Veronese's enormously scaled architecture in the painting is fantastical enough, even if it also references the pale stone and *all'antica* architectural language of Palladio's new building at San Giorgio.

Despite the vast extent of the picture surface, it is not big enough to contain the entirety of the painted buildings. The lower parts and bases of the columns on the nearer arcades disappear behind occluding figures, meaning that no clearly defined or logical ground plan can be established. This sectionalization further serves the effect of visual amplification common to many Veronese compositions. Following his approach in his frescoes for the Villa Barbaro, Veronese took the example of Palladio's architecture only as his starting point, pushing its expansive and monumentalizing principles much further in order to imagine an entire ideal cityscape.[25] But this classicism is not based on firm, geometric foundations. The perspective generated by the shadowed edges of the receding columns and entablatures does not add up in strictly mathematical or optical terms, perhaps serving instead to accommodate multiple, shifting viewpoints.[26] Veronese's abandonment of an objectivized one-point perspective system à la Alberti and other Renaissance theorists serves as another indication of his conception of painting as a fundamentally self-sustaining entity that works its effect beyond the control of rational co-ordinates.[27] Rather than making his vast picture dependent on objective measurements derived from the exterior world beyond itself, he presented it as a knowingly fictive pictorial invention that is primarily subject to its own laws.

The status of the *Cana* as a semi-independent imaginary must always have been understood and accepted by the Benedictine monks who sat before it in their comparatively plain and unadorned refectory at San Giorgio. Many of these original viewers would have been from patrician or aristocratic families and would thus have been familiar enough with the delights of a lavish meal. But Veronese's painting must nonetheless have appeared to them as substitutive or compensatory. It is true that mouths are kept closed throughout the painting, but we can be in no doubt of the noisiness of the scene: conversations among the guests are implied, and the hubbub of the servants is evident enough, above the ongoing music. Veronese reportedly painted a (now lost) fresco on the wall of the vestibule at the door of the refectory that featured two angels holding up a placard inscribed 'SILENTIUM'.[28] But his painting itself is alive with sound, perhaps symbolized by the parrot held by the dwarf: a bird renowned not only for its imitative skills but for its garrulousness. Veronese's noisy auricular world triumphs over the surrounding silence, proposing another, semi-licit – at least from the point of view of Benedict's founding Rule – social world, which recalled the one that its primary audience had, at least officially, foregone. In his painting, visual appetite predominates, but is strongly supported by sound, touch, taste and even smell – Aretino's roses, or the dogs – that combine to thicken the sensual effect. All is in support of a marriage: that other great social institution forbidden to the viewing monks in the refectory.[29]

The more recent attempts to justify Veronese against the charge of undue decorativeness from an iconographic point of view have led to a strong re-emphasis on the way Christ is made central to the composition, serving symbolically as its still, fixed or anchoring point. His figure is aligned – in a verticalized, spatially flattening and symbolically charged way – with the hourglass below him, and the butcher with raised meat-cleaver above. A suddenly different, non-sequential and non-diachronic ordering of time is proposed, which might recall the alterity of the non-worldly perspective Christ himself opened up in his harshly rhetorical words to his mother at the marriage feast: 'Woman, what have I to do with thee? Mine hour is not yet come' (John 2:4). This contrasting, non-linear alignment is reflected too in the temporal anomaly that the meat-choppers above Christ introduce. The nuts and fruits currently on the table suggest that the meal has already been eaten, corresponding with the point in chronological time at which the wine ran out towards the end of the feast. But this makes the continued preparations of the meat course above appear anomalous. We are encouraged to understand the butchers' activity in alternative, symbolic and theological terms: as a prefiguration of Christ's own upcoming death which is also, of course, symbolized by the turning of water to wine.

Despite the apparent otherness of this non-naturalistic sacred zone or lozenge, and its placement at the centre, it vitally does *not* serve to invalidate the everyday goings-on, or the multitudinous appearances roundabout it. Christ's relationship with all that surrounds him is presented as non-judgemental and non-exclusive, his embeddedness or submergence not intended to comment critically on the synaesthetic worldliness of the wider pictorial display.[30] As is typical in Veronese's paintings, margin and centre – or surface and depth – are conceived in a non-hierarchical relationship with one another, or held in a subtle state of balance and inter-dependence. Having spotted the partially buried theology in the *Marriage at Cana*, the viewer must return once again, and without prejudice, to enjoyment of the visual details, however trivial or digressive, taking them on their own terms – as compelling and fascinating, valuable in their own right. The way in which Christ's alternative hieratic mode is enfolded into its endlessly expansive material context indicates that this latter domain is not to be understood as 'lesser' or secondary, or as a deceptive distraction from a singular and deeper spiritual truth. That kind of dualistic moralizing from a thematic point of view is inimical to Veronese. Christ's centrality might indicate his final control over all else depicted. But this is also a painting through which the eye is invited to wander at will: to delight in the sensual pleasures of an aristocraticized vision of luxury, already reimagined by the artist in terms that go beyond extant social reality, as also beyond the bounds of the text that is apparently illustrated. Vitally, the narrative is not permitted to dominate, as it might in a sacred painting by Titian, Tintoretto or Bassano.

THE *CANA* MUSICIANS AGAIN: VERONESE AND TITIAN

At the lower foreground centre of Veronese's painting two musicians are highlighted, their richly clad forms establishing the lower wings of a figural pyramidal with Christ himself at its apex (illus. 3). As we saw in the Introduction, these two are likely to be a self-portrait of Veronese alongside a portrait of the elderly Titian. Veronese's depiction of himself collaborating with the revered older master as if he were his chosen artistic son and heir is significant. He had broadly modelled his 'noble' artistic persona as a courtly painter on Titian's own, even if he had not been knighted by a royal patron and could not match the range of the older master's international aristocratic patronage. He frequently referred to Titian's paintings in his own works, suggesting continuity and overlap between his style of painting and that of the revered older master. Veronese's decision to depict himself in close physical proximity to Titian in the *Cana* thus appears understandable enough. His imagery in this passage suggests that the two artists, old and young, worked closely together, creating a finely harmonized kind of painting equivalent to music. Ridolfi might have drawn on this polemical passage in the *Cana* when asserting that Veronese thought of Titian as 'il padre dell'Arte' ('the father of Art'), and conversely that Titian thought of Veronese as his natural artistic successor, and as the embodiment of 'nobility and decorum' in painting.[31]

It is, though, difficult to find much evidence for this close mutual relationship in historical reality.[32] It seems likely that Titian was among the painters who came to see Veronese's great refectory picture at San Giorgio within a few years of its unveiling, as recorded by Benedetto Guidi, a monk of the monastery.[33] But it might also be that the old master was less than happy with his representation in the painting: as a mere hired help at an aristocratic feast, shown working with his hands. Nor would Titian have been so very content with Veronese's self-serving depiction of him as a special supporter, given that he envisioned his own son and current workshop manager, Orazio Vecellio (1525–1576) – also legally ennobled under the terms of the 1533 decree – as his artistic heir and successor. In his own later self-portraits of the 1550s and '60s Titian showed himself in opposite terms: as a powerfully independent painter-aristocrat, typically sporting the gold chain awarded to him by the emperor Charles V on his ennoblement. This all-powerful royal patron, so Charles's courtiers complained, treated Titian as an equal, and certainly not as a mere entertainer or servant.[34]

Veronese was not alone among the younger painters working in Venice in attempting to prove that he had Titian's particular favour, or that he was first in line to succeed him as the leading master in the city.[35] His depiction of himself in front of other potential artist portraits in the musician group – Tintoretto, Bassano and even Palladio have been suggested – who are only half-seen behind Veronese's resplendent figure, might equally have served to prove that he was Titian's chosen heir to the throne of Venetian painting. So much tends to contradict Ridolfi's ideal image of Veronese as a reticent and non-competitive master noted earlier. The depiction of painter-musicians at the feast suggests that Veronese was, after all, every bit as ambitious and pushy as his rivals. But the wider appearance of the *Cana* has little in common with Titian's sacred works. In his feast scenes, at least, Veronese did not closely follow Titian's pictorial lead. Even when at his most Titianesque in certain altarpieces and portraits Veronese typically returned to Titian prototypes made decades earlier in the 1520s, rather than to his more recent experimental works of the 1550s and '60s. Rather than attempting to follow the ageing master's increasingly complex, passionate and unsettling existential visions of physical, emotional and spiritual struggle, Veronese's mature style remained independent, exuding visual certainty and worldly confidence, based on ever-greater chromatic intensity and material splendour: features all apparent enough in the *Cana*. In his mature mythologies and allegories, too, Veronese drew back from the troubling intensity of the older master's more recent works in that pictorial genre. And even in the final decade or so of his career, when his paintings became significantly darker in tone – both literally and metaphorically speaking – he responded more closely to the later styles of Tintoretto and Bassano.

LAST SUPPER/FEAST IN THE HOUSE OF LEVI

To what extent did Veronese's more generic idea of a grand feast win out against any more specific definition of a biblical event of this kind? Asking this question does not mean arguing that Veronese paid no attention to the texts he illustrated. In the *Marriage at Cana*, he subtly enfolded theological meaning without compromise to the principle of pictorial splendour. But many elements in these feast scenes are nonetheless shared, perhaps reflecting the specific requests of his monastic patrons, who had seen and admired existing versions, and wanted very similar-looking works for their own refectories. Specific pictorial motifs, but also larger compositional ideas, were readily carried across from one Veronese feast to the next, so that subject-specificity gives way, to some extent, and the new work appears like a variation on an earlier one. In his first banqueting scene for a monastic refectory, the painter tellingly remained independent of any one biblical account, freely combining elements from all four gospel texts (illus. 41).[36] And in a refectory painting for the Servite monastery of Monte Berico at Vicenza of 1572 (in situ) the theme of the painting itself insisted on overlap or slippage between two grand feasts held centuries apart: the Church Father Gregory the Great is shown re-enacting the Last Supper, having invited thirteen poor pilgrims to come and dine with him.

At the Dominican monastery of Santi Giovanni e Paolo in 1573, it was Veronese's free approach to his subject-matter that caught the interest of the Catholic Inquisition, even if there is no indication that the interview was called after they had seen his earlier works of this type (illus. 44).[37] Quite understandably, given the appearance of Veronese's recent painting, the inquisitors could not identify which subject had been depicted.[38] Veronese had (almost certainly) painted a Last Supper as a replacement for a work with the same subject by Titian, destroyed in a fire two years earlier, and thus resisted the inquisitors' suggested alteration of the foreground dog into a Mary Magdalene, which would have transformed it into a 'Feast in the House of Simon'. It was this initial refusal that led to a summons to appear before the tribunal in the *chiesetta* of St Theodore, adjacent to St Mark's, on 18 July. From the surviving transcript it emerges that the inquisitors were concerned not only about the obscurity of the subject of the painting, but about the very prominent secondary figures placed in its foreground. Their line of questioning indicates that they suspected that some of these had a hidden heretical religious meaning. They also found these figures ugly and vulgar, and thought that they unduly distracted from the sacred subject. Veronese's answers to their questions are concerned with justifying his inclusion of these accessories.

Asked why he had depicted a man with a bleeding nose and two armed Germans, Veronese replied 'we painters take liberties, the same way as poets and lunatics do.' Here he evoked the ancient Roman ideas of Horace, Cicero and others to the effect that poets (and by extension painters) were animated creatively by a divinely inspired madness that took them beyond ordinary social expectations, conventions and responsibilities.[39] Shakespeare's line 'The lunatic, the lover, and the poet are of imagination all compact,' from *A Midsummer Night's Dream* (V.1), indicates that such ideas were current enough in the period. Veronese's figures were

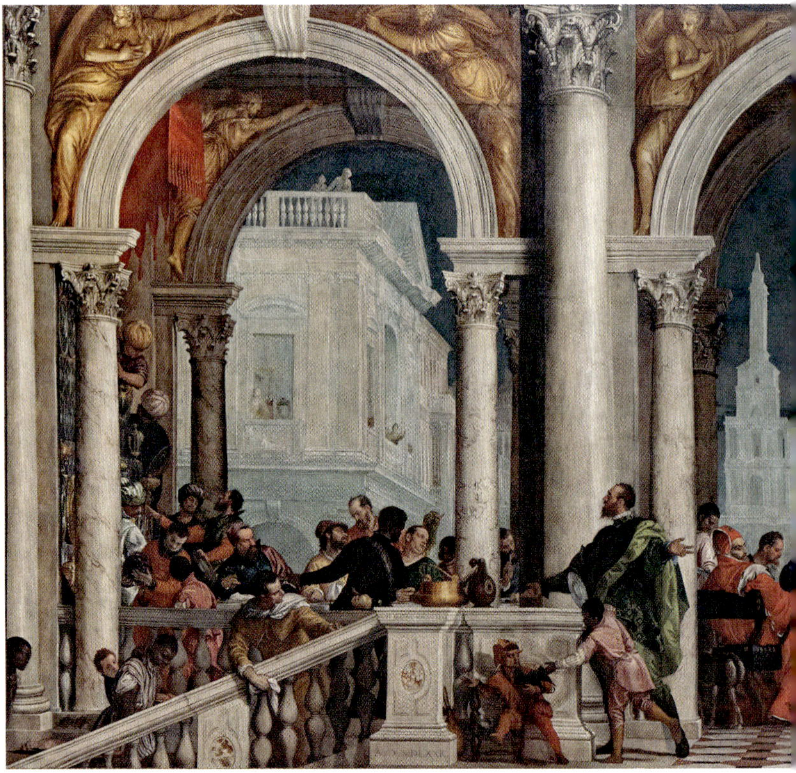

thus to be understood and enjoyed as the free inventions of his fertile artistic *fantasía*, rather than as more widely meaningful or as an implied heretical attack on Catholic orthodoxy. Such figures, he went on to suggest, were necessary to properly tell the story. The two soldiers would have been in the service of 'the owner of the house', as might several of the other foreground figures. With this explanation, Veronese casually introduced the conventional idea of a legitimate pictorial exegesis or embellishment of a sacred text noted above. But the *richezza* of the man hosting the Last Supper is certainly not implied in the biblical accounts, suggesting that Veronese was not making a closely text-based

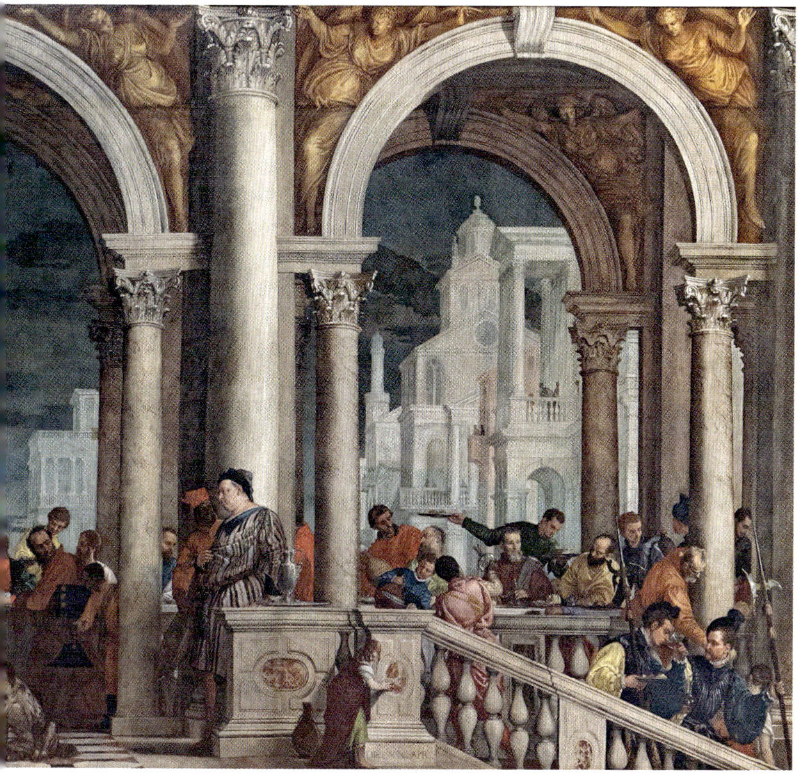

defence of his approach. Rather, he refers to his own generic idea of the setting for any grand feast. He thought it likely that someone laying on a lavish supper would, by definition, have been 'a rich, important man', and therefore would have employed many servants or hangers-on.

Questioned further about why he had depicted a jester-dwarf holding a parrot, Veronese replied succinctly and perhaps tersely: 'for ornament, as one does' ('Per ornamento, come si fa'). His use of the word *ornamento* might again seem to refer to the conventions of biblical exegesis, but there is tellingly no further symbolic or thematic unpacking on the painter's part. It is more likely that

44 Veronese, *Last Supper/Feast in the House of Levi*, 1573, oil on canvas.

he is saying that the dwarf and parrot were included for their own sake, with the viewer's pleasure in an entertaining imitative depiction primarily in mind (the bird might symbolize his own abilities to 'parrot' nature in such visual descriptions, as it did in a number of his other works). The limit to iconographic meaning in his accessory figures is made clearer still in Veronese's next reply, when he explains that if there is an empty space in a picture, it his habit to 'adorn it with figures'. His subsequent attempt to deflect the inquisitors' criticism is more defensive, even if it reflects repeated Venetian criticisms of Michelangelo's *Last Judgement* fresco in the Sistine Chapel dating back to the 1540s.[40] If Michelangelo's impious inclusion of nudes in this work is acceptable to the authorities, Veronese asks, then why should he be blamed for including such 'ornamental' foreground figures? His questioner testily replied that 'there is nothing that is not spiritual' in Michelangelo's painting: 'there are no jesters, nor dogs, nor weapons, nor similar buffooneries.' Veronese does not hazard a reply but then offers a final defence of his accessory figures, claiming that they do not disrupt the overall composition: 'I never thought of causing disorder, the more so as the buffoons are outside the part where our Lord is.' Veronese suggests here that the enormous three-arched loggia that he had painted to frame the scene effectively divides Christ from the low performers in the foreground and thus maintains overall visual and thematic decorum.

This final justification is Veronese's most interesting response, but also his most disingenuous. As was the case in the *Feast at the House of Simon*, Veronese's painted architecture is much more porous than he claimed. As many as 21 servants of different sorts, and even a dog, have infiltrated the supposedly reserved sacred space under the loggia. A second Black page busy serving the guests under the loggia mirrors the foreground figure at the top of the steps, while one disciple is glimpsed idly picking his teeth (illus. 45), like the woman in the *Cana*. The worlds of high and low, serious and mocking, textual and non-textual, depth and surface, interpenetrate more freely in the picture than Veronese admits. The inquisitors certainly had a valid point when noticing the way in which the accessory figures win out, in purely visual terms, against the sacred-historical ones. It is hard enough to see many of those seated beneath the loggia, whose forms are – admittedly apart from Christ himself – half-concealed by columns, or by those of the 'buffoons' in front of them. To a still greater extent than in the *Cana*, these minor figures *do* distract the viewer's attention, and their visual dominance lies behind the ongoing confusion about the exact subject-matter.[41]

While it is intricately connected to the scene beyond, the supplementary foreground space has a random or adventitious quality. If it is populated by *buffoni* then that is not immediately apparent, even if all those shown are low on the social scale. Some of these people certainly belong to the house: the major-domo dressed (like the one at the foreground left of the *Cana*) in emerald green silks and satins undeniably does, as too the equally finely attired Black page boy in salmon pink who threatens the jester-dwarf with a raised plate. The man has apparently just struck another, who retreats down the steps with a bloody nose.[42] The two figures stand like loyal sentries at the top of the blind arcade of steps, seeming to guard the raised central place where Christ sits from a lower kind of unruly street poor who threaten the house (the dwarf's begging bowl may indicate that he is an untrustworthy outsider on this occasion).[43] But speculation inevitably creeps in, especially on the steps to the right, given that the two boys shown there (one Black, one white, like those on the opposite side) are bona fide servants of the household. Veronese himself identified the soldiers further down the steps as such, and their placement in front of a poor woman who receives alms from an apostle reaching round a column further indicates their connection with those seated beneath the loggia (illus. 46).[44] It may be that

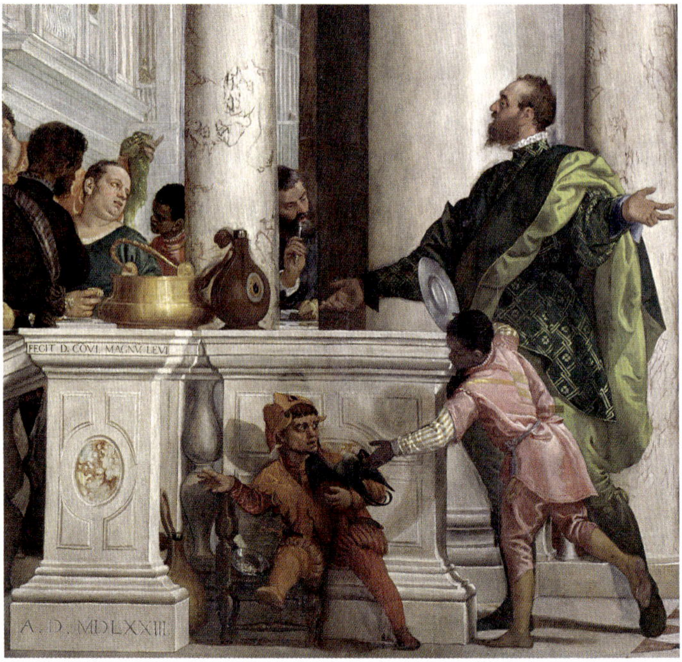

this charitable action to the right was intended to contrast with the repeated motifs of expulsion and control to the left, perhaps recalling the similar balancing act maintained by two Dominican deacons seen dispensing charity in the lower foreground of an altarpiece by Lorenzo Lotto (*c.* 1480–1556/7) for the same church (the *St Antoninus Giving Alms* of 1541–2). There is, though, nothing so very ideological in Veronese's entropic foreground, where precise meanings and identities have a habit of escaping their moorings, and where the painter's artistic licence holds sway.

Despite the simplification of his last answer, it seems likely that Veronese was telling the truth when answering his questioners, rather than playing some obscure game of double bluff. If any putative association with heretical Protestant imagery suggested by the Tribunal can be discounted, then a specific or sustained

45 Veronese, *Last Supper/Feast in the House of Levi*, detail.

connection with Catholic theology seems equally unlikely, or at least only a matter of suggestive but loose and fleeting connection. Veronese describes at least one of these figures – the jester-dwarf – as a pictorial *ornamento*, rather than as an iconographic indicator, a point to which we will soon return. But that does not make these contentious figures any more secondary to the viewer's experience. The accurate way in which the inquisitors cite details in the picture suggests that they had examined it very closely in situ at Santi Giovanni e Paolo, and their focus on the offending details reflects their careful close looking. Veronese's visual emphasis *was* on those lower down the social hierarchy after all, as it had been, albeit it to a lesser extent, in the earlier feasts discussed in this chapter. In the end, the inquisitors did not require the painter to erase them to facilitate a better view of the sacred actors under the loggia. Instead, it was decided that the painting could, without any other alterations, stand as another biblical supper altogether: the rarely depicted Feast in the House of Levi.

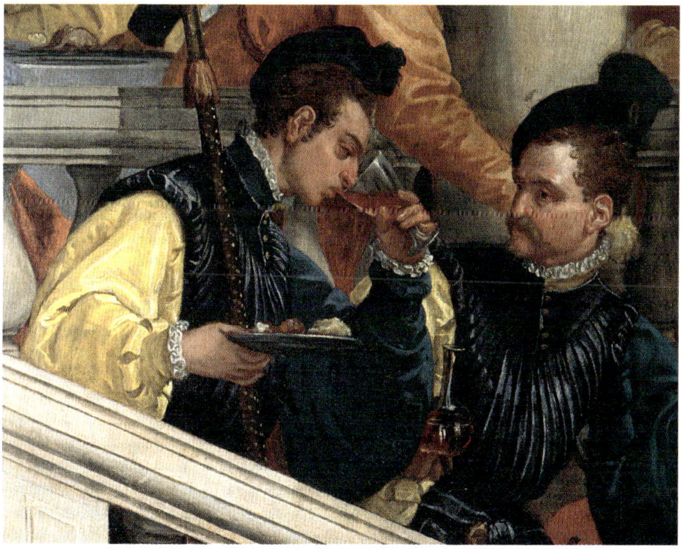

46 Veronese, *Last Supper/Feast in the House of Levi*, detail.

The solution was neat enough, given that this was a much less important event than the Last Supper in theological terms, and that it was, according to Luke, attended by 'a great company of publicans and of others that sat down with them' (Luke 5:27–9). Veronese was simply instructed to add the inscription along the base of the loggia facade identifying the new subject and its precise textual source. The slightness of this required change may indicate Veronese's then very high artistic reputation in Venice; the persuasiveness of his answers to the Inquisition; or the latter's relative lack of any very pressing concern about the heretical meaning of this painting or any others in Venice at the time.[45] The painter was subsequently able to continue his artistic career without any major ill-effects, although it is notable that he did not venture to paint any further lavish feast scenes for monastic refectories after the interview. And in a late Last Supper for a parish church, he seems to restrain or 'correct' his pictorial manner in accordance with his rival Tintoretto's pious approach to the subject (illus. 63). However, the very failure of the authorities' attempt to control or erase the imagery in the Santi Giovanni e Paolo version remains telling enough. While the appended words proclaim the master's close adherence to a specified governing text – 'LUCAE CAP[VT] V' – his picture continues to show a different scene altogether.

While the inquisitors were explicitly concerned about the potentially heretical elements in Veronese's painting, their negative reaction to the socially low foreground figures also indicates their implicit class prejudices. As high-ranking members of the nobility, they were shocked and surprised by Veronese's extended visual presentation of such disgraceful riff-raff.[46] During the interview, Veronese tried to settle their qualms by picking up and running with their identification of his figures as 'buffoons'. As such, he says, they are of little significance and offer no threat to the underlying order of the painting. But their visual prominence and ubiquity in his painting indicate otherwise. They clearly played a key role in his work, even if their presence does not explicitly offer a direct criticism of the exclusions of the existing social order. Serving as a badge of wealth, the lowlife types might have helped to establish the importance and high status of the main actors, as Veronese suggests in one of his answers to the inquisitors.[47] Even if they are not always shown as part of the household, their presence as bystanders provides a sense of ongoing everyday life that adds an air of truth to the given narrative, as such occasional types had, too, in earlier Venetian narrative paintings by Gentile Bellini (1429–1507) and Carpaccio.[48] They do not perform in quite the same way as the main actors. Their movements are typically freer and less dignified or pre-considered: to borrow Michael Fried's terms, they are more 'absorbed' than 'theatrical', insofar as they are less aware of being seen by the viewer.[49]

There is also a measure of equalization inherent within Veronese's approach to picture-making which pushes against his use of such low types merely to replicate or restate existing conditions of social hierarchy, othering or alterity. The interview of 1573 suggests that some influential contemporary observers, at least, found Veronese's careful and extended interest in such figures *indecorous*, from a hierarchical institutional perspective that was both religious and social. The inquisitors were right to notice how 'the buffoons' occlude the given iconography, their spontaneous actions offering a measure of free visual play that does not always point towards the sacred story. Veronese's *buffoni* might have been justified as large-scale equivalents to the irreverent drolleries painted in the margins of medieval manuscripts. But unlike these, they are given undue visual prominence, seeming to attack or displace the authority of the sacred text at the centre and to obscure its meaning.[50] This was a matter of balance between the debts owed to the pictorial and to the textual. If the presence of such figures was not in itself a problem, then the extent to which they are allowed to divert the viewer's attention away from the underlying theme certainly was. Veronese's marginal figures were too distracting, too insistently *there*.

Their presence constantly hints at the artist's own freedom or licence to invent. The nature of the disobedience they seem to intimate is hard to define but certainly reflects Veronese's insistent pictorialism as described in the discussions above, and its implicit resistance to the close control of externally derived meanings sanctioned by the authorities. These types were, after all, derived from the painter's own artistic armoury rather than from the narrative he was asked to represent. Veronese's answers to his questioners consistently indicate that these figures were originally intended as artistic creations with no wider meaning beyond themselves, and there is little reason to doubt that he was telling the truth about this. If he accepted the inquistors' upper-class dislike of such lowlife figures, even adopting their dismissive terminology, his *buffoni* must also have meant something different for him, given the care with which he painted them. As we have seen, these figures often seem to come with associational meanings: if they are not the carriers of hidden heretical ideas against the Catholic Church, then they certainly carry social meaning insofar as they are taken as bona fide representatives of ordinary, contemporary people lower down the hierarchy. But too ready or strong a reading of Veronese's marginals as 'meaningful' would obscure their status as independent pictorial signs that resist a close indexical relation to any reality beyond themselves, or beyond the picture that they appear in. As Veronese's despicable lowlife figures enter the world of his painting, they are redeemed by his visual effort, subsumed into his all-determining pictorial assemblage: to some extent relieved of their final responsibility to all iconographic or social meanings.

FIVE

Mythologies and Allegories

It is something of a surprise to find that Veronese did not turn to the well-established genre of erotic cabinet painting until the 1560s. The type was particularly connected to court culture, and thus to the kind of high-ranking aristocratic patrons he often worked for. And these smaller-scale works were typically commissioned to be hung in their family palaces: a context in which the painter had been especially active since the outset of his career. Moreover, such works usually featured mythological subjects from classical antiquity, functioning as a vehicle for the expression of the kind of *all'antica* values that Veronese was especially alive to. The type, as it had developed in Italian Renaissance painting of the later fifteenth and sixteenth centuries, was underpinned by certain visual conventions that would have been particularly conducive for the 'pictorial' Veronese. Many earlier examples had been presented in a planar fashion that deliberately recalled ancient relief or frieze sculpture, and that avoided close imitation of the rapidly shifting appearances of nature. The figures in these works displayed proportionate anatomies, closely defined within firm formal contours, to give a presiding effect of physical beauty. The mythological body, at least by comparison with the sacred one featured in Christian art, remained inviolate, self-contained and impenetrable, defined by its agglomeration of sensuous surfaces rather than its revelation of inward spiritual depths.[1]

Mythological paintings of the Renaissance, at least before Titian's groundbreaking series known as the *poesie*, typically demonstrate a reduced interest in psychological, emotional or moral expression, and a heightened one in externalized displays of formal perfection and sensual pleasure. Similar characteristics are, as we have already seen, evident enough in many of the religious paintings and portraits by Veronese discussed so far. His subjection of natural appearances to the demands of the given composition has been noted, as has his avoidance of the disturbances attendant on narrative action. In these ways, Veronese's underlying pictorialism made him a natural candidate for the further development of mythological painting. As the works discussed below demonstrate, he rapidly made up for lost time, finishing an impressive succession of such paintings over the course of the 1560s and '70s. In a closely related sequence of allegorical works, certain of which were made with court patrons from northern Europe in mind, he drew closely on these efforts, albeit that in these intellectualized examples he modified the erotic tone to foreground abstract moral themes.

A RETREAT FROM TITIAN'S *POESIE*

Veronese's initial slowness in taking up this kind of imagery is, however, telling enough. It might reflect the relative limits to his patronage in his earlier period: although he often worked in the private residences of leading aristocratic families, these commissions apparently provided relatively few opportunities for cabinet-sized oil paintings with mythological subjects. While the taste in Venice for such mythological works dates back to at least the opening decade of the century, Veronese was initially admired more for his abilities as a fresco painter who worked on larger-scale, multi-picture decorations, even if the pagan gods and goddesses were sometimes featured in that context (illus. 12, 28, 30, 31). And then there was the continued domination of the more famous Titian in the production of paintings of this type: between circa 1552 and 1562 the older master was busy creating a groundbreaking cycle of Ovidian mythologies for his royal patron, King Philip II: the so-called *poesie*, sent away periodically to various locations of the Habsburg court in northern Europe and Spain.[2] These ultra-exclusive, visually unique and bespoke works increasingly departed from the Renaissance conventions for the picture type that Titian himself had helped to establish in his earlier career. Painted in Titian's visually complex late style, the *poesie* defied rather than encouraged emulation by other painters, destabilizing and subjectivizing pictorial space while showing the pagan protagonists as prey to the cruel vicissitudes of implacable Fortuna. Titian now admitted expressional qualities more familiar in Christian imagery – physical and psychological suffering and a presiding sense of worldly transience and its pitfalls – into the previously timeless pleasure dome of erotic mythological painting. Faced with this recent example, so antithetical to his own pictorial approach, Veronese may initially have felt daunted or confused. It is notable that in his own early attempts, Veronese instinctively retreated from Titian's new example, restating an approach that has more in common with Renaissance conventions for the type, but that also allowed him to apply his own, by now well-established, visual priorities.

Comparison of his erotic mythologies of cabinet type from the early 1560s with Titian's recent mythologies for Philip indicates the younger master's hesitancy in the face of their dynamic expressive and narrative mode. In a painting featuring *Venus and Adonis* that offers a direct commentary on Titian's *poesia* of the same subject (*c.* 1553–4, Madrid, Museo del Prado), Veronese's approach to his source is equivocal (illus. 47).[3] Veronese closely followed Titian's departure from Ovid's original account in the

Metamorphoses, in which the two protagonists, divine and mortal, do not appear together as intimate paramours. This visual motif of paired lovers was destined to remain as a fundamental starting point in many of Veronese's subsequent works of this kind. But he also downplayed the dramatic, temporally driven and psychologically disturbing aspects of his model. The idea of Adonis's immanent departure is still suggested, but Venus nonetheless repossesses something of her usual placid authority in erotic mythologies. If, in Titian's work, Venus's inner psychological torment is expressed by the extreme torsions of her body, in Veronese's version she is more confident and relaxed, her back-turned posture recalling famous models from the earlier Cinquecento, such as the heroine in *Jupiter and Io* of 1532–3 by Correggio (1489–1534).[4]

Hinting at the familiar idea that the feminine persuasions of 'Love' will win out against the masculine temptations of the hunt, Veronese already seems keen to reimagine the classical world as an ideal and secluded domain, reserved from the depredations of time, as also from the horrors of bodily destruction and emotional suffering. So much was, after all, in keeping with his visualizing approach more generally. It may be that Adonis will abandon Venus in the end to meet his dark fate (he was killed by a boar). But Veronese does not further indicate the scene of the hero's death as Titian did at the background right of his *poesia*, keeping his viewer's attention fixed on the foreground present. This was to re-emphasize the power of the presiding goddess while reducing her male lover Adonis to a conflicted figure, caught in a moment of mortal weakness or uncertainty about whether to go or to stay. His dithering subtly shifts the painting back towards a comedic approach, a levity of tone supported by details such as the humorously defeated expression of the greyhound held in Cupid's childish headlock.[5]

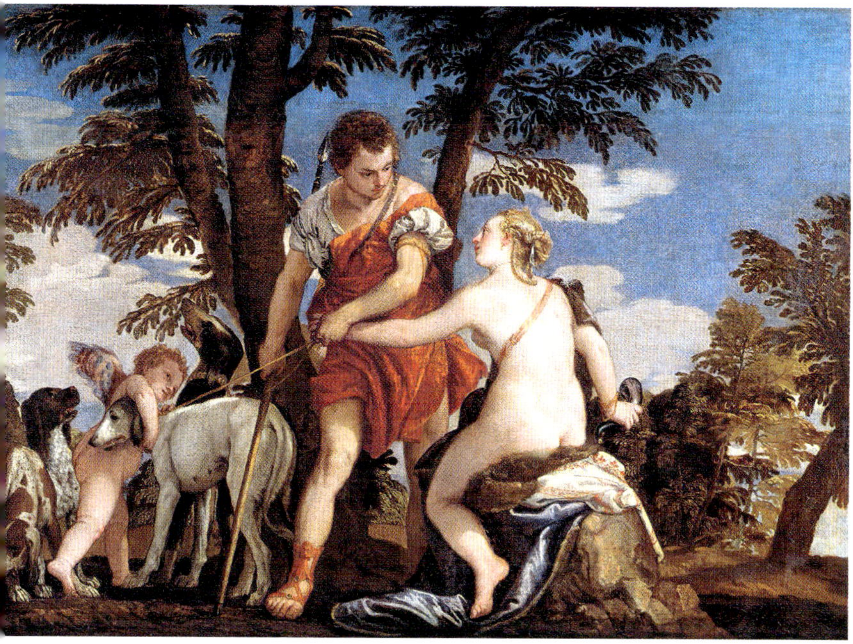

RAPE OF EUROPA

In the *Rape of Europa* painted for the Venetian palace of the leading patrician collector Jacopo Contarini, probably in 1573, Veronese departed still more determinedly from Titian's *poesia* of the same subject (illus. 48).[6] There is accordingly no suggestion that Europa is being (or is about to be) physically assaulted against her will, or that the bull's intervention is unanticipated and unwelcome. In order to calm troubled waters, Veronese chose an earlier moment in the narrative that allowed him to recover an ancient Roman ideal conception of a classical or *all'antica* 'rape' which drew on positive patriotic, familial and epithalamic meanings, rather than implying the crime of forced sexual intercourse.[7] His richly clad nymph alights willingly on the bull's back, her side-saddle position, with legs closed, further implying her control over the docile

47 Veronese, *Venus and Adonis*, c. 1560–65, oil on canvas.

animal beneath her (he is, of course, the god Jupiter in disguise). Even if the pacified beast is permitted to suggestively lick her foot – a detail not included in Ovid's text – this action leads him to bow his head, in deferential fashion, as if in homage to the supreme power of her civilizing beauty.

Ovid devoted many more lines of poetry to the nymphs playing on the shores of Tyre than to the precipitous journey across the sea to Crete that followed, but this latter nonetheless provided the narrative climax to the story. Veronese's avoidance of it is in keeping with his wider tendency not to show the main event, or to present the moment just before it occurs. It also allows him to still the action and present the beautiful young heroine as dominant over her masculine counterpart. This reversal of gender roles, with the feminine presence dictating proceedings, is one of Veronese's most telling departures from Titian's *poesía*, in which the maddened desire of the impassioned bull so terrifyingly undermines the young woman's equilibrium. Instead, Veronese concentrates on the preparatory or lead-in scene, as the chosen nymph is carefully made ready for her upcoming journey by her female companions who consequently become much more significant (they are reduced to tiny background figures in Titian's painting). Reviving an archaic simultaneous narrative technique to show the pair of lovers disappearing across the sea at the background right, Veronese makes the potential dangerousness of the future ride disappear. Europa remains comfortably upright on her mount, who retains a respectful passivity. Veronese's painting may have been made in celebration of a patrician marriage: the heroine is pictured as the beautiful and god-favoured 'bride' being prepared to depart with her divine 'groom' by her waiting women. Special emphasis is laid on the cladding of Europa's body, downplaying her sexuality in order to secure her determining power against a viewer's gaze that might otherwise be understood as prioritizing a voyeuristic male perspective.[8]

The relaxed and leisurely pastoral scene is closer to the gentle intimacy of his *Finding of Moses* (illus. 40) with its similarly feminine dramatis personae.[9] If such works featured contrasting sacred and pagan subjects, then that distinction was smoothed away by Veronese's use of them as vehicles for the depiction of the domestic lives of the women (both royal and serving) of his own place and time.

It is also true that Veronese maintains an air of artificiality that delimits the idea that his work is simply naturalistic. Its presiding effect of planar and static *all'antica* beauty was established, in part at least, at the expense of human interaction or interiority. His picture encourages a sophisticated acceptance that what is

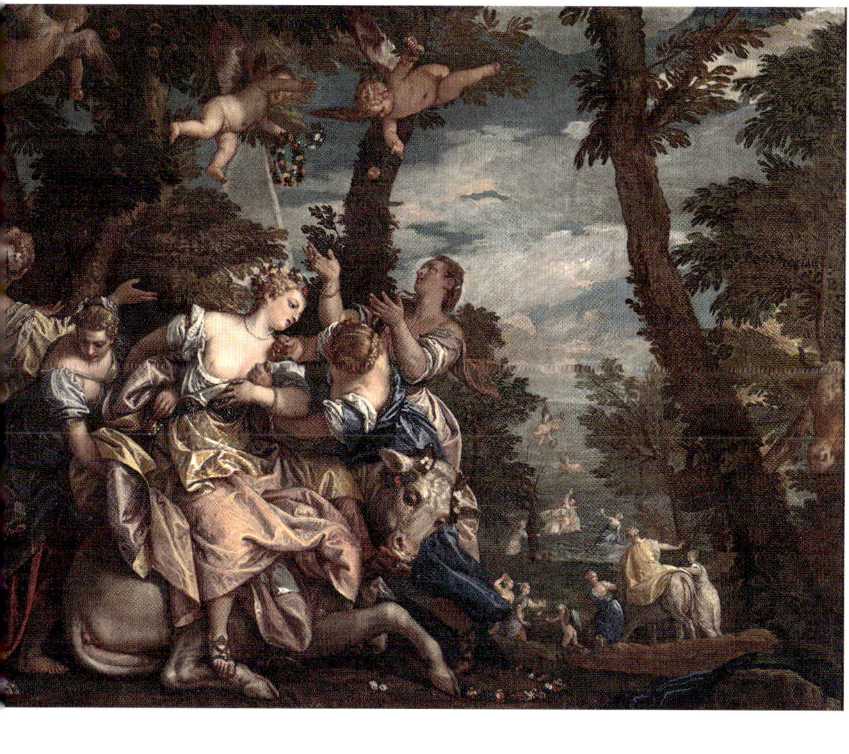

48 Veronese, *Rape of Europa*, *c.* 1573, oil on canvas.

shown to us within this reserved or iconic pictorial realm is not to be mistaken for a direct or inductive transcription of reality. Veronese's Ovidian works are more self-consciously 'artful' than Titian's, downplaying the old master's emphasis on sudden transformations, while relocating his female-dominated cast to a safer domain, where pleasures can be enjoyed in a privileged vacuum, without further consequence. Even these 'pleasures' are made a matter of subtle inference or euphemistic suggestion: the bull's foot-licking, for example, or the generative suggestion of Europa's bared breast, linking her to the ancient Venus Genetrix. Narrative itself, with its destabilizing – as well as masculinist – potentials, might still be implied. But it is also reduced to a kind of unrepresented 'off-stage' echo. The scrupulously mediated and differentiated domain of Veronese's mythologies offers itself to the viewer as a delicious release from reality. This approach sanctioned the artistic licence that Veronese appealed to – and implicitly championed – in his replies to the Inquisition in the interview perhaps held in the very same year that he worked on the Contarini painting. If Veronese's mythologies certainly evoke the classical texts they depict, then the imagery presented is not narrowly determined by any one of them. It was Titian, rather than Veronese, who was criticized by one contemporary for making an undue departure from Ovid's account by placing the lovers together in his *Venus and Adonis*.[10] But the younger master took this pairing of lovers as his starting point in many of his mythological and allegorical works in a way that granted his imagery a measure of freedom from the specific text he represented. As he did so, his sensually aroused young couples became generic markers of the authority of his own visual world.

TWO PAINTINGS OF VENUS AND MARS

Veronese was understood by his first major biographer as an abstracting and idealizing Neoplatonic painter, and it is tempting to interpret his repeated depictions of subjects such as Venus and Adonis and Venus and Mars in this light.[11] To some extent, these formally iterative paintings reflect an underlying 'Idea', perhaps fundamentally based on Virgil's famous proclamation: 'Omnia vincit Amor'. Veronese's paintings might even suggest his reduction of wider or more complex meanings altogether, assimilating these to a singular simplified trope, with his mythologies consequently released from the kind of burdensome expressive depths suggested in Titian's *poesie*. Veronese was apparently uncomfortable with Titian's fiercely Aristotelian *imitatio*, offering a pictorially self-contained version of mythological painting that reflects his knowledge of the recent vernacular translations of Neoplatonic texts published in Venice.[12] When applied to painting, Neoplatonism encouraged visual play beyond the constraints of *imitatio*, and in Veronese's works of this kind formal invention enjoyed a particularly free rein. It would matter relatively little whether Veronese depicted one pair of lovers or another, and to this extent Venus's paramours became increasingly interchangeable in both visual and semantic terms. Insofar as the message in many of his works of this kind is simply that Love will overcome, then the story of Venus's affair with Mars, the god of war, proved especially conducive. But in one depiction of this subject, probably dating from the early 1560s, Veronese's approach contradicted his later ideal presentation of Love's inevitable victory (illus. 49).[13] In this little work, perhaps made for a local patron in Venice, Veronese's mythological imagery is closer to Tintoretto's, who took a satirical approach to the pagan gods, presenting his puppet-like protagonists as driven by degrading sexual desire.[14] There is likewise something furtive and potentially ridiculous about the adulterous love dance performed by the 'false gods' featured in the Turin painting.

Laying aside the more usual Neoplatonic inflections in his mythologies, Veronese allows his gods to appear as commonplace adulterers, recalling Aristotle's 'satyric' mode of theatrical presentation mentioned in his newly popular *Poetics*.[15] Their lustful liaison assigns them a moral level beneath that of the spectator. Although the background sky seems to suggest that the scene is set in a high tower, the descent of Cupid leading Mars's horse down winding spiral steps simultaneously suggests the opposite: that we look downwards into a lower room or even a basement: fitting setting for the 'low' activities enacted there.[16] Veronese's use of cold ice-blue for the drapery concealing Venus's genital area operates as a tonal deflection, signalling by way of contrast the underlying theme of hot passion interrupted, still revealed by the brash scarlet of the labia-like folds of the bed drapes. The god of war is a risible figure, appearing as squat and dark-skinned, his back-turned, bent-kneed posture, with hoof-like foot, made satyr-like. His animalistic crouched posture, as if about to spring, and Venus's corresponding, irritated twist of her head as the imminent taking of her pleasure is thwarted, only add to the mockery. The reappearance of Mars's warhorse breaks the sexual spell, revealing the less than poetic or ideal nature of the lovers' appetites. The introduction of the animal into the bedroom intimates that there is, after all, something still warlike – or better, *horse-like* – about their encounter, and that physical passion might not be the same thing as 'Love' in its more elevated sense. The timeless mythological idyll is, in this painting, interrupted by the constant suggestion of the physical act of coitus, and the lovers' passion might not be entirely free from future consequences. Cupid's unexpected intervention serves as a reminder of the illicitness of the gods' affair. Instead of the boy with the horse, it might easily have been Venus's cuckolded old husband Vulcan limping down to the chamber to discover his wife's affair, and to put in train the adulterers' capture in a net and subsequent exposure to the ridicule of the gods.[17]

By the 1570s, however, Veronese had arrived at a much grander and more monumental manner for his mythologies: an elevated presentation in which the pagan gods – or at least the female ones – are allowed to appear as dignified by their passions, the one-on-one liaison generating wider allegorical meanings. In the *Venus and Mars United by Love* (New York, Metropolitan Museum of Art) the scene is translated to a suitably pastoral or Arcadian

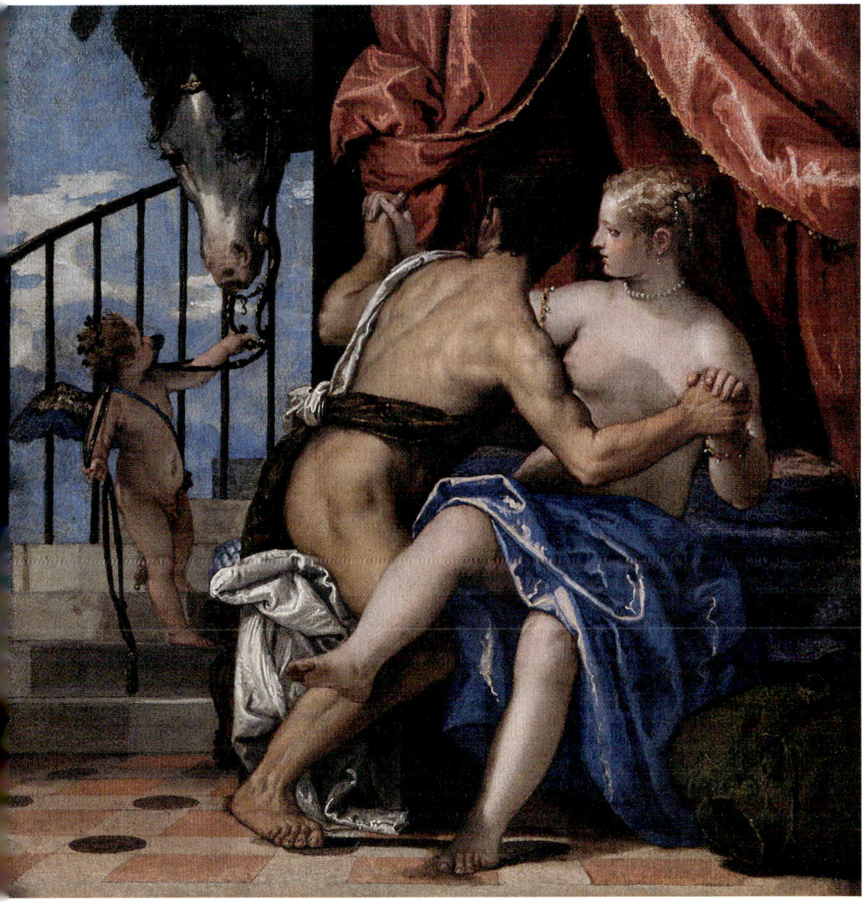

49 Veronese, *Venus and Mars*, *c.* 1560–65, oil on canvas.

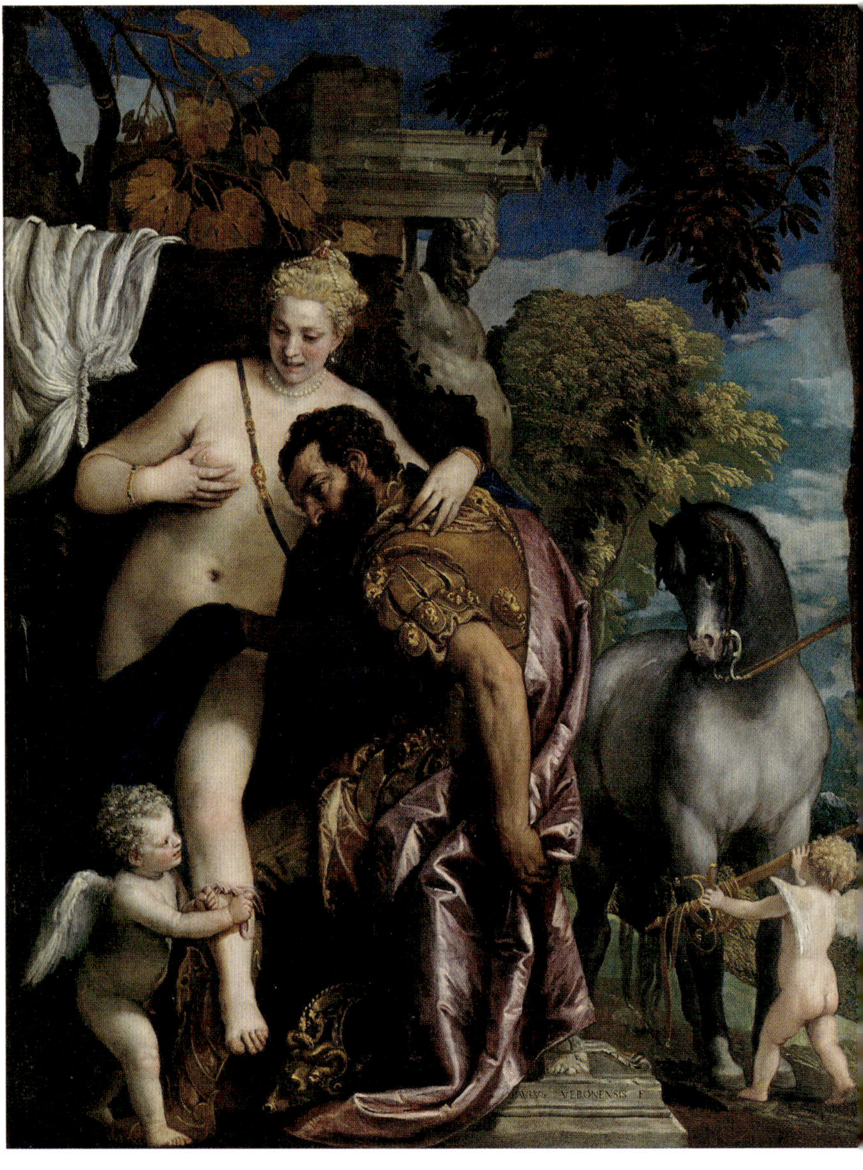

50 Veronese, *Venus and Mars United by Love*, *c.* 1570–75, oil on canvas.

outdoor setting and is partially allegorized (illus. 50). Mars, dressed as a soldier, appears as a heroically powerful (though also defeated) figure, lightly bound by a golden tassel to his mistress by one cupid, while another reverses the motif in the Turin painting, intervening to prevent the horse from disturbing the pair with the god's own sword. Mars's feelings towards his lover are elevated to a higher register through the cupids' double interventions, the one keeping his sexual ardour at bay, while the other binds him to a non-physical principle of Love, now more clearly symbolized by the shining-fleshed figure of Venus. The dangerous, all-absorbing narcissistic physical engagement of the lovers in the Turin painting is replaced by Mars's decorous subordination, which means that he must sit passively below his resplendent standing mistress, whose breast milk – mirrored by the nearby flow of the fountain – expresses her endless fertility.

Veronese's Neoplatonism is, however, playful enough, as the less-than-pleased expression of the god of war indicates. He seems to submit to his fate, but the turn of his dark, shaggy head away from his lover is not only deferential; it suggests too his displeasure in the face of her imposition of a new supra-sexual hierarchy of Love. As in his other allegorizing mythologies, Veronese is careful to suggest that something more than the apparent moral theme is in play. Mars's slumped posture may suggest his new-found doubts about the morally hazardous adulterous affair he has embarked on. But it indicates too his parallel awareness of what he must give up to avoid the derisive laughter of the gods (and of his viewer). There must at least be a chance that this still physically all-powerful god will rebel against the cupid's insubstantial binding of the lovers' legs; or that the background infant's tepid intervention with Mars's little sword against the still eager and pressing horse will not sustain for too long. The lecherous satyr featured in a pagan sculpture just above him – apt symbol of Mars's truncated or thwarted sexual urge

– might be reduced to inertia by his stoniness. But still he seems to turn his head interestedly towards the embracing pair, as if he understands that all is not quite so decided.[18]

THE CHOICE BETWEEN VIRTUE AND VICE/WISDOM AND STRENGTH

In two paintings of the mid-1560s Veronese had already adapted his mythological mode towards the allegorical, making the underlying moral meaning hard to miss (illus. 51, 52).[19] Abstract ideas are more pressingly insisted on, as indicated by the supply of the guiding inscriptions: '(H)ONOR ET VIRTUS/POST MOTEM FLORET' ('Honour and Virtue Flourish after Death') and 'OMNIA VANITAS' ('All is Vanity'). To a still greater extent than in his other paintings, Veronese's painted *all'antica* statues serve here as negative markers, their broken truncated limbs reflecting their failed authority in the morally superior Christian present. The fulsome sculptural female nude at the upper left of *The Choice between Virtue and Vice*, placed just below the moralizing inscription, is also associated with the active living figure of Vice below, while the second statue of a sphinx, with a knife between her breasts concealed behind Vice's back, speaks of her treachery and cruelty.

The un-Veronesian moral tone of these two paintings is supported by the painter's taught and crisp handling, in which contrasts in local colours are made particularly intense, and the finish unusually high. These qualities are probably explained by the fact that the two works were made with a northern royal court patron in mind.[20] They are probably identifiable with the paintings listed (among others) by the art dealer Jacopo Strada (active in Venice) for sale to Albrecht II of Bavaria in 1567.[21] As such, they are likely to be the first works that Veronese made for export to the European courts, and display an interesting modulation of his normative style for an anticipated audience north of the Alps. In keeping with the predilections of his anticipated German patron, Veronese loosely modelled his *Choice between Virtue and Vice* on Dürer's engraving of the *Choice of Hercules* (1498) although he also transposed the scene into an apparent present day, dressing his actors in fashionable clothing, jewellery and coiffure. The young nobleman's dash away from Vice's lap into the arms of Virtue is presented as particularly precipitate, even if it was intended to offer a behavioural example to a young aristocrat or ruler. His undignified haste suggests that his decision has only just been made, and that it was a close-run thing. He glances worriedly over his shoulder, still sensing the physical proximity and allure of Vice, who has left her mark, quite literally, on his left calf, where his ripped stocking reveals a bloody gash from the talons she displays on her right hand. If we can take it that he has made the right decision, then he does not enter Virtue's arms unscathed.

In the other painting, Strength's *all'antica* identity as Hercules – he is dressed in the skin of the Nemean Lion and his massive figure recalls the Farnese *Hercules* in Rome – seems this time to consign him to defeat. He looks bleakly downwards towards the earth, his semi-nudity speaking of worldly transience rather than strength and making a suitable contrast with the lavishly dressed, heaven-blessed and heaven-gazing figure to his right. Squeezed out of the main picture space, his awkward and unresolved leaning posture contrasts with the easy elegance of Wisdom's pose. As such, he appears to be a precursor of that other ancient strong man featured as a defeated figure in the New York painting of *Venus and Mars*, as also in the later version in Edinburgh (*c.* 1580 National Galleries of Scotland). In the latter painting, Veronese shows the god of war as a darkened and relatively slight secondary figure, easily outshone by his paramour. In a surviving preparatory drawing for this painting, Mars is not included at all, indicating that he was a late addition, perhaps even an afterthought.[22] In

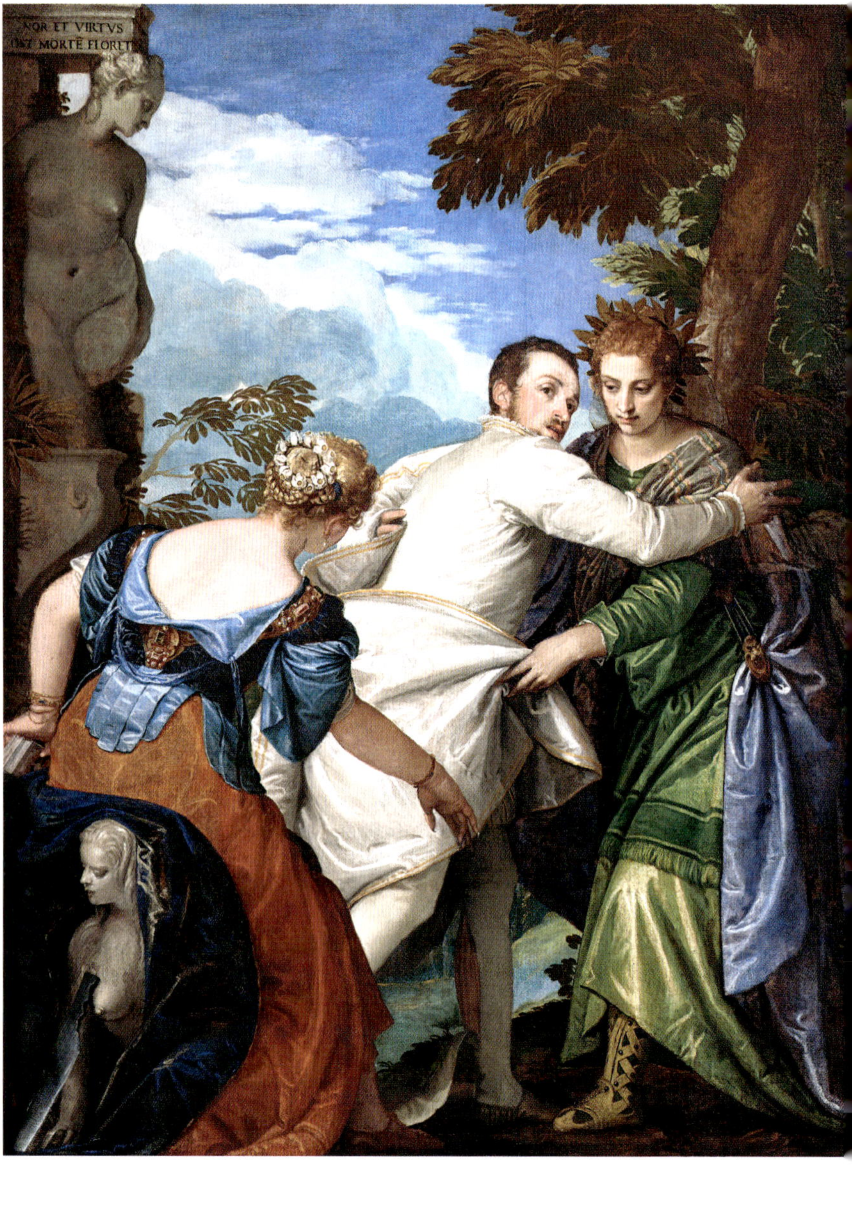

51 Veronese, *The Choice between Virtue and Vice*, c. 1567, oil on canvas.

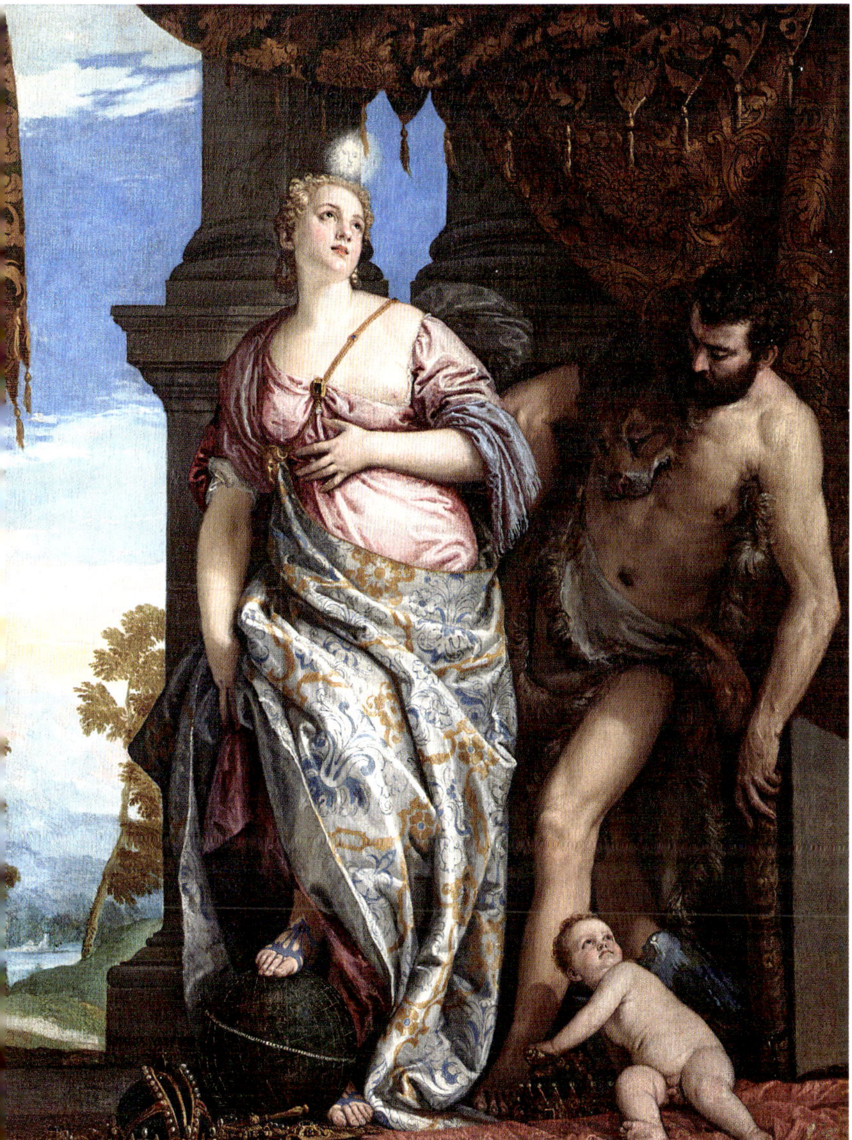

52 Veronese, *Wisdom and Strength*, *c.* 1567, oil on canvas.

the Frick allegory, Strength is similarly marginalized, making him an equivalent to these 'miserable Mars' figures and encouraging a modicum of sympathy with his emasculation, beyond the allegory's simplifying demands. To make things worse, Veronese's careful attention to Wisdom's dress seems to indicate that her dominion is not exclusively otherworldly, heavenly or future-orientated. If her upper and inner garment are historicized, pointedly recalling the traditional colours of the Virgin herself, then the lavishly patterned silken draperies of gold and silver that appear to slide sensually off her lower body, forming sweeping folds along the surface in Veronese's usual manner, are more secular and contemporary in their range of reference. A similar point can be made about the very richly worked and expensive lime-green and blue costume sported by Virtue in the other allegory, held together with an expensively carved gold brooch; or about this figure's especially elaborate footwear, which might serve to piously cover her flesh, but also signals her material *richezza*. Even in these most ethical of allegorical works, anticipating the added piety of a north European royal patron, Veronese's pictorial mode – his sense of the debt owed to sumptuously manufactured materials – presses against the binary terms of the theme. Both paintings are, after all, lavish in appearance, self-consciously fashioned and jewel-like works of art that would be at home in any northern collector's cabinet of curiosities. And if Veronese's still sensual approach does not undermine abstract, hierarchical meanings then it nonetheless demonstrates his refusal to sacrifice surface values to expressive depth, even in his most explicitly moralizing pictures.

THE ALLEGORIES OF LOVE

In a series of four paintings probably made to decorate the ceiling of a Venetian palazzo around 1577–8, Veronese's visual performance more confidently overpowers his commitment to the simplifications of a fixed allegory, or his expression of abstract moral principles.[23] As a consequence, the exact meaning of these works has remained obscure for centuries, their appearance seeming to defy a simple translation back into ideas derived from the non-visual or non-pictorial realm.[24] Louis François Dubois de Saint-Gelais' identification of the four scenes as 'Respect, Love, Scorn and Unfaithfulness' in 1727 is still typically followed.[25] But these titles were always tentative, given that Dubois also noted that the paintings had 'allegorical subjects that everyone explains according to their own way of thinking'. There were certainly precursors to Veronese's approach in previous Venetian paintings of the sixteenth century. His series further developed the local idea of secular paintings as freely conceived 'poetries' or *poesie*, in which received or fixed meanings were laid aside in imagery made intentionally elusive, ambiguous and suggestive. Trying to reconstruct a consistent meaningful narrative for the series is a bit like trying to establish a watertight meaning for a painting by Giorgione, or a late mythology by Titian. Any such attempt would run the risk of contradicting the underlying aim of the work, even if such interpretative projections are encouraged by the imagery.[26]

If these paintings were intended as closely explicatory 'Allegories of Love' then Veronese's pictorial approach resists or defeats this clarifying aim, given that they do not finally deliver an underlying, singular or overarching meaning. Bravura visual performance constantly intervenes to undermine the expression of bounded or consistent abstract ideas. It would be easy to imagine that the imagery follows a now lost iconographic programme, and that its ambiguity will disappear once this is rediscovered.

But we know from the problems surrounding the feast scene for Santi Giovanni e Paolo that Veronese's paintings had a habit of escaping from their precise iconography. It is more likely that in this series he again worked beyond the authority of a given text or a closely defined written programme, inventing pictorially in accordance with his own predilections. But this is certainly not to argue that his imagery therefore becomes meaningless or trivial. The four paintings especially repay close looking, offering a subtle and shifting exploration of the complex and often fraught power relationships between young men and women. Avoiding pat answers and simple distinctions, Veronese's paintings engage the complex existential questions raised by 'Love' but do so in ways that are '*poesie*-like' in that they do not offer final resolution or even intellectual coherence around a theme. In these works, as in certain others discussed in this chapter, Veronese certainly engages ethical questions. But each image continues to defy reduction to an abstracted hierarchical schema.

Women are granted a determinative control over proceedings. In what might be the opening scene, Dubois' proposed title, *Unfaithfulness*, is particularly questionable (illus. 53). The naked young woman between her two clothed suitors controls the dance of desire: the performance is accompanied by music, as the dolorous cupid at the virginals indicates. The entire left side where he plays appears to be winning out, in accordance with the woman's glance, suggesting her impulse towards higher things. The musical cupid with heaven-derived wings contrasts with the more earthbound seated one without them, who half-attempts to restrain his mistress's leanings. The man that the woman seems to choose by passing him a note pointedly looks away from her upwards towards heaven. Perhaps he is poet rather than a second suitor, whose eyes remain fixed on divine and eternal matters. It is tempting to read all this as a Neoplatonic allegory, with the woman playing the role of the goddess of love, shown as caught between her contrasting heavenly and earthly natures: Venus Caelestis and Venus Naturalis. But if she learns from, and leans towards, all to her left, then it is the staring bearded man with the dark curly hair to her right who she will be constrained to deal with in the other paintings in the cycle. Her alluring nudity, blonde hair, elaborate fashionable coiffure and strings of pearls at neck and wrists bring her back down to earth, suggesting that she is a contemporary woman. The surreptitious passing of the note indicates her continued connection to the duplicitous sensual world that she seems inclined to reject. Double-sidedness – and double-dealing – plays an inevitable part in the shifting merry-go-round of relations between these young people, suggesting

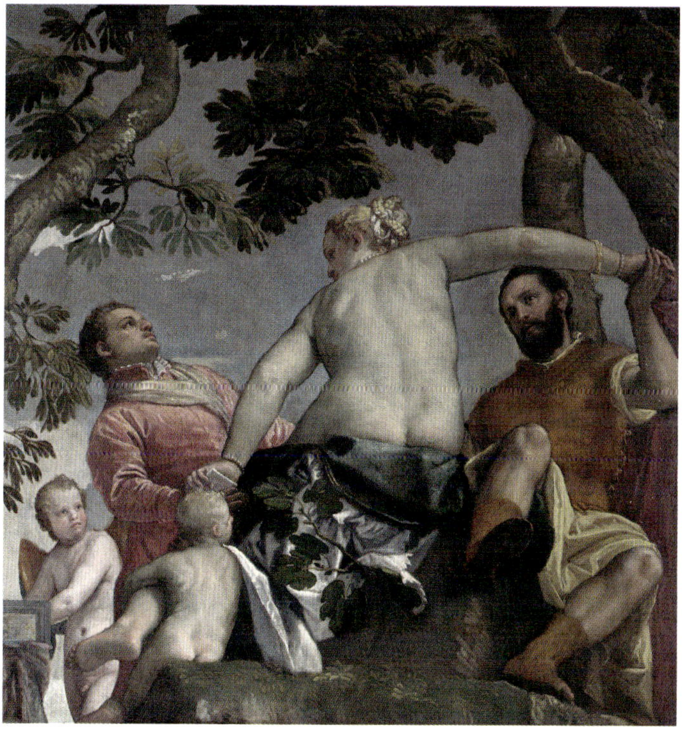

53 Veronese, *Unfaithfulness*, from the 'Allegories of Love' series, *c.* 1577–8, oil on canvas.

the essential fluidity of love and passion beyond the control of the neat philosophical Neoplatonic hierarchies. Dubois' idea of the unfaithfulness of a married or engaged woman seems too prescriptive and judgemental. But her determining power is not in question, and is, in fact, reiterated in each of the subsequent paintings in the cycle.

In *Scorn*, the Veronesian inversion of the male order is at its most explicit and unyielding, as the expected hero is quite literally laid on his back by the power of his desire for the woman who returns only her contempt (illus. 54). A delicate little cupid dances victoriously on his chest without fear and is about to clout him again with his bow, dispensing with the relative subtlety of the usual arrow.[27] Humour often plays through the imagery of the *Allegories* but somehow without trivializing it. The dismembered antique satyr and the cut section of a ruined Pan sculpture provide a mocking commentary on the man's already defeated carnal desires, while the broken-down cornice he lies on is an apt indicator of the inversion: how far the once masculine high and phallically vertical has fallen! Veronese's bathetic imagery works hard to resist the conventional idea that the disempowered sprawling figure is inevitably redeemed by his all-powerful emotion of 'Love', further cancelling the prospect of the kind of elevating release hinted at in the New York painting (illus. 50). Comparison with this work reveals the extent to which Veronese domesticates and contemporizes the scene in the four London paintings: and this despite the precipitous *di sotto in su* view up into each one, or the broken and fallen remnants of ancient sculpture and architecture, which speak of the precarious moral positions of the main protagonists vis-à-vis one another. Rather than safely distanced classical gods, or simplified personifications, we witness a performance much closer to home, put on by ordinary mortals of the present day, its outcome uncertain rather than safely resolved.[28] The undignified subjection of the man on his back in

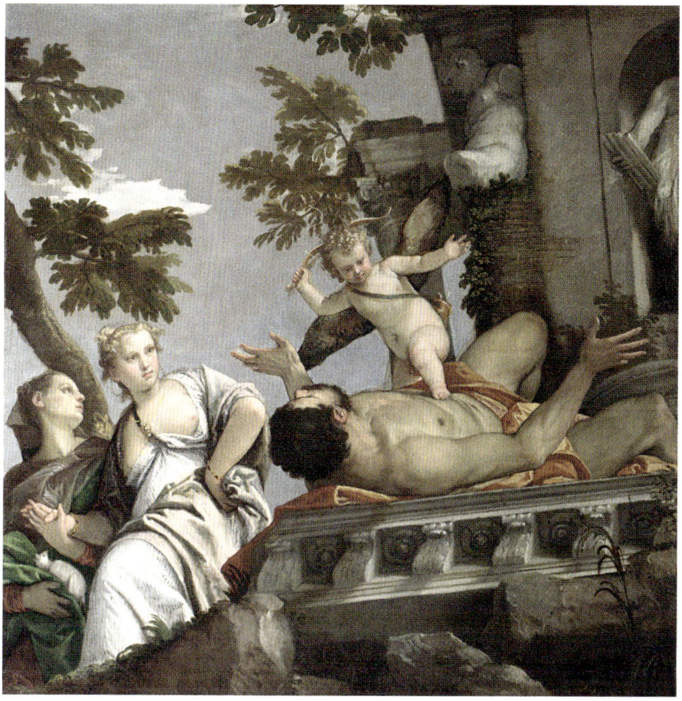

Scorn guarantees very little, as the fierce and disbelieving stare of the object of his passion warns us.

In *Respect*, Veronese reverses the gender roles, with the man shown as clothed and upright and the woman as naked and supine (illus. 55). This was superficially to resurrect the more conventional positions of male and female in earlier erotic mythological painting in Venice, pioneered by Giorgione and Titian, with its implication of a hierarchical power relationship between an active and projective observing male and a passive, reclining female who is viewed (and desired) beyond her control and without her consent. In many such works, typically featuring Venus or one of her eroticized types, the immobile horizontalized woman accommodates the view of the – typically unrepresented – phallically

54 Veronese, *Scorn*, from the 'Allegories of Love' series, *c.* 1577–8, oil on canvas.

verticalized man who observes her with impunity from beyond the frame.[29] But in *Respect*, one such 'viewer', at least, is already admitted into the painting, his gaze on his love object deflected heavenwards, in response to the apparent theme. How far this cancelling of the man's conventionally privileged view can delimit the spectator's own seems now to be the question raised by the picture, even if the answer remains elusive. The *Scorn* had already inverted the usual viewer-image construction, empowering the woman; the man's broken view in *Respect* intimates something similar, proposing a deferral or disruption of the normative proprietorial male gaze.

Drawing on Titian's imagery of problematic or forbidden male viewing in his *poesía* showing *Díana and Actaeon* of 1556–9, Veronese's

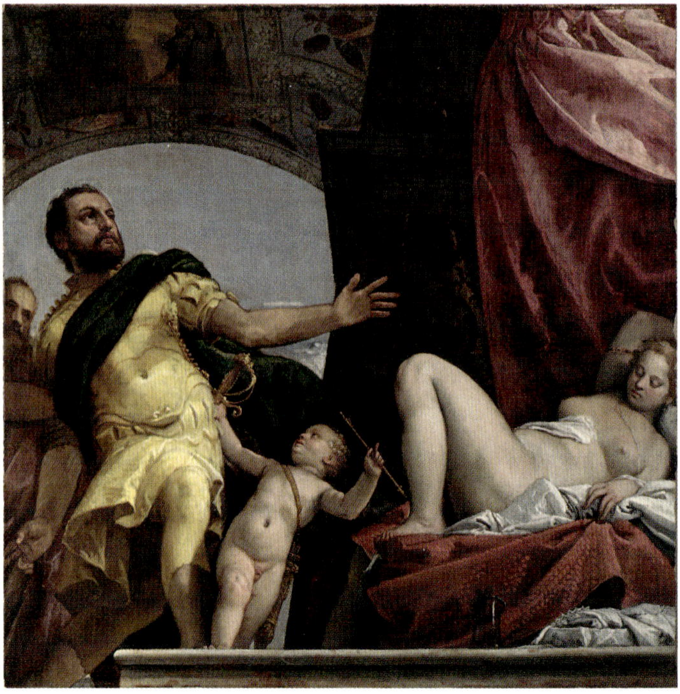

55 Veronese, *Respect*, from the 'Allegories of Love' series, *c.* 1577–8, oil on canvas.

Respect again puts things on a knife-edge. We are shown an unanticipated and potentially rapacious male entering the private bedroom of an appealing young female reclining on her bed who has not permitted him to enter and is unaware of his presence. But what will be the outcome? The positioning of her fleshy body – the upper part a memory of Giorgione's supine *Sleeping Venus*, the lower recalling Titian's various versions of Danaë – is provocative enough, even if it must be taken as an innocent movement in her sleep.[30] If she has not registered or sanctioned the man's entry into her chamber, then he has certainly already laid eyes on her, as his halted stride and exaggerated posture of self-control indicate. Will his chaste or 'noble' deferral of illicit looking be enough to win her approval or forgiveness? However that future drama might play out – and a return to 'Scorn' seems a possibility – the invasive gaze of the viewer remains very much in play, at least insofar as this onlooker is imagined as a man. The spectator's eye is not constrained to follow that of the respectful one depicted, straying readily across the painting surface to take in the woman's soft, exposed flesh, and detonating an inevitable erotic charge in the process. Can the male viewer learn from the interrupted stride of his surrogate hero of restraint to the left of the painting? Might the unreformed invasive gaze from beyond the frame even throw doubt on the truth of the depicted one's histrionic reform? After all, we have just seen him sprawling naked on his back in a paroxysm of yearning.

The moral questions raised by male desire and looking in *Unfaithfulness*, *Scorn* and *Respect* might seem to be answered in *Happy Union* (Dubois's 'Love'), which appears to resolve the difficulties of the previous paintings through a final marriage (illus. 56). But is a resolution or explanation really what we see? If the naked woman straddling the globe, her legs parted as she does so, is really meant as 'Fortuna', then is she capable of granting the couple before her release from the vicissitudes of passion (deferred or otherwise) that they have previously been driven by? There is anyway something more generic about the imagery in this painting, as Veronese returns again to one of his favoured compositional schemas, showing a kneeling or genuflecting person on some steps before a raised crowning authority figure, in front of a grand facade that extends vertically out of the upper part of the picture. The iterative qualities of the painting suggest that Veronese was less interested in resolving the questions raised by the imagery in the other three paintings in intellectual or moral terms than in presenting a visually alluring but still ambiguous *mise en scène*. Veronese notably gendered this imagery of triumphal coronation as feminine, in a manner that recalls his

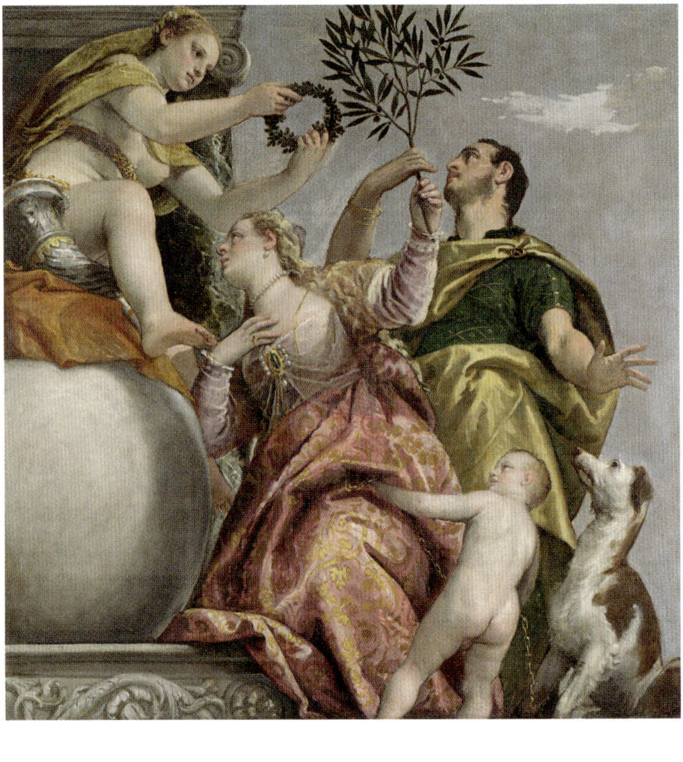

56 Veronese, *Happy Union*, from the 'Allegories of Love' series, *c.* 1577–8, oil on canvas.

altarpiece for the Augustinian nuns of Santa Caterina (illus. 39). The (mostly) naked crowning figure, plumb and fleshy rather than abstracted and idealized, retains certain qualities of Venus, even as her position astride a huge stone globe, suggesting her rule over the world, suggests she is 'Fortune'. She mirrors the richly attired woman kneeling at her feet before her. It may be no accident that this young mortal looks adoringly towards the naked goddess's belly rather than meeting her eyes: staring intently towards her womb, seat of feminine fertility. The coronation of one generative woman by another with a myrtle wreath – more strongly associated with Venus than Fortune – displaces the olive branch held jointly by the couple on the steps, even as this latter signifies their peaceable marriage. The male presence to the right – as represented by the groom, cupid and dog – is consigned to a supporting role that might remind us of Strength and Mars in the works discussed earlier in this chapter. The handsome dark-haired man may seem to have at last got his prize, having learned the lesson on Respect. But his secondary role in the denouement recalls his earlier unedifying appearances as the hapless victim of deceit, and of his own abject desire, pictured in the other paintings for the cycle.

A sole surviving pen, ink and wash drawing tells us that Veronese conceived all four paintings together, and in close relation with one another (illus. 57). The sheet defines the compositions with extraordinary concision, establishing the relationship between the figures within each group as also their spatial relation to a projected viewing position from below. Only the sprawling man in *Scorn*, repeated five times towards the centre, seems to have caused Veronese much trouble in this regard, as he attempted to establish the exact angle of foreshortening required. It thus seems likely that this sheet of sketches was made very rapidly on site, perhaps all on one occasion, as an aide de memoire for the paintings made later in the workshop. The sheet

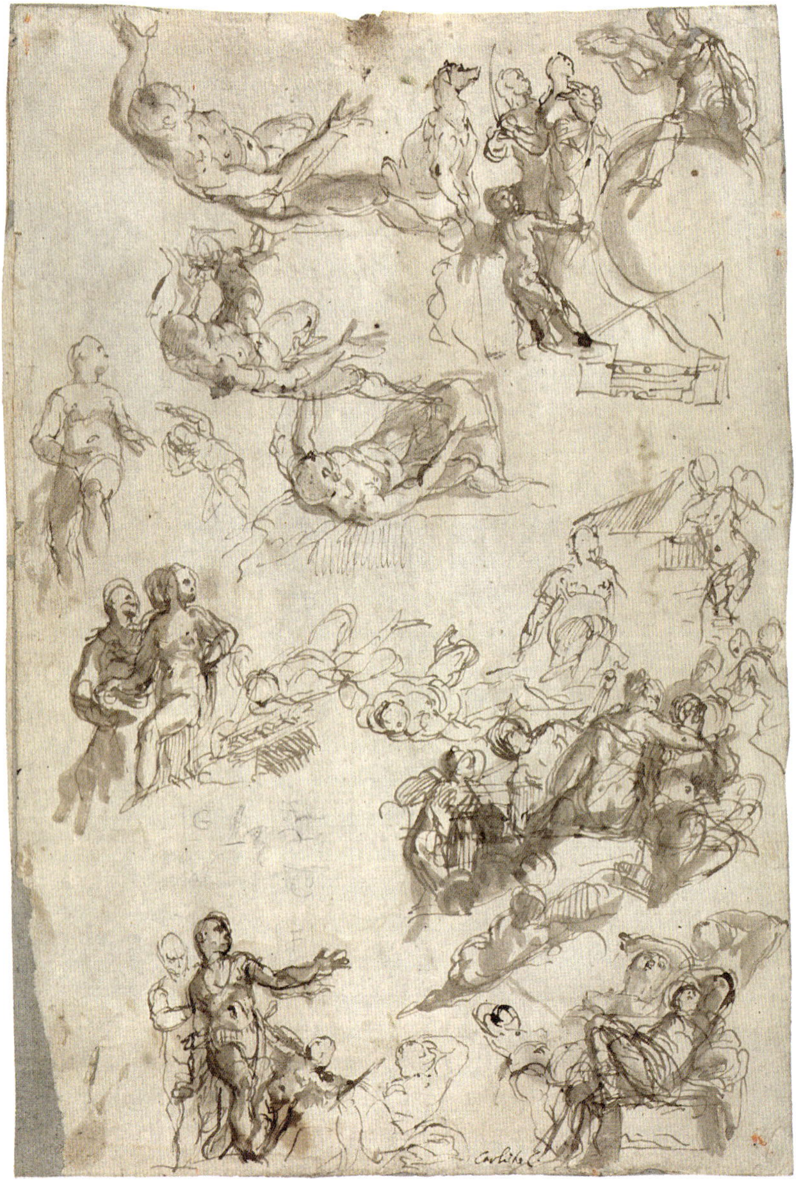

57 Veronese, *Studies for the 'Allegories of Love'*, *c.* 1577–8, pen and brown ink, brush and brown wash on paper.

must surely be a chance survival from a much more extensive process of preparation. Its visual economy is nonetheless striking, as is the closeness of each grouping to the final work. If the earlier sheet of studies discussed in Chapter One (illus. 15) indicates the painter's habit of simultaneous movement between ideas for different paintings, this later one is more closely focused on the immediate task in hand, suggesting greater specificity and accuracy in relation to the paintings concerned. Like the other surviving sheets of pen, ink and wash drawings from his later period, it indicates that Veronese's graphic approach gradually became less synoptic or digressive over time. If, by the mid-1570s, he did more studies of this kind, sometimes for the use – or with the help – of his growing workshop, then they also became more closely tied to the specific task in hand.

VENICE, JUSTICE AND PEACE

Despite this, Veronese's habit of allowing his paintings to overlap in visual and semantic terms continued into the 1570s, with compositions and ideas being readily adapted from one commission, picture type or subject-matter to another. It is noticeable that the sketch for the *Happy Union* developed at the upper right of the drawing is reversed. It follows the directionality of a larger ceiling painting for the ceiling of the Sala del Collegio in the Ducal Palace, suggesting that the Allegories of Love series followed rather than preceded the works for the Collegio ceiling, which date from 1575–7. In the *Venice, Justice and Peace* a raised enthroned woman is placed at the upper right, while two others approach her on some steps to the lower left (illus. 58). The enthroned woman is 'Venetia', although the curve of the globe beneath her throne suggests her subsidiary identity as 'Fortuna'. Venus is also evoked, given that this goddess was, like the city itself, born from the sea. The dominant woman – synthetic image

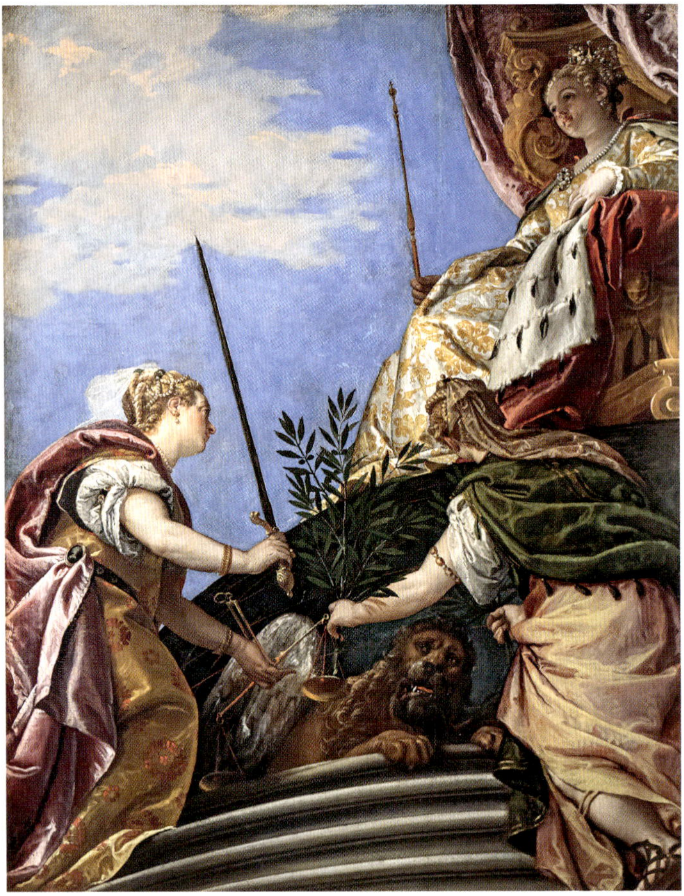

of the Venetian state – is lavishly enrobed and holds an upward-pointing sceptre to indicate her royal status and heavenly connection. As in his other paintings for the Sala del Collegio, Veronese made little attempt to emulate the flickering drama of Tintoretto's near-contemporary ceiling paintings for the Sala Capitolare of the Scuola Grande di San Rocco. Instead, he took care to maintain continuity with his own earlier ceiling paintings,

58 Veronese, *Venice, Justice and Peace*, 1575–7, oil on canvas.

placing his bulky figures in precipitous forward planes and draping them in an array of contrasting brightly coloured and patterned fabrics that hold the eye close to the surface. His adaptation of imagery to the official context and to the presiding myths of Venice as the perfect state was relatively seamless.[31] The personifications featured in the *Venice, Justice and Peace* are identified as the *Custodes libertatis* (Custodians of Liberty) in a nearby inscription. But as in the presumably private commission for the Allegories of Love, the figures work their effect through the semantic overlap or slippage generated between different identities.

Whether he worked on a sacred scene for a church ceiling (illus. 17); a High altarpiece showing a popular saint for a convent (illus. 39); a sensual and ambiguous *poesia* for a private palazzo (illus. 56); or, as in the current work, a political state allegory, Veronese maintained a consistent visual template that could be adapted to specific iconographic needs as they arose. Very often, a singular, internally generated, compositional idea can be seen to have underwritten Veronese's approach across several decades. Some of Veronese's preferred visual schemas were admittedly tied more closely to specific picture types or to related subject-matters, such as the biblical feast scene for a Monastic refectory, or the two-lover model applied to erotic mythologies and allegories. This template approach nonetheless gives his paintings a generic quality, lending a meta quality to his visual thinking that allowed him to operate beyond the specific demands of varying patrons, picture types and iconographies. Taking this approach had certain practical advantages, allowing the painter and his growing posse of assistants to work quickly and efficiently in the completion of many commissions. It also served to protect the visual consistency of his art against external pressures or contingencies. In the compositional type noted here, the enthroned figure is typically female, whether she is identified as the Virgin Mary, Fortune, Venus or Venice, or is worshipped by adoring figures of a secular young woman, a queenly saint, or personifications of leading biblical virtues.[32]

APOTHEOSIS OF VENICE

Following a further fire in the Ducal Palace in 1577, Veronese's career as a state painter was extended into the early 1580s, when he and his workshop worked alongside those of Tintoretto, and the younger masters Palma Giovane (1544–1628) and Francesco Bassano (1549–1592), on an extensive pictorial enterprise of re-decoration in the main state rooms. Veronese, as Ridolfi was keen to point out, seems to have enjoyed a position as *primus inter pares*, winning the commission to paint a vast Paradise on the tribune wall of the Sala del Maggior Consiglio.[33] Although Veronese produced several presentation sketches (*modelli*) for this painting, the final work was only completed by Tintoretto in the years following his death in 1588. Veronese did complete a major work for the Sala, however: the huge central ceiling painting showing the *Apotheosis of Venice*, which was finished in 1582 (illus. 59).[34] In this work, he revisited many of the visual motifs and ideas that he had developed over the course of the earlier decades, although these were now stage-managed or synthesized – undoubtedly with the help of his brother and two painter-sons – on a still grander scale. Veronese's painting was both a culminating answer to his patrician patrons' social and political aspirations and a self-reflexive exercise in independent pictorial design.

Veronese's imagery of the crowning of Venetia draws most immediately on the recent *Venice, Justice and Peace* although it is further expanded and monumentalized. If the dominant female figure in that work is seated then this becomes less clear in the *Apotheosis*, given that she floats free of the massive architecture behind her. In this detail Veronese reprised his own earlier depictions of the Coronation and Assumption of the Virgin, dating back as far as the mid-1550s at San Sebastiano (illus. 16).[35] The apparent overlap between secular and sacred iconographies was apposite in ideological terms, recalling as it did the accepted (though mythic) foundation date of Venice, 25 March 421, the Feast of the Annunciation to the Virgin. But Veronese's reference to the city he celebrated was characteristically indirect, at least in architectural terms, insofar as the enormous facade does not recall any existing structure in Venice. The grandiose architecture is supported by giant twisting Solomonic columns similar to those Veronese had seen in Giulio Romano's frescoes at the Palazzo Te in Mantua in the early 1550s, and had reprised in his frescoes in the upper nave at San Sebastiano and, in a private context, at the Villa Barbaro.[36] Insofar as this structure also takes on qualities of a triumphal arch, then it recalls the buildings of ancient Rome, as Giulio's painted columns in Mantua already had. So much was, in fact, in accordance with the programme Veronese was asked to illustrate.[37] This entailed imagining one city in terms of another, equating the apotheosis of Venice with the appearances of the Eternal City.[38] It was to make the Republic appear as a court: a suggested transposition which, as we have seen throughout this book, was central to Veronese's successful visualization of the social ambitions of the Venetian patriciate. If Veronese pictures Venice in terms of Rome, then he also goes further, given that the latter city had no hereditary governing family. In the fantasized world of Veronese's painting, Venetia is depicted as an ascending queen, holding her sceptre of command, about to be crowned by Victory. Showing her in this guise, Veronese once more engaged the age-old idea of Venice as the Venus-like 'Queen of the Sea'. But he also took care to update this idea by substituting an idea of Venice as a royal court for its older identity as a mercantile Republic.

Something of this secondary regal and courtly reimagining, beyond the conventional mythic narratives of the city, is evident from the leisured seated or reclining postures of Venetia's higher

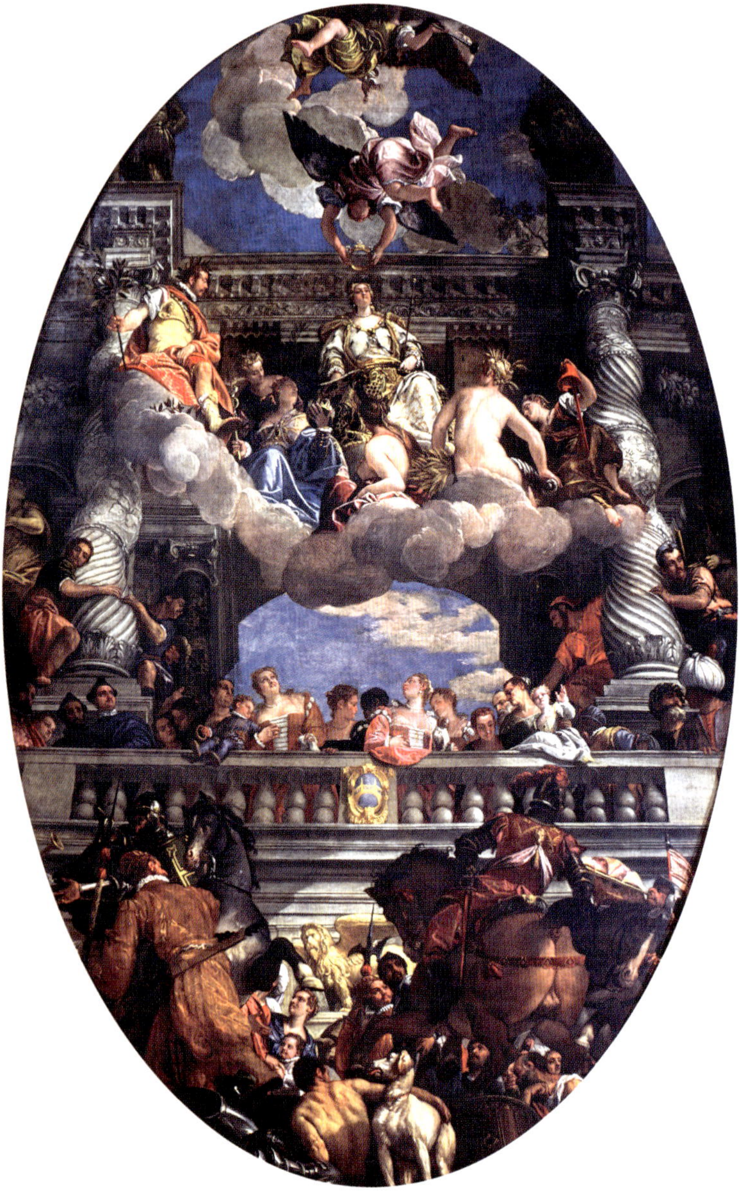

59 Veronese, *Apotheosis of Venice*, 1579–82, oil on canvas.

coterie of Virtues, who are richly attired and float on clouds just beneath her. This elite circle of six, including two semi-naked – though decorously back-turned – figures of Felicity and Abundance, is dominated by women. Only Peace with the olive branch (but still sporting his tell-tale cuirass) to the left breaks the pattern of female dominance in the upper region of the painting.[39] The personification of Venice as a woman was centuries-old at the Palace, but Veronese nonetheless greatly expands upon the idea, in accordance with the wider feminizing propensities already noted in works such as the *Venice, Justice and Peace*. Venetia is, too, the visual offspring of his earlier female authority figures such as Latona at the Villa Barbaro (illus. 28), 'Wisdom' in the Frick allegory (illus. 52) or Venus in the mythology in New York (illus. 50). Two tiers down, in an intermediary zone that is both idealized and worldly, Veronese fills a balcony with contemporary women and children of the city: denizens of the once private and hived off domesticated spaces of the city are now given centre stage in a state allegory. One of the most prominent figures with her lapdog sat on the balustrade and a servant to the right, this time holding her child, strongly recalls the family imagery on the fictive balcony scene at Maser (illus. 29). She is probably no longer identifiable as a specific wife, but seems (like the other patrician women depicted) to serve a similar purpose within the wider scheme of Veronese's imagery: promoting the idea of such noblewomen as the fundamental mainstay not only of Venetian private life, but of the state itself. It is the domestic world of women, children and their servants (including a Black boy) that is now made the visual synecdoche of Venice, their figures standing in for the entire city. This represented something of a departure from many other state allegories or depictions of official occasions in paintings or prints, in which women do not appear at all, are historicized or allegorized, or are barely glimpsed, peering out of enclosing windows as they watch the men process in the public spaces of the city.[40]

In Veronese's *Apotheosis*, the women push aside the men on the intermediary level to take centre stage, their appearances closely mirroring those others relaxedly floating on the clouds above. Below them, at the lowest level in the painting, a comparatively shadowy and violent male-dominated action scene unfolds, as soldiers on rearing horses suggestive of warfare crowd into an amorphous and chaotic foreground space, beyond the bounding architectural wall of 'Venetia' itself, guarded by the familiar winged lion of St Mark.[41] The terms of the allegory make it clear enough that the peaceable and civilized family life enjoyed by those above is secured by this grimly conflictual masculine world below. The otherwise anachronistic personification of 'Peace' as an armoured man near to Venetia above seems to suggest as much. But in visual terms the women are imagined as elevated and superior to the men below them, who are by contrast condemned always to struggle and fight. Those on the balcony do not gaze admiringly or gratefully down on those who act on their behalf. Instead, they look upwards, like feminized apostles, watching another woman – Venetia – ascend, and aspiring like her to a place in the heavenly sphere at the top of the painting.

SIX

Late Works

Veronese died on 19 April 1588 of a pulmonary infection, apparently contracted after he had participated in a religious procession near his country home near Treviso on the *terraferma*. He was just sixty years old, and thus did not have time to develop an old-aged style comparable to those of Titian, Tintoretto and Bassano. He did, however, have a 'late style', given that, from around 1580 onwards, at least away from the Palace, his palette darkened, and his approach became more expressive and dramatic. This meant laying aside the jubilant pictorialism that was for so long characteristic of his approach, while newly admitting elements of narrative urgency, sometimes with tragic dimensions, that he had previously avoided or eschewed. The causes of this development are hard to pin down, but must in part reflect changes in taste among his patrons, themselves a reflection of the darkening cultural climate in Venice: one marked by fires, disease and increasing political adversity, as also by a creeping sense that the city's sumptuous lifestyle had brought down the wrath of God himself. Even in his most sombre and serious works from this last decade, however, Veronese typically managed to accommodate the new concern with suffering and transience without abandoning altogether his established pictorial principles. If shadows now more readily encroach on Veronese's lavish play of surfaces, and the full light of day is replaced by expressive gloaming, then his earlier insistence on joyful visuality is not forgotten. The Veronese style instead proved elastic in its ability to incorporate alternative effects, becoming dialectical in its fluid movement between surface and depth, sanguinity and seriousness.

TWO LATE MYTHOLOGIES AND A DEVOTIONAL WORK

In a pair of mythologies from circa 1580–81, Veronese allowed darker elements to infiltrate the once charmed and trouble-free idyll of his imagined classical world (illus. 60, 61).[1] In the *Venus and Adonis*, Veronese stills the narrative in his usual manner, presenting the two lovers as intimately sequestered as they enjoy the unfettered sensual bliss of the classical Arcadia. By comparison with Veronese's earlier depiction of this subject (illus. 47), the possibility of the hero's departure for the hunt is further downplayed, as he lies sleeping on Venus's lap.[2] This was to adapt a visual motif usually associated with Mars rather than Adonis in Renaissance paintings, in which it typically signifies positively: as an indicator of sensual post-coital bliss or of the ultimate victory of Love over War. But in the Madrid painting, where the motif is adapted to the ill-fated mortal Adonis, it takes on more ominous overtones. The hunter might be presently relaxed, but his unconsciousness also contains a darker allusion to his upcoming death, drawing on well-established period conventions that saw sleep as death's brother, mirror or precursor.[3]

In this work, Veronese belatedly turns to facial expression to set the tone. Venus's surprised mien suggests her emotion of sudden realization, and perhaps dread, as she has a powerful premonition of her lover's dark fate. Her head twists suddenly away from her torso to emphasize the immediacy of this inward apprehension, as she becomes aware of the significance of Adonis's eager hunting dog, and of the mortal intimations of his sleep. There are other instances of the importance of facial expression in Veronese's oeuvre, although it had long been his preference to downplay such indicators of inward emotion, subsuming the individual figure into larger figural masses to maintain the viewer's primary attention on surface qualities.[4] In the Prado painting, Venus's face, with its implication of inner fear or doubt, intervenes against the surface calm. But this is made a matter of fine balancing between contrary modes, given that her look does not quite overreach or undermine the enjoyment of more immediate pleasures. Nonetheless, things are on the turn. As in the Augsburg version, the ever-supportive Cupid boy-hugs the hound in an attempt to defeat its bloody instincts, still implying light-heartedness.[5] But the joke has faded. His struggle with the dog might only delay the inevitable, as the goddess, with her divine foreknowledge of the future, already understands.

When viewed alongside its pendant, showing *Cephalus and Procris*, this sense of foreboding would have been more apparent still, given that in this other work death becomes the explicit subject (illus. 61). The *Cephalus* provides a compositional mirror image, focused on twinned upright and reclining figures, though with genders reversed, an effect that would have been more apparent still when the pair were originally viewed together on the walls of a private home, with the *Adonis* to the left and the *Cephalus* to the right. In the latter work, the tragic husband helplessly watches the colour drain from the body of his jealous wife, whom he has accidentally killed with the arrow she gave him while hunting. His sorrowful explanation and pleading are wholly lost on his unintentional victim. Even as their fingers lovingly entwine in one final moment of intimacy, her other hand goes limp, releasing the fatal arrow from its grip. Veronese's inclusion of a dying body at the front of his painting is very similar to his placement of the recently dead Christ in a near-contemporary devotional painting of the *Pietà* (illus. 62). In both works, looming shadows encroach upon the figures, while the gesturing angel in the *Pietà*, replete

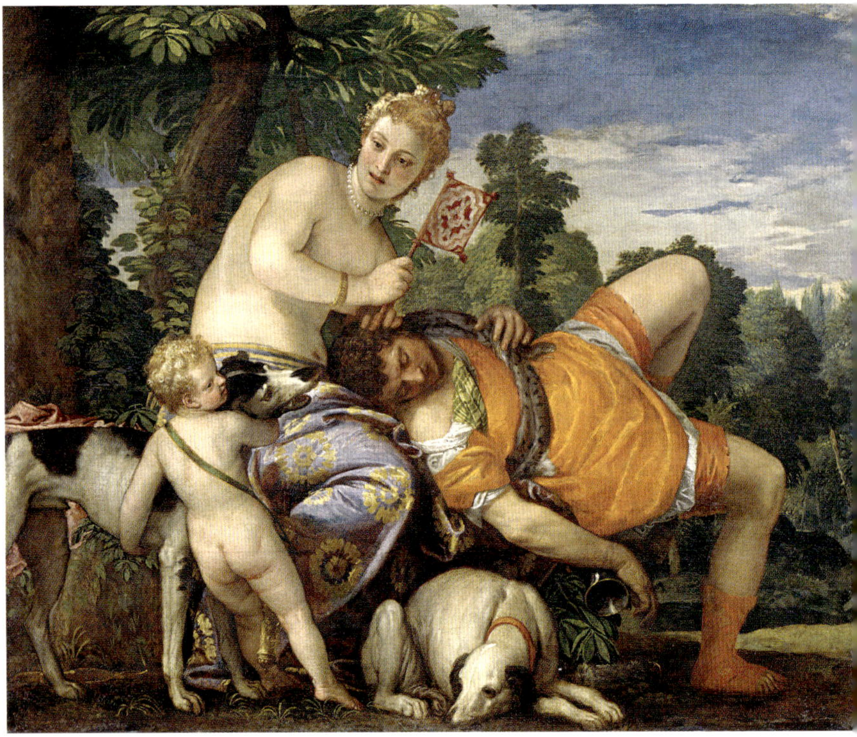

with classical hair and footwear, parallels the figure of Cephalus, indicating Veronese's ready play between sacred and secular image worlds. The emotive motif of interlocking fingers between the angel and Christ was easily adapted to – or from – the mythological setting. The dying woman lies parallel to the picture plane, retaining a planar *all'antica* dimension.[6] But if the white-gold brocade of her dress allows her fallen figure a residual effect of lavish material *richezza*, all that seems about to fade away as the colour drains from her face. The heroine's expression mirrors to some degree that of Venus in the pendant, although now her open mouth and rolling eyes indicate upcoming death much more explicitly. Even her luxuriant garment seems to blanche, the

60 Veronese, *Venus and Adonis*, *c.* 1580–81, oil on canvas.

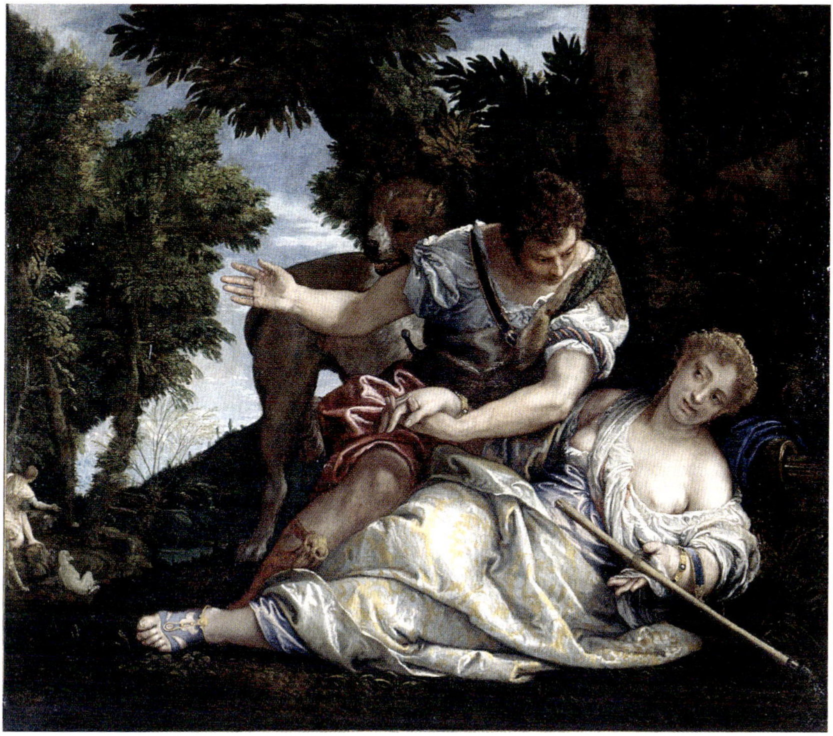

washed-out tones suggesting that it might soon be transformed into a pale winding sheet like the one on which Christ reclines in the *Pietà*.

The *Pietà* – sometimes known as the 'Dead Christ' given that it is unclear that the protagonist really does recline on his mother's lap – is a characteristic example from the increasing number of private devotional works that Veronese completed in the last decade or so of his life. In these pointedly pious works, Veronese modulated his usual flamboyant style, typically featuring the naked body of Christ, shown as highly lit in the foreground, in a way that deliberately recalls the frontal mode of traditional sacred icons.[7] In these works, simplicity of presentation and iconographic

61 Veronese, *Cephalus and Procris*, c. 1580–81, oil on canvas.

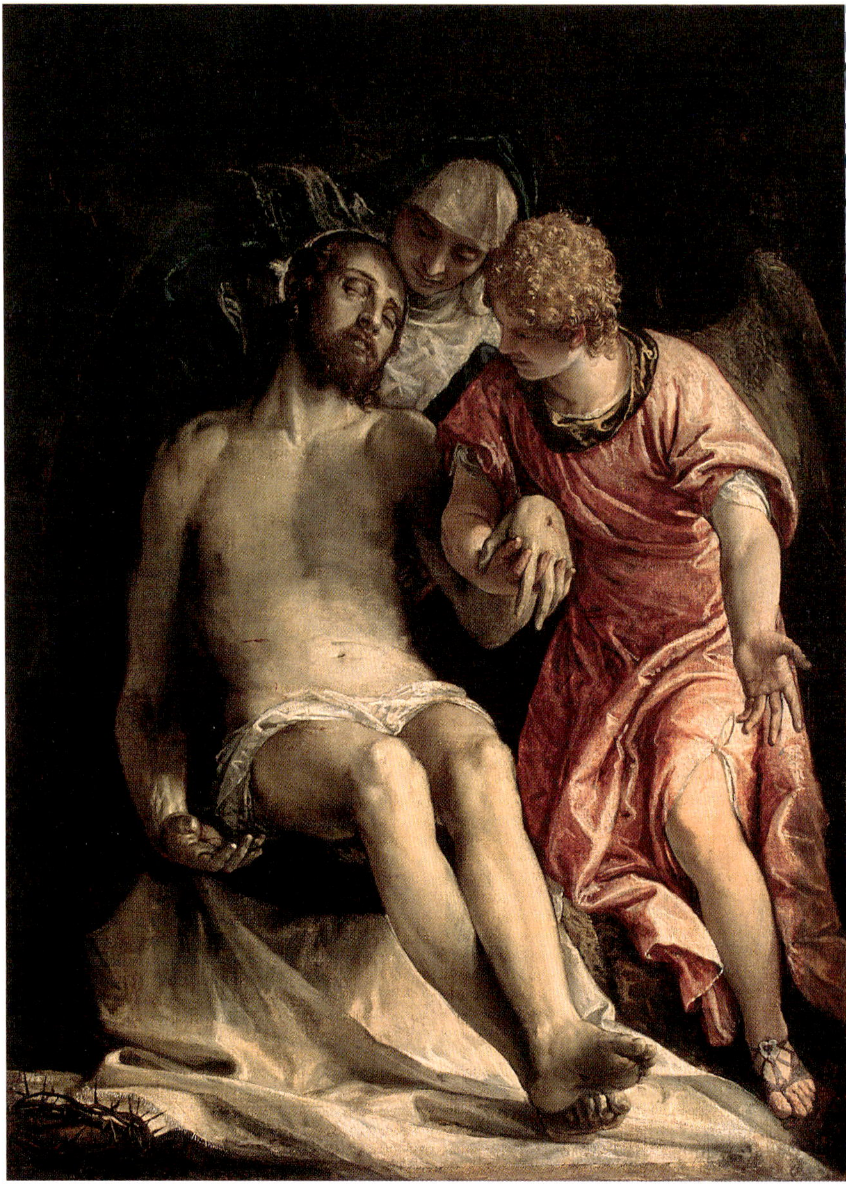

62 Veronese, *Pietà* (*Dead Christ*), *c.* 1581, oil on canvas.

explicitness replace pictorial digression, with distracting accessory figures or anecdotal vignettes excluded. The visual dominance of the saviour's body in the *Píetà* is typical of such works. It occludes that of his mother in a manner that may recall Michelangelo's pointedly reformist arrangement of the equivalent figures at the top of his *Last Judgement* in the Sistine Chapel. A tendency towards Christocentric imagery had anyway become de rigueur in Venice, as leading patrons in the city sought to demonstrate their Counter-Reformatory piety.[8] In the *Píetà*, Veronese pointedly departed from his usual compositional planarity, replacing surface values with an emphasis on spatial depth that served to mark its spiritual equivalent. Christ's feet poke upwards and outwards, in ungainly fashion, revealing their dusty soles, in a manner that recalls the paintings of Jacopo Bassano, with a similarly (unpleasant) olfactory implication. The body beautiful is no longer pictured as the conduit to the unseen world of spiritual life, as it had been in so many of Veronese's paintings. Instead, the work admits the possibility of a paradoxical alliance between outward physical awkwardness, or even ugliness, and inward sacredness.

VERONESE'S FINAL *LAST SUPPER*

In several large-scale religious paintings of the 1580s, Veronese also adapted his style towards a chastened alternative to his previous emphasis on decorative values. In these works, he quite demonstrably turned to the later spiritualizing mode of Tintoretto and Bassano, who had both arrived at a dramatic, chiaroscuro-based manner, incorporating powerful naturalistic elements.[9] Their recent work suggested values of worldly and pictorial humility in response to the powerful currents of popular piety that had spread through Venice and the Veneto. In a final *Last Supper* of circa 1585 (illus. 63) Veronese offered a kind of retraction of his visually digressive mode in his earlier feast scenes.[10] Just seven accessory figures remain and are easily outnumbered by the biblical actors: the twelve disciples and Christ. The lavishness of the triple-arched, proscenium-like loggia in the 1573 version of this subject (illus. 44) is replaced by a much plainer, even lowering, architectural setting that allows a clearer view of the figures within it. There are just two columns supporting the structure, but they are left unornamented, their decorative capitals pointedly excluded. The Supper now takes place in a humbler abode commensurate with the indications given in the gospels

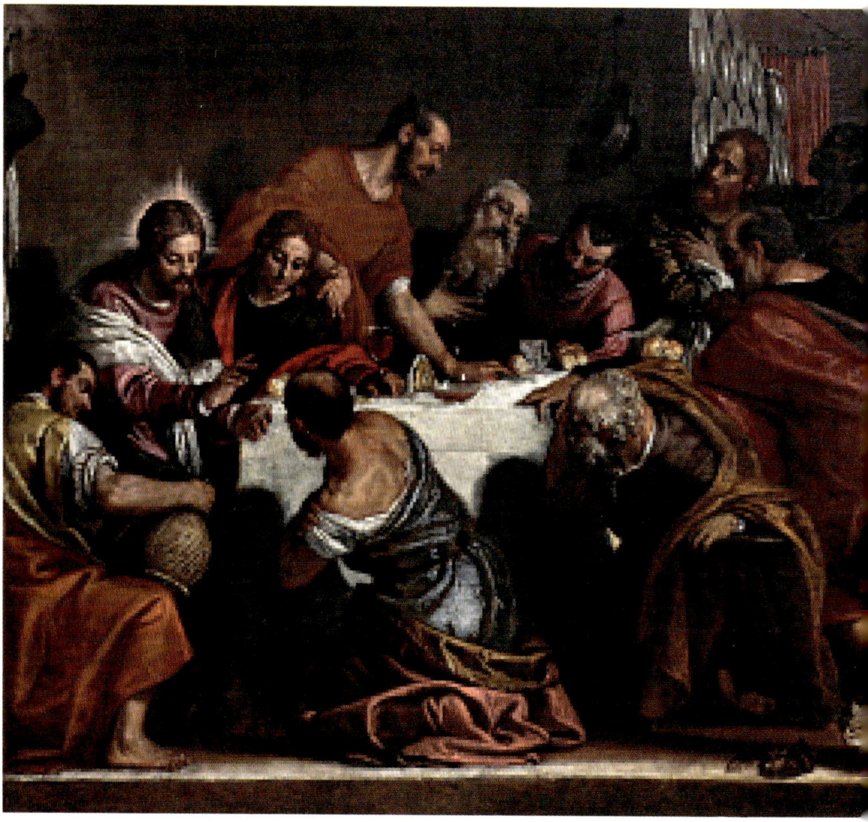

of Mark and Luke.[11] It may be that the 'goodman of the house', mysteriously ready to follow Christ's instructions in the gospel accounts, is depicted at the extreme right of the painting, where he sits writing at a table.

Veronese studiously downplays implications of material wealth or lavishness, using the extreme horizontality of the picture shape to suggest spiritual humility. Rich local colours do not draw attention to themselves, as in many of his earlier works, and there is no display of contemporary-looking Venetian manufactured fabrics

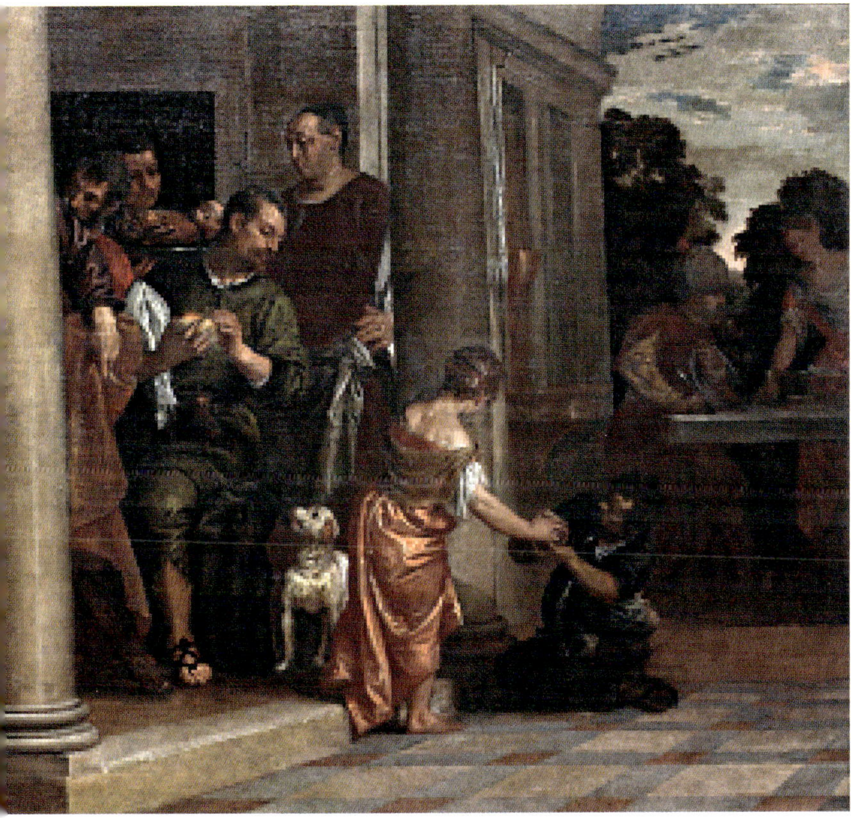

63 Veronese, *Last Supper*, *c.* 1585, oil on canvas.

or jewellery. Some, at least, of these differences can be explained by external factors of patronage and location. For the first (and last) time, Veronese produced a Supper scene for a humble parish church rather than a grand refectory in a wealthy, patrician-backed monastery. His late *Last Supper* hung on the contra-facade of the little church of San Sofia, above the place where a local lay confraternity of super-pious parishioners – a so-called Scuola del Sacramento – met to discuss the proper upkeep of the Eucharistic sacrament between masses. Tintoretto had exploited this burgeoning area of confraternal artistic patronage in Venice, repeatedly producing horizontally shaped *laterali* showing the Last Supper and related subjects for these parish Scuole from the 1540s onwards. The Tintorettesque arrangement that Veronese adopted for his new picture indicates his knowledge of these works, and can be taken as an admission that he had strayed into his rival's patronal territory, accepting a commission which he might earlier have eschewed as too 'humble', or as beneath his consideration as a supposedly high-born Caliari. But times had changed. Veronese's willingness to modulate his usual aristocratizing manner towards one that was popularizing entailed the sacrifice of material *richezza* to the newly prevalent idea of sacred poverty (*sancta povertà*). Following Tintoretto's recent paintings of the subject for the churches of San Polo and San Stefano, Veronese angled the sacred table or *mensa* sharply away from the picture plane, and showed Christ towards the picture margins, as if to emphasize his humility, where he feeds a kneeling disciple a sacramental wafer. Again following Tintoretto's lead, Veronese foregrounded the doctrinal moment of the Institution of the Eucharist at the Supper, rather than the dramatic one of the Annunciation of the Betrayal, in accordance with the special concerns of his local patrons with this key sacrament that had been challenged by the Protestants.[12]

The viewer's eye moves into depth from foreground left to background right, through the bunched apostles on either side of the column, past the two beggars, towards the turbaned man at the extreme right. The two columns, like the spatial recession itself, serve to mark gradations between high and low in both the spiritual and social order, a device that Veronese had deployed in his very first supper scene (illus. 41). As in that work, however, the division is made porous or incomplete, its implication of a fixed hierarchy challenged by other elements. Christ's charitable example in offering the salvific wafer is mirrored by the disciple at the opposite end of the table, to the right of the column, who turns away from his master to engage directly with the poor. Almsgiving is present in more than one of Veronese's earlier feasts, but here it is given much more attention, with particular emphasis laid on charity in its more active, social guise as *amor proximi* ('love thy neighbour'). In this area, two more servants appear, as also a dog looking up pleadingly as the newly symbolized bread is distributed: a motif that again addressed his patrons' concern over the proper reservation of the sacrament between the masses.[13] The mirroring action of an impoverished young girl who passes the bread selflessly on to a disabled male beggar crouching near to her extends the charitable flow from left to right, beyond the second column. And then our eyes arrive at the background man and woman at the table mentioned earlier. His dress identifies him as a Muslim Turk, and thus as an even greater outsider to the Christian Eucharistic rite than the desperate street beggars: a point reiterated by his placement furthest away from Christ himself in the picture space, and by the fact that he seems to take no notice of what goes on inside the room.[14] But although he has pen in hand, he has also paused from his writing and seems to intuit the fact that something very significant has just happened at the other end of the painting. Whether or not this outsider will understand the importance of Christ's action, and convert to the 'true faith', his inclusion in the painting extends the wave of sympathetic and culturally inclusive actions across the painting that it sets in train.

ADORATION OF THE SHEPHERDS

In a late altarpiece for the family chapel of the leading patrician Marino Grimani in the Venetian church of San Giuseppe di Castello, Veronese turned instead to the work of Jacopo Bassano, a master whose style had increasingly engaged the theme of Christian humility, albeit it primarily with reference to the supposedly simple life of the peasants in the countryside (illus. 64). Marino was the son of Girolamo, the prominent patrician cardinal who had reportedly taken Veronese to Rome earlier in his career.[15] A portrait of Girolamo (who had since died) in his cardinal's robes as the church father St Jerome is included to the left, and the Christ child pointedly looks in his direction rather than at the rustics to the right. The inclusion of Girolamo's figure, like Christ's special attention to his image, makes the usual kind of Veronesian concession to patrician family values. But in other ways this work is far from the Romanism that might have been expected in a commission from a leading *papalisti* family, whose taste for all things *all'antica* was well-established. By the 1580s, however, this more secular, imperial and pagan style would have appeared too exclusive and even as morally questionable, at least for a church altarpiece.

In an attempt to counteract any such implication, Veronese abandoned his usual models for altarpieces, such as Titian's Pala Pesaro, presenting instead a humble, chiaroscuro-darkened rural scene that closely reprises Bassano's imagery of peasant piety in the countryside. Veronese's figure of the kneeling shepherd with his back turned, who appears like a surrogate for the viewer in prayer before the altarpiece, was based on an equivalent one in Bassano's *Adoration of the Shepherds* (*c.* 1568, Bassano del Grappa, San Giuseppe). Veronese's attention to the surfaces of his coarse and dirtied clothing makes a particularly stark contrast to his usual display of finely manufactured silks and satins. In Bassano's polemically charged depictions of local rural life, the condition

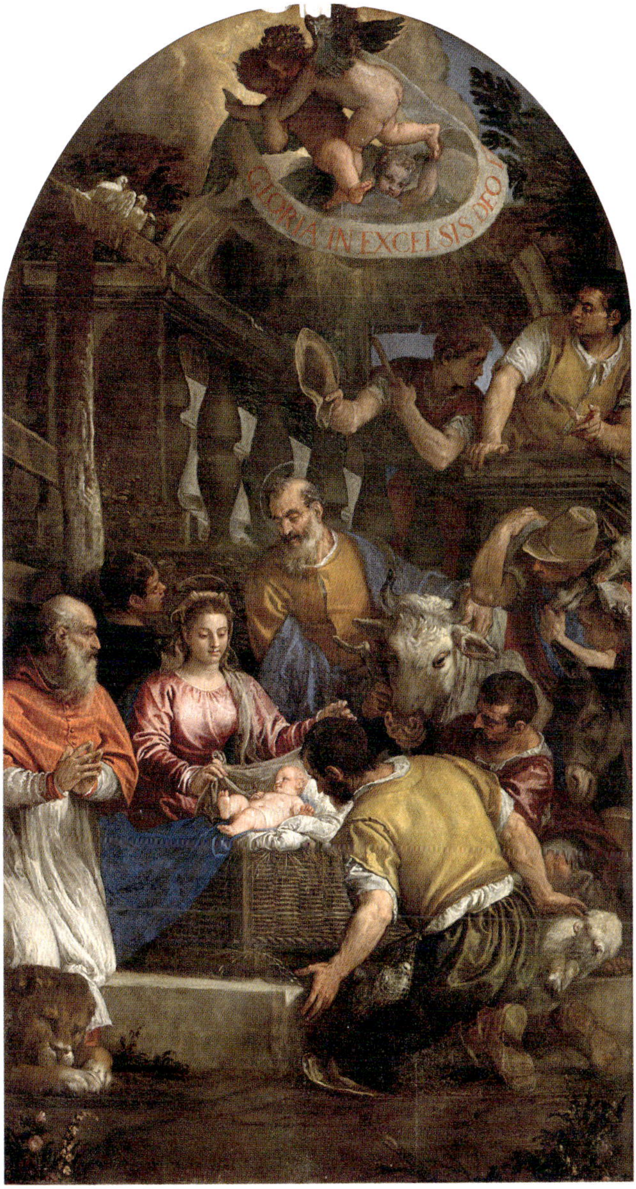

64 Veronese, *Adoration of the Shepherds*, 1582–3, oil on canvas.

of material want suffered by the peasantry was pictured as drawing them close to Christ and the saints, while also making a pointed moral contrast with the worldly opulence of urban *all'antica* painting in the metropolis, championed above all by Veronese himself. But Veronese had long been interested in Bassano's rhetorically humble approach, paying special attention to his trenchantly naturalistic depictions of domestic animals (see illus. 13, 14). In the final decade of his life, he responded more directly and comprehensively to Bassano's imagery of the rural poor, engaging in several works with the older master's prevalent idea that simplicity and poverty were the fundamental preconditions for true Christian piety.[16]

In the Grimani *Adoration*, Veronese fills the right side of his altarpiece with rustic types: there are as many as five shepherds with their animals crowded into this area, while his usual elegant and socially elevated actors – other than the donor-like cardinal – are nowhere to be seen. The shepherds' very lowliness grants them privileged access to the Christ child. The heavenly domain, which often plays such an extended role in Veronese's mature altarpieces (see illus. 36), is reduced in scale and elaboration, so that the immediate earthly and earthy one below becomes all-dominant. If the patronal type might have encouraged Veronese's modulation of his usual style in the San Sofia *Last Supper*, then the example of the San Giuseppe altarpiece indicates that the social rank of his clientele was not all-determining. Even his most elite patrician patrons were eager enough to promote the new taste for 'humble' religious imagery that masked the ongoing reality of their high social position and great material wealth. The late cardinal Girolamo Grimani, so carefully painted in the guise of his onomastic saint at the left, might at first appear to be a lofty outsider to the warm press of shadowy peasant and animal bodies crowded in at the right. But he looks on at these lowly figures admiringly, taking on a role equivalent to that played by a mediating saint in a *sacra conversazione*, as if supplying an official church sanction to the recalibration towards Christian humility that their innocent piety portends.

A LATE PORTRAIT

In the sacred works discussed above it is Veronese's move towards the moralized later styles of Tintoretto and Bassano that is most notable. In other paintings from the 1580s, however, he remained truer to his earlier approach. In a portrait of a member of the Soranzo family of circa 1585 Veronese deployed a darkened but still glimmering and velvety palette of dark olive greens, viridian blue and coal black, set against cold, silvery whites, to generate subtle colouristic harmonies beneath the darkening cloak of his chiaroscuro (illus. 65). Veronese again worked for a patrician family with whom he had long been associated (illus. 4), and this might have given him the confidence to persist, in certain ways, with his earlier pictorialized approach to portraiture, even if the effect of material *richezza* is now reined in. So much is evident from the diagonal arrangement of the seated figure, which recalls that deployed in his seated portrait of *Daniele Barbaro* of circa 1556, albeit the Soranzo painting is now extended to full length. A very careful black-and-white chalk drawing on blue paper records the sitter's drapery, but not his head, perhaps indicating that Veronese also continued his earlier habit of making a portrait in two consecutive stages (illus. 66).[17] It may be that he took his sitter's likeness before turning to the detailed study of his clothing at a later point, when Soranzo himself was no longer present. The dress would have been modelled by a workshop member and would eventually serve to carry the main expressive effect of the work.

Even in this late 'expressive' example, with its muted colour scheme and air of solemnity, Veronese's subtle allowance of an equality of attention between head and clothing remains evident

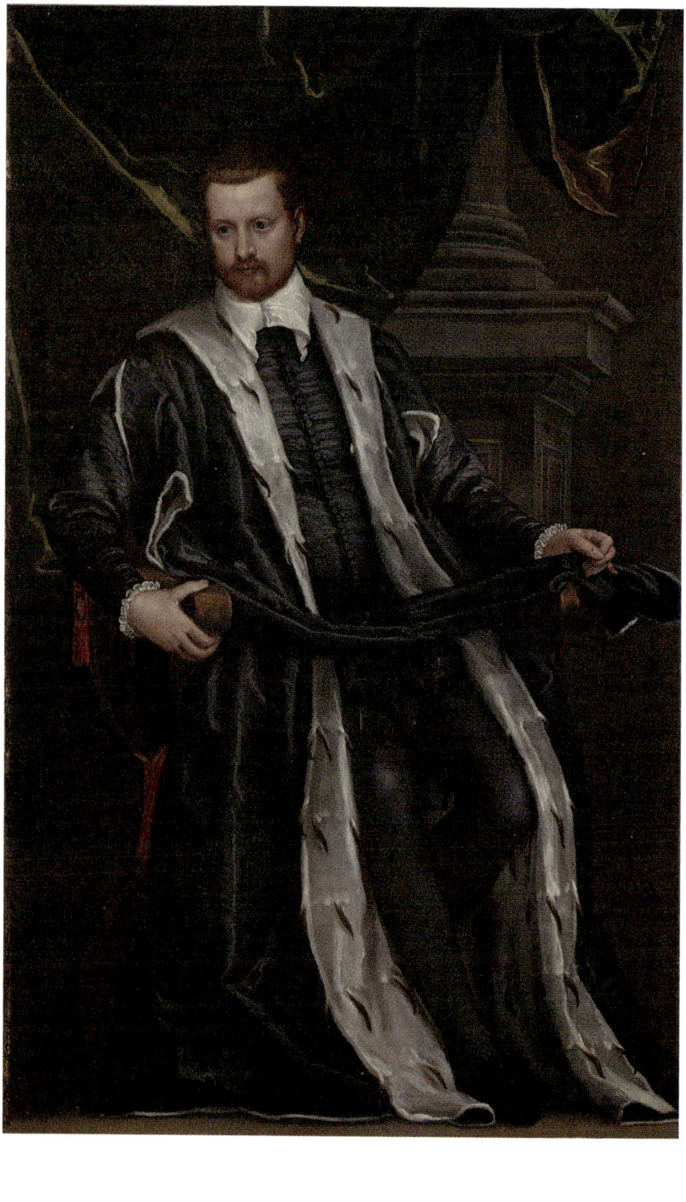

65 Veronese, *Portrait of a Gentleman of the Soranzo Family*, c. 1585, oil on canvas.

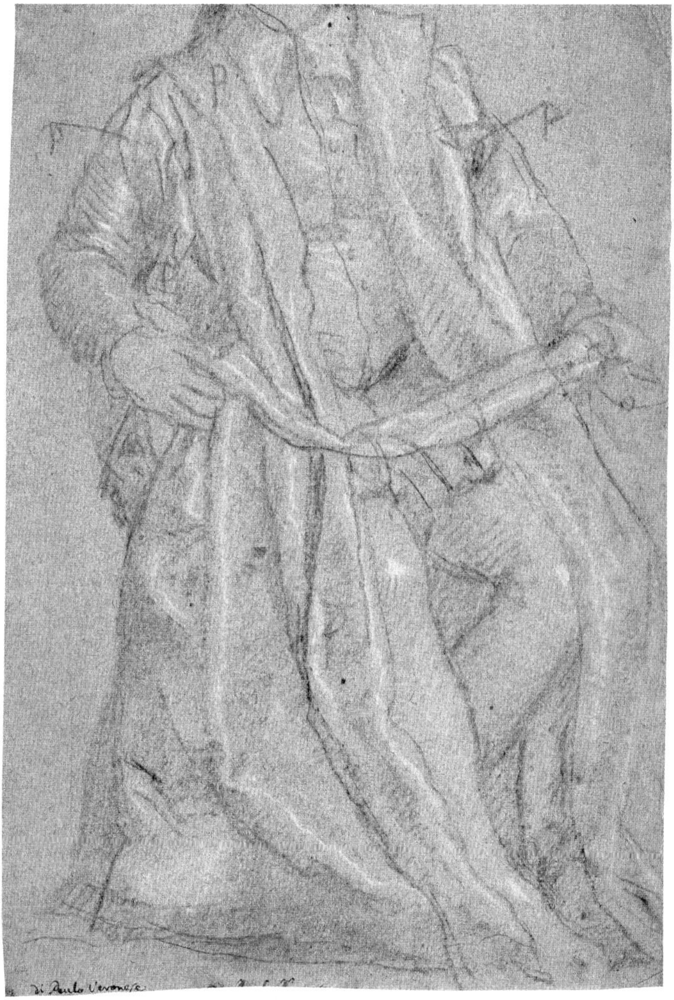

enough. Perhaps it is still more than that, given the smallness of the man's face relative to his costume and the picture dimensions, and the quiet impassivity – rather than imperiousness – of his deflected gaze. The viewer's eye must spend more time on the

66 Veronese, *Study for the Portrait of a Gentleman of the Soranzo Family*, c. 1585, black chalk heightened with white chalk on paper.

dramatic downward flow of his ermine-edged drapery, which even flows outwards beyond his feet to form two little tubular curlicues as it meets the floor. If this top to bottom directionality, upper left to lower right, predominates, it is also interrupted, somehow vitally from a compositional point of view, by the sash draped loosely across the arms of the chair. Dividing the upper and lower parts of his body, its horizontality holds the eye up (at least momentarily) against the gravitational pull of the drapery, initiating the same kind of internalized drapery play evident in Veronese's earlier works. If the sash serves to maintain some interest in the upper part of the picture, and thus in the sitter's upper body and head, then this is not allowed to be absolute or all-absorbing. The expensive costume, however far it is downplayed by the submergence of local colours and surface texture, more completely conceals the man's bodily contours beneath than it does in the drawing, with liquid highlights playing across its subtly pigmented surface. But even this is not finally explainable in formal terms. As the downward flow of fabric wins out, it generates an air of melancholy or pensiveness that threatens to undermine the high-ranking sitter's confident sense of control and material ease.

TWO LATE PAINTINGS OF PIOUS WOMEN

In several late paintings featuring heroic and pious women, Veronese again maintained elements of his earlier approach, even while he adapted this to the more tragic tone favoured in the 1580s. In these works he extended further his long-standing preoccupation with women, but showed them as isolated, suffering figures, subject to the cruelties of the world of men, rather than as serenely victorious over them, as in many of his earlier mythologies and allegories.[18] In a portrait-like painting showing Lucretia, the virtuous wife of ancient Rome who had (in the account of

Livy) been raped by Sextus Tarquinius, the emphasis is certainly on the sadness of her lonely suicide (illus. 67). With downcast head and lowered eyes, she is shown at the moment when she drives a dagger – vicious consequential substitute for Sextus's invasive penis – into her soft body. Colour tones are muted and the space beyond her figure to the left painted black, generating a sharp contrast with her translucently pale flesh. But in other ways, Veronese's painting retains a quiet sumptuousness: the new expressivity is not allowed to undermine our attention to rich and complexly arranged materials arrayed near to and across the picture surface. The viewer's eye is constantly led away from the dagger towards the subtle colour harmonies, with sophisticated modulations of green between the fabrics she holds up across her body and the richly patterned drapery and scarf to the right. The worldly and fashionable contemporary designs in this latter area, with stripes and surface patterns of pomegranates and flowers, contrast with the simpler, more historicized, draperies around Lucretia's body itself. They nonetheless draw attention to themselves, generating something of the all-over *richezza* of surface effect characteristic of Veronese's style. It is hard to decipher the exact position of Lucretia's body in space beneath the play of draperies, which constantly draw the eye back to their varied textures close to the forward plane. There is similarly no retreat from his favoured emphasis on lavish jewellery. Lucretia is particularly extravagantly bedecked, with a pearl and ruby headdress and necklace and matching gold bracelets decorated with cameos, probably featuring profile heads of other heroic women. The colour of the huge ruby nestling in her hair might give notice of her action below as she forces the dagger into her chest. But this climactic action is nonetheless downplayed, made easy enough to miss, the fatal blade cast into shadow as it nestles among the complex softening folds of the surrounding draperies. There is only the slightest indication of blood flowing from her wound.

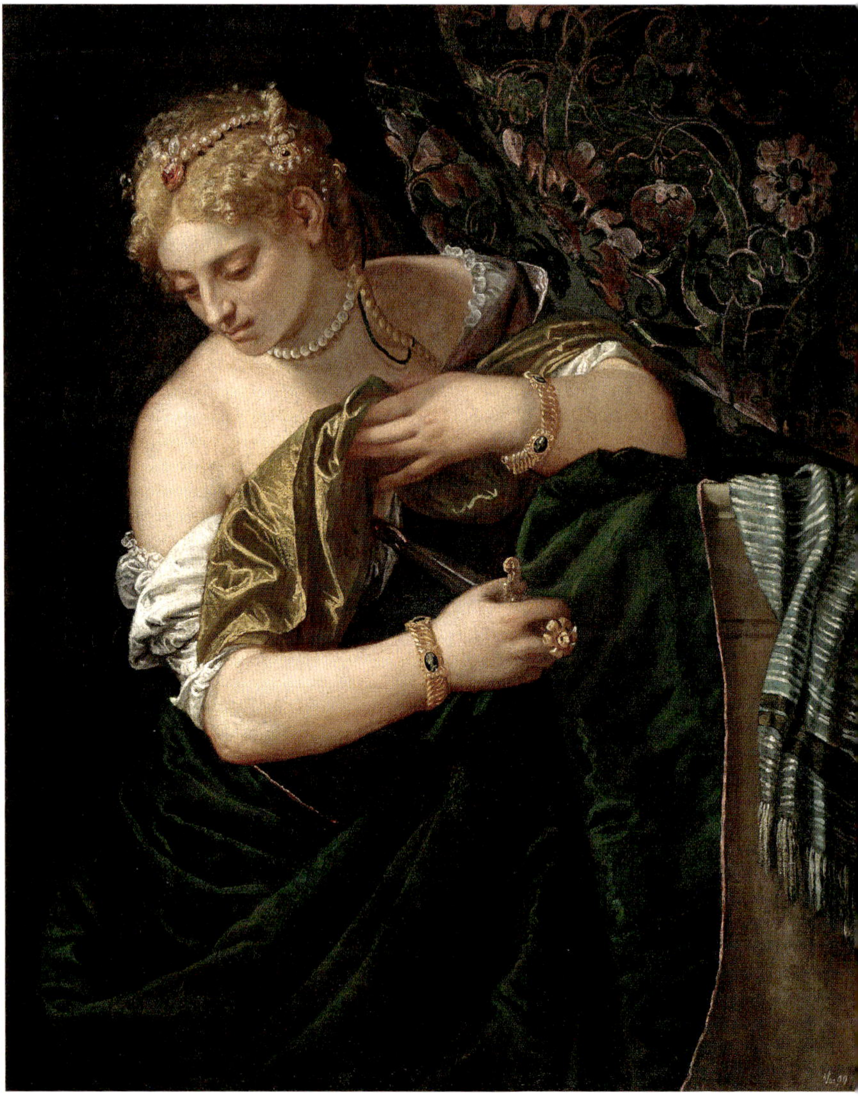

67 Veronese, *Lucretia*, *c.* 1583–5, oil on canvas.

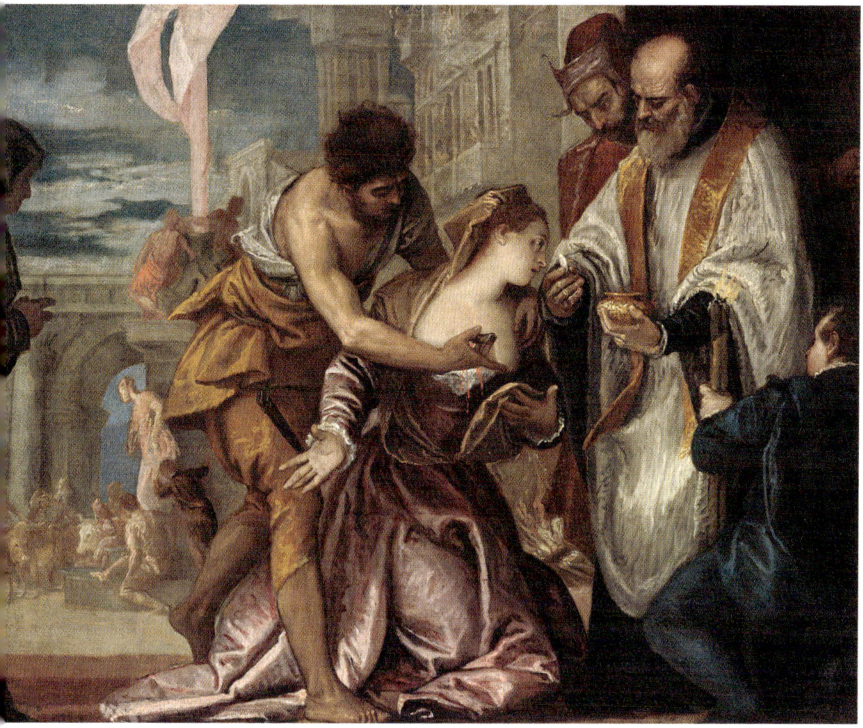

If Veronese's Lucretia is at the mercy of harsh and unjust masculinity, she does not lose her physical beauty, poise or self-control. In Titian's depiction of this story (1571, Cambridge, Fitzwilliam Museum), we see the moment when she is physically overpowered by Sextus. Veronese, as was his want, avoided that climactic moment of physical violation, choosing the later one in which Lucretia has regained command, even if this means – under the patriarchal terms of her marriage – the taking of her own life. But that action, as we have noted, is reduced in visual terms, shown as just one element in a resolved pictorial composition that retains a core principle of decorativeness. The *Lucretia* indicates just how successfully Veronese could negotiate changing tastes

68 Veronese, *Martyrdom and Last Communion of St Lucy*, *c.* 1585–6, oil on canvas.

in his final decade, accommodating the call for greater seriousness and depth while remaining true to his established approach to picture-making. In a still later painting, the *Martyrdom and Last Communion of St Lucy*, Veronese returned to his old habit of moving freely between different moments in the story to generate a visually powerful composition (illus. 68). In a late altarpiece showing the *Conversion of St Pantalon* (1587, Venice, San Pantaleon), explicit emphasis is laid on the intercessory role of the church by the inclusion of a portrait of the commissioning parish priest, Bartolomeo Borghi, who is permitted to participate in the dramatic action. Ridolfi tells us that the *St Lucy* was, instead, a confraternal commission by the Scuola del Croce for the church of Santa Croce in Belluno (demolished), where it hung on the left wall of their chapel. But the elderly man administering the last rites to the saint also appears portrait-like and may again be an image of the local parish priest, although his name is lost to posterity.[19]

In its brief proclamations on visual imagery of 3 and 4 December 1563, the Council of Trent had demanded simplicity and directness in church imagery, so that the sacred work could be easily understood by the worshipping faithful, serving to stimulate pious thoughts regarding the sacred prototypes, without ever, of course, being confused with them. Certain aspects of Veronese's *St Lucy* seem to conform to this directive. The elaborate architecture and distracting supporting cast of observers typical in his earlier works have all but disappeared: there are just three onlookers beyond those directly engaged in the drama that dominates the foreground. The secondary scene, set in a hazy distance, illustrates earlier moments in Lucy's story, when unsuccessful attempts were made to drag her to a brothel and to burn her alive.[20] But these harrowing scenes are made difficult to see. And although there is little to distract us from the scene of her death by stabbing, Veronese makes it easy enough to miss this violent climactic and finalizing action. Lucy kneels before the priest in submission to his authority but nonetheless dominates the scene in visual terms. Her genuflection is one last rendition of his much-favoured visual template discussed in earlier chapters: a graceful aristocratic and courtly action of submission before a sympathetic authority figure. The moment of Lucy's violent end is certainly the theme, but as the executioner's knife is thrust into her chest it is – in a fuller realization of the deflecting solution offered in the *Lucretia* – concealed from view by his hand and by a deft foreshortening of the dagger itself.

The spilling of blood demanded by the gory theme is, in this way, once again downplayed, reduced to a few small splashes that hardly interrupt the scene in visual terms. Narrative attention might seem to fall instead on the key doctrinal moment of the reception of the sacramental wafer into the martyred saint's dying body (see illus. 1). But here, too, Veronese's penchant for visual deflection survives to maintain the visual integrity of the painting. The dying Lucy's mouth opens slightly to receive the host, but that action is only half-suggested. Instead, the priest holds up the wafer close to her eyes, invoking an earlier incident in her sad story, in which she had puritanically plucked them out to stop her lover praising their beauty. The possibility is suggested that she is already blind and cannot physically see the proffered wafer, her salvation made dependent on one final leap of faith. None of that, however, is allowed to undermine our prevalent sense of her physical beauty and actorly self-possession as she so gracefully gives up the ghost.

Analysis of the late paintings discussed above indicates just how successful Veronese's modulation of his style away from his usual visual flamboyance in his final decade could be. But in these years, too, the Veronese manner increasingly took on supra-personal dimensions, as his brother Benedetto, now joined by his two painter-sons Gabriele and Carlo (Carletto), came to play increasingly active roles in the supply of paintings from the workshop. The studios of Tintoretto and Bassano developed in an equivalent way, such that the styles of all these masters, once boldly offered as individualistic and unique, morphed into communal or shared stylistic envelops into which their family members and many other workshop followers could seamlessly slip. Many works (including some drawings) from the later period of Veronese's career document this collaborative enterprise in the supply of a large quantity of paintings. Following the master's sudden death in 1588, it comes as no surprise to find that his family of painters – the *Haeredes Pauli* (Heirs of Paolo) as they called themselves – stayed together to continue the successful family business.[21] The collapse of this enterprise in 1598 certainly reflects the recent deaths of 'Carletto' and Benedetto, but perhaps its viability always had certain inbuilt limits. The ability of Paolo's followers to translate or generalize Paolo's style was already questionable prior to his death, given the production of chaotic and lifeless workshop altarpieces from the 1580s for the Venetian churches of Santa Maria Maggiore and the Ognissanti (both Venice, Gallerie dell'Accademia). Although the Haeredes undoubtedly understood Paolo's style as a readily translatable, communal or shared entity, it quickly proved to be fatally wedded to himself.

Conclusion

Veronese's visual domain was fundamentally aspirational in kind, never quite offering a straightforward representation of a pre-existing reality. He envisioned an alluringly sensual but also gracious pictorial world that, although robustly material, seemed to exist just above, beyond or apart from the more mundane one beyond the frame. In many examples, Veronese features protagonists who are a little more heroic, well-behaved, better dressed or beautiful; ornately carved architectural settings that are a little grander and finely made fabrics and jewels that are a little more sumptuous, than those of reality. This is the case in many of his religious, mythological and allegorical works, as also in his portraits, typically presented as lavish works in which the sitters sometimes appear in costumes and jewellery that may have been suggested or even half-invented by the painter. In his subject paintings – and not only those for ceilings – we are usually required to look slightly upwards into the fictive space towards raised theatre-like architectural structures before or beneath which graceful actors perform their allotted parts. In several paintings – and beyond the stricter demands of a given picture type or subject-matter – we have the sense that we are watching a carefully choreographed social performance put on by an elegant ruling elite. In this drama, the interactions of the main actors are presented as iterative or repeatable pictorial tableaux. Typically avoiding the narrative climax, Veronese often shows a decorous arrival before a seated, enthroned or standing authority figure, set on some elegant steps leading up to a grand portal. The underlying import of the painting is carried by a gracious courtly genuflection or a magnanimous gesture. Certain elements in that set-up were undoubtedly swept away in the more expressive modulation of his style in the final decade of his life. But even in a late work such as the *St Lucy* much more than a mere vestige of Veronese's long-standing courtly visual template survives to underpin the presentation.

The majority of Veronese's paintings have a sacred subject-matter – a higher proportion even than Titian or Tintoretto – and this has served those arguing that his work is always deep and meaningful very well.[1] But it would be easy to overestimate this painter's susceptibility to religious ideology or to wider external or contextual pressures. Something of the courtly flavour pertains even when an Old Testament heroine is featured in a church nave (illus. 17); when a bowing saint approaches the Virgin in an altarpiece (illus. 39); or when one is about to be martyred (illus. 36, 68). It does not follow from this, however, that Veronese's courtliness made his pictorial domain a socially exclusive one. The lesser figures arrayed so carefully towards its edges command attention. In his portraits, children are joyously set free of the usual familial and dynastic constraints that control their representation in many Renaissance paintings.[2] In his sacred paintings, non-Europeans and non-Christians regularly appear. Although they usually take up positions towards the sides or back of the picture, they often come to play a significant role in visual and even thematic terms. Veronese's careful drawing of a boy's head illustrated in Chapter Three, made *dal vivo* (from life), offered his doubly marginalized subject – a Black child – a new visual profile (illus. 38). In the *Finding of Moses*, the foreground man with a picnic hamper might seem to be included merely as an indicator of place, given that the setting is in Africa (illus. 40). But he, like the responsive dwarf opposite, is allowed an active role in progressing the sacred narrative. Even if such types are typically more passive in their relation to the main actors, they are also made similar to the viewer, at least in so far as they too are pictured as interested spectators, watching on intently. In the *Family of Darius before Alexander* (illus. 2) a chained monkey turns its back on the edifying action to the right, but a nearby dwarf is granted a prime view of the event and is deeply engaged by it. Such 'low' types were familiar enough as slaves or servants in sixteenth-century Venice. But in the improved world of Veronese's painting they are partially released from the prejudice and bondage that they endured in social reality.

A paradigmatic work in this regard is the *Last Supper/Feast in the House of Levi* of 1573 in which Veronese's habit of equalizing through visualizing was deemed to have got out of hand, at least by his iconographically obsessed and socially snooty inquisitors (illus. 44–6). At one point in the interview Veronese suggested that he had included his lowly accessory types to illustrate the wealth of the rich man who had held the banquet. But in the picture itself they take on a more independent visual identity. In his earlier *Marriage at Cana*, the numerous servants had already been promoted in both numerical and thematic terms, getting ahead of their social superiors in their understanding and furthering of the unfolding narrative (illus. 43). In his very first feast scene, marginal types are subtly linked to the given theme, illustrating its ethical reach beyond a mere display of the *richezza* of an aristocratic feast (illus. 41). And then there is the question of Veronese's promotion of women in works of many kinds, painted throughout his career. It would be easy enough to remain sceptical of the grounds for Veronese's approach. In a number of his paintings, women are granted a presiding agency or power, seamlessly dominating the space and controlling the narrative. But how far was Veronese able to capture the realities of feminine experiences?

After all, like so many other old master painters, Veronese was constrained to offer only a *masterly* – and therefore to some degree voyeuristic or compensatory – viewpoint. His effort might even appear as an example of the cultural process known by anthropologists as inverse symbolism, whereby a group who are discriminated against or excluded in social reality are comfortingly promoted or centralized in the fictive or symbolic domain of representation.[3]

Veronese's presiding focus on the depiction of nobility, or of what it was to live and behave in a properly 'noble' manner, must in any case have encouraged or necessitated greater female visibility in his work, as in Venetian culture of the sixteenth century more widely.[4] Venetian society already understood – and often represented – itself in 'feminine' terms, following patriotic myths in which the city appears as Venetia, as the Venus-like 'Queen of the Sea', or is specially associated with the Virgin, due to its projected foundation on the feast day of the Annunciation. In the fast-developing realm of art theory in this period, Venetian art was often interpreted using feminine words or concepts such as *grazia* (grace), *leggiadria* (lightness) or *venustà* (charm) as a means of distinguishing it from the more masculine qualities of the central Italian artists.[5] All this might seem to make Veronese's approach normative, merely typical or representative of Renaissance Venice and its artistic culture. It is also true that in many of his works no women are present, and that in others, such as the *Darius*, they appear as passively subject to the will of all-dominant men. But many of the contrasts that I have drawn between Veronese's works and those of the other leading masters in the city – Titian, Tintoretto and Bassano – indicate that he went much further in the promotion of femininity in his painting than they did.

This aspect of Veronese's work provides a further means of getting at the defining qualities of his pictorial style. It might help to explain his discomfiture with the presentation of narratives and texts themselves, the majority of which were, after all, written or generated in the dominant cultural world of men.[6] Veronese's visual promotion of women further facilitated the wider pictorialism or decorativeness of his approach. Understood in formal rather than merely social terms, his avoidance of arguably masculine qualities, such as sharp outlines or contours, clearly defined and anatomically correct bodies, or of optically accurate perspectival effects, is also pertinent. The pervasiveness of feminine qualities – at least as these have been conventionally conceived – can be read in the details of his paintings, such as the emphasis he laid on domestic and cosmetic culture: luscious fashionable fabrics and textiles, jewellery and ladies' coiffeur; children, household pets and other domesticated animals (his undermining approach to the heroic masculine horses of the Leonardesque tradition is relevant). As in so many other cases in art history, gender was to some extent intersected by social or economic rank, so that the prominent position of women in Veronese's paintings does not, after all, offer a challenge to the established hierarchies, and might easily be seen as further supporting them. It is nonetheless fruitful enough to allow that Veronese's feminization of painting had a significant relationship to his equally careful depiction of those others excluded from society's top table: servants, Black people, Muslims, dwarves, mimes, animals and the outcast poor.

It would be easy, however, to exaggerate the extrinsic aspects of Veronese's visual equality: not because he was ultimately an elitist who sought only to flatter his high-ranking patrons by glorifying their social dominance, but because of the special authority he granted to the picture itself. His intrinsic attitude to picture-making is evident from one of his more frustrated replies to the inquisitors in 1573, when he explains that his accessory figures were included 'for ornament'. Seeing an empty space, Veronese was inclined to paint in a figure, regardless of any wider social or iconographic meaning it might have. Like his great rival Tintoretto, he was visually voracious, intent on filling the buildings of Venice with his paintings, beyond the expectations or practical needs of his patrons. As the critical Reynolds observed, Veronese preferred to depict 'at least forty figures' when far fewer were needed to tell the story. But Veronese's pictorial loquacity does not mean that his many painted figures have no significance at all. Rather than being inert or irrelevant, they function as vital components in the visual ensemble, operating (to some extent) as non-indexical signs. In this way, they threaten to shed their original responsibility to context altogether. Veronese's pictorialism underpinned the unusual consistency of his style, beyond or despite the immediate local impacts or conditions of picture type, medium or subject, making the accurate dating or chronology of his work notoriously difficult to establish. It encouraged his development of iterative visual templates, and it determined his graphic approach, which served to secure the transfer of his figural inventions onto the given painted surface. Veronese's respect for the authority of the picture plane, for so long misunderstood as making his work semantically superficial, was carefully maintained against the depredations of perspectival depth, with its implications of masculine optical science, narrative resolution, and profound meaning. And this truth to his visual medium was studiously managed even in the more expressive works of his final decade.

The leading painters of the rhetorically pictorial Baroque, such as Rubens and Van Dyck, instinctively understood the implications and potentials of Veronese's expansive and capacious visuality. But it was only in the eighteenth century that a painter emerged who was fully able to respond to the internal world of the picture that he had opened. It may be an exaggeration to say that for Giambattista Tiepolo (1696–1770) 'Veronese was painting.'[7] There remain differences enough between the 'animality' of Veronese – so well observed by Ruskin – and Tiepolo's twinned effects of airiness and immateriality. Yet looking at Tiepolo's paintings nonetheless offers a primer on how to look at Veronese's. Tiepolo's obsessive attention to the margins of his pictures is telling, given that these liminal areas were also those most vulnerable to invasion from the polluting realities of the non-pictorial world beyond. Filling his unstable edges with figures and objects allowed Tiepolo to release his gravity-defying imagery beyond such worldly dictates. Veronese was always more bound by his sense of materiality and of the weight of gravitational bodies, and his picture centres typically retain their visual authority. But he too enlivens and invigorates the borders of his compositions, granting new visual privileges to figures that were not always sanctioned by the given subject-matter.

Like Tiepolo's, Veronese's figures are typically gathered into difficult-to-read clusters that are already altered from their original shapes, or half-hidden and extended by draperies that bind them to the painter's will. His dense patterning of form is to some extent internally driven, respecting the demands of richly coloured and patterned surfaces against the occular-centric seeing-through of three-dimensional anatomy or perspective. What results in the art of both painters is the imagination of a partially self-sustaining 'othered' world of painting, always marking its difference from anything prior to or beyond itself. Tracing Veronese's artistic process as revealed by his drawings, we sometimes see obsessively repeated figures that point to this absorbative process, as a *dal vivo* form or group is made over into the terms set by his composition. Colour is similarly transmogrified, as local tones are modulated beyond natural appearances to generate new combinations within the picture. Such examples trace a characteristic movement away from the merely imitative towards the integral and semi-independent realm of painting. Within this field, nothing is left to chance or remains quite true to its original pre-pictorial identity or meaning. If Veronese's pictorial materials come trailing darker clouds of signification from the world beyond, then these will soon be scattered or dissolved by the powerful sunlight of his visual realization. And in this way, too, Veronese's painting redeems and ennobles all that it shows.

CHRONOLOGY

1526	Titian completes his Pesaro altarpiece for Santa Maria Gloriosa dei Frari, Venice
1527	Sack of Rome by the troops of the Holy Roman Emperor, Charles V
1528	Paolo Veronese born to Gabriele Bazaro and Caterina Caliari in Verona
1532–5	Giulio Romano's frescoes in the Palazzo Te, Mantua
1541	Veronese in the workshop of Antonio Badile in Verona
1544	Veronese probably in the workshop of Giovanni Caroto in Verona
1546	Veronese's first known independent works: the *Raising of the Daughter of Jairus* and the *Virgin and Child with Sts John the Baptist and Louis of Toulouse* (the Pala Bevilacqua) for churches in Verona
1547-8	Tintoretto's *Miracle of the Slave* for the Scuola Grande di San Marco in Venice
1550	First edition of Giorgio Vasari's *Lives of the Artists* published in Florence
1551	Veronese completes his first known commission in Venice: the *Virgin and Child with Sts Joseph, John the Baptist, Catherine, and Anthony Abbot* (the Pala Giustinian) for the church of San Francesco della Vigna
1552	Veronese at work on the mainland, where he completes the *Temptation of St Anthony* for the Duomo in Mantua and the da Porto portraits for the Palazzo Porto in Vicenza, a building designed by Andrea Palladio
1552–62	Titian works on a series of Ovidian mythologies for King Philip II of Spain known as the *poesie*

1553–5	Veronese moves to Venice
1554–5	Veronese works alongside the mainland painters Giambattista Ponchino and Giambattista Zelotti in the rooms of the Council of Ten at the Ducal Palace in Venice. Death of Veronese's father, Gabriele Bazaro
1555	15 January: Veronese is living in Venice in the Corte della Candela, Cannaregio 3 June: names himself 'Paolo Caliaro Veronese' on a contract for an altarpiece for the Duomo at Montagnana 23 November: Veronese completes ceiling paintings in the sacristy at San Sebastiano
1556	Daniele Barbaro's Italian translation of Vitruvius's *Ten Books on Architecture* is published. Veronese completes the nave ceiling at San Sebastiano
1558	Veronese works on frescoes for upper walls of the nave at San Sebastiano and begins work on the interior of the Villa Barbaro at Maser
1559	Death of Michele Sanmicheli
1562	6 June: Veronese contracted to supply a huge feast scene for the refectory of Palladio's new church of San Giorgio Maggiore in Venice. Veronese paints the High altarpiece at San Sebastiano and begins work on paintings for the presbytery walls 17 August: his mother, Caterina, is living with him in Venice
1563	3 and 4 December: final session of Council of Trent, under the auspices of Pope Pius IV, which discusses the role of images in Catholic churches
1564	18 February: Michelangelo dies in Rome
1566	17 April: Veronese marries Elena Badile at Santa Cecilia in Verona. He later moves from San Felice in Cannaregio to larger premises on the Salizada San Samuele
1568	Second revised and expanded edition of Vasari's *Lives* published in Florence, including a short account of Veronese's career to date 7 September: Baptism of Veronese's first son, Gabriele
1570	20 July: Baptism of Veronese's second son, Carlo ('Carletto')
1571	7 October: Venice is part of the Holy League, which defeats the Ottomans at the Battle of Lepanto

1573	20 April: Veronese completes a Last Supper for the refectory of the convent of Santi Giovanni e Paolo in Venice 18 July: Veronese interrogated by the Tribunal of the Inquisition
1575	Veronese living in Padua, probably to escape the devastating plague in Venice. He completes a High altarpiece showing the *Martyrdom of St Justina* for the church of Santa Giustina there in the autumn
1575–7	Veronese works on paintings for the ceiling of the Sala del Collegio in the Ducal Palace, Venice, following a fire
1576	Death of Titian in the plague
1577	20 December: second fire at the Ducal Palace destroys certain of the main state rooms
1579–82	Veronese works alongside Tintoretto,Palma Giovane and Francesco Bassano on the ceiling of the Sala del Maggior Consiglio at the Ducal Palace. He wins the commission for a vast *Paradise* to hang on one of the Sala walls, eventually completed by Tintoretto after Veronese's death
1580	Death of Palladio
1582	Veronese owns property and land near Treviso
1584	Publication of Raffaello Borghini's *Il Riposo* in Florence; it includes a short biography of Veronese. Veronese paints an altarpiece featuring the *Annunciation* for Philip II's El Escorial in Spain
1585	3 March: Veronese provides drawings for costumes for the opening of Palladio's Teatro Olimpico in Vicenza
1588	19 April: Veronese dies at his home on the Salizada San Samuele

REFERENCES

Introduction

1 See Sir Joshua Reynolds, *Discourses on Art*, ed. R. R. Wark (London, 1975), pp. 63–4. For early criticisms of Veronese in the French academy of the 1660s see Richard Cocke, *Paolo Veronese: Piety and Display in an Age of Religious Reform* (Aldershot and Burlington, VT, 2001), p. 21.

2 Henry James, *Italian Hours* [1909], ed. John Auchard (London, 1992), pp. 55–6.

3 See Fry's letter of 18 March 1934 in *The Letters of Roger Fry*, ed. Denys Sutton (London, 1972), p. 688.

4 Michael Levey, 'Review of *Le Pitture di Paolo Veronese nella chiesa di S. Sebastiano in Venezia* by Terisio Pignatti', *Burlington Magazine*, CIX/770 (1967), p. 314.

5 Cocke, *Paolo Veronese*; Fabrizio Biferali, *Paolo Veronese tra Rifroma e Controriforma* (Rome, 2013). For an iconographical account see, for example, Alessandra Zamperini, *Paolo Veronese* (London, 2014).

6 John Garton, *Grace and Grandeur: The Portraiture of Paolo Veronese* (Turnhout, 2008), pp. 137–8; Giorgio Tagliaferro, 'Drafting Characters: Action and Enactment in Veronese's Creative Process', in *Paolo Veronese Giornate di Studio*, ed. Bernard Aikema, Thomas Dalla Costa and Paola Marini (Venice, 2016), pp. 111–24.

7 For the increased visual splendour of at least some Venetian art influenced by the Counter-Reformation in the late sixteenth century see Marie-Louise Lillywhite, *Reforming Art in Renaissance Venice* (Cambridge, 2025).

8 According to a letter written by the humanist Pietro Bembo in 1506, Giovanni Bellini did 'not like to be given many written details which cramp his style; his way of working, as he says, is always to wander at

will in his pictures, so that they can give satisfaction to himself and to the beholder': see D. S. Chambers, ed., *Patrons and Artists in the Italian Renaissance* (Columbia, SC, 1971), no. 72, p. 131.

9 Terisio Pignatti and Filippo Pedrocco, *Veronese*, 2 vols (Milan, 1995), vol. II, p. 556, doc. 22.

10 T. J. Clark, 'Veronese's Higher Beings', in *Heaven on Earth: Painting and the Life to Come* (London, 2018), pp. 166–204, notes 'his art's effortless difference from language' (p. 171).

11 For Veronese's concern with luxuriant surfaces as an intellectual or mental activity see Michael Podro, *Depiction* (New Haven, CT, and London, 1998), p. 13.

12 Bernard Berenson, *The Italian Painters of the Renaissance* (London, 1952), p. 174.

13 See, for example, the arguments over the subject of the early painting usually described as the 'Conversion of Mary Magdalene' (London, National Gallery) but occasionally as 'Christ Healing a Woman with an Issue of Blood'. See Nicholas Penny, *The Sixteenth Century Italian Paintings*, vol. II: *Venice, 1540–1600* (London, 2008), pp. 334–43.

14 For Veronese's Venetian-style *colorito* see David Rosand, *Paolo Veronese*, ed. Mary E. Frank (London and Turnhout, 2023), pp. 19–20.

15 See Hans Dieter Huber, *Paolo Veronese: Kunst als soziales System* (Munich, 2005), whose otherwise persuasive discussion of Veronese's painting as an independent system is weakened by his attempt to abstract it from its historical context.

16 For sixteenth-century *maniera* painting as a 'stylish style' see John Shearman, *Mannerism* (Harmondsworth, 1967).

17 Xavier F. Salomon, ed. and trans., *Lives of Veronese: Vasari, Borghini, Ridolfi* (London, 2014), p. 182. Antonio Zona illustrated Ridolfi's anecdote in the large-scale history painting *Titian Meets the Young Veronese on the Ponte della Paglia* (*c.* 1857–60, Venice, Gallerie dell'Accademia).

18 Pierpaolo Brugnoli, 'Nuovi documenti su Paolo Veronese e la sua famiglia', *Verona Illustrata*, XIII (2000), pp. 11–19.

19 Pignatti and Pedrocco, *Veronese*, vol. II, p. 553, doc. 5, 11 March 1553.

20 Ibid., pp. 553–4, doc. 7, 15 January 1555 ('Paolo Veronese'); doc. 9, 1 December 1555 ('Paolo da Verona'); doc. 8, 3 June 1555 ('Paulo Caliaro Veronese').

21 Caterina is recorded living in Veronese's house at San Felice in Venice on 17 August 1562: see Brugnoli, 'Nuovi documenti', p. 14.

22 For a useful family tree see Xavier F. Salomon, *Veronese*, exh. cat., National Gallery, London (2014), p. 220.
23 Frederic C. Lane, *Venice: A Maritime Republic* (Baltimore, MD, and London, 1973), p. 266.
24 Pignatti and Pedrocco, *Veronese*, vol. II, p. 561, doc. 61.
25 Ugo Tucci, 'The Psychology of the Venetian Merchant in the Sixteenth Century', in *Renaissance Venice*, ed. J. R. Hale (London, 1973), pp. 346–78.
26 Lane, *Venice*, pp. 202–94.
27 '[T]he skill in discerning social ambition lies at the heart of Veronese's achievement': Garton, *Grace and Grandeur*, p. 11.
28 Charles Hope, 'Titian as a Court Painter', *Oxford Art Journal*, II/2 (1979), pp. 7–10; Tom Nichols, *Titian and the End of the Venetian Renaissance* (London, 2013).
29 Sociologists have sometimes seen the aristocratization of the *haute bourgeoisie* as a more general phenomenon of the later Renaissance: see, for example, Alfred von Martin, *Sociology of the Renaissance* [1932] (London, 2015).
30 Claudia Terribile, 'La "Famiglia di Dario" di Paolo Veronese: la committenza, il contesto, la storia', *Venezia Cinquecento*, XV/29 (2005), pp. 63–107.
31 Penny, *The Sixteenth Century Italian Paintings*, pp. 367–8, argues that the kneeling women are ideal types rather than portraits.
32 Bernard Berenson et al., *Palladio, Veronese, e Vittoria a Maser* (Milan, 1960), pp. 9–10.
33 Terribile, 'La "Famiglia di Dario"', pp. 81–2. See also her *Del piacere della virtù. Paolo Veronese, Alessandro Magno e il patriziato veneziano* (Venice, 2009).
34 'opera veramenta di disegno et gentile': Anselmo Guisconi, *Tutte le cose notabili che sono in Venetia . . .* (Venice, 1556), A viiij v. The description recurs in the expanded 1561 edition of the guidebook, published under the name of Francesco Sansovino (see 20v).
35 Veronese shared commissions with painters from his home city and elsewhere on the mainland at the villa Soranzo at Treville in 1551, the Duomo at Mantua in 1552 and the Ducal Palace in 1553.
36 For an extended treatment of the rivalry between the leading painters in Venice see Frederick Ilchman et al., *Titian, Tintoretto, Veronese: Rivals in Renaissance Venice*, exh. cat., Museum of Fine Arts, Boston, and Musée du Louvre, Paris (Farnham, 2009).
37 Philip Cottrell, '"Thence comes it that my name receives a brand": Tintoretto's Nickname Reconsidered', in *Jacopo Tintoretto: Identity,*

Practice, Meaning, ed. Marie-Louise Lillywhite, Tom Nichols and Giorgio Tagliaferro (Rome, 2022), pp. 13–46.

38 Rosand, *Veronese*, p. 14, describes Veronese and Tintoretto as 'starkly competing', but their frequent borrowing from one another, like their shared ability to bring to completion vast schemes of pictorial decoration, suggests that the two painters had much more in common than is at first apparent.

39 Salomon, ed., *Lives of Veronese*, pp. 128, 181.

40 Leonardo describes the elegant painter, 'arrayed in the garments he fancies', contrasting him with the artisanal sculptor, whose face is 'pasted and smeared all over with marble powder, making him look like a baker': ed. Jean Paul Richter, *The Literary Works of Leonardo da Vinci*, 2 vols (London, 1970), vol. I, p. 91.

41 For the identification of the musicians as painters see Marco Boschini, *Le ricche minere della pittura veneziana, Seconda impressione con nove aggiunte* (Venice, 1674), p. 755.

42 Ridolfi reports that Veronese placed '6,000 scudi [ducats] in the banks': see Salomon, ed., *Lives of Veronese*, p. 80. He also owned properties on the *terraferma* and beyond in later life.

1 Earlier Works

1 For Veronese's supposed struggles in his native city see Ridolfi in Xavier F. Salomon, trans. and ed., *Lives of Veronese: Vasari, Borghini, Ridolfi* (London, 2014), p. 55. For the more recent emphasis on the formative and lasting impact of Verona see Paola Marini and Bernard Aikema, *Paolo Veronese: L'Illusione della Realtà*, exh. cat., Palazzo del Gran Guardia, Verona (Milan, 2014); Diana Gisolfi, *Paolo Veronese and the Practice of Painting in Late Renaissance Venice* (New Haven, CT, and London, 2017), pp. 7–69.

2 Xavier F. Salomon, *Paolo Veronese*, exh. cat., National Gallery, London (2014), pp. 39–40.

3 Gisolfi, *Paolo Veronese*, especially pp. 41–68.

4 See the fragments of the frescoes Veronese completed at the villa La Soranza and the Palazzo Canossa in Verona (*c*. 1550). Ridolfi reports that Veronese painted many internal and external frescoes on the walls of private houses in Venice, such as the Palazzo Bellavite in Campo San Maurizio: Salomon, ed., *Lives of Veronese*, pp. 66–7.

5 For Palladio's increasing influence on Veronese's painted architecture after 1550 see David Hemsoll, 'Veronese's Painted

Architecture: Vocabulary and Application', in *Paolo Veronese Giornate di Studio*, ed. Bernard Aikema, Thomas Dalla Costa and Paola Marini (Venice, 2016), pp. 175–87.

6 See John Marciari, 'The Drawings of Veronese', in *Paolo Veronese: A Master and His Workshop in Renaissance Venice*, ed. Virginia Brilliant and Frederick Ilchman, exh. cat., John and Mable Ringling Museum of Art, Florida (London, 2012), pp. 194–207 (p. 196), who notes that 'there is perhaps no Italian Renaissance artist of Veronese's ability or fame for whom the date of so many works is so uncertain.'

7 The related painting hung in the chapel of the Avanzi family in the church of San Bernardino in Verona.

8 For illustrations of these paintings see Salomon, *Veronese*, p. 51.

9 Veronese drew on Sanmicheli's recent buildings in Verona such as the Palazzo del Podestà and Palazzo del Capitanio.

10 Two members of the commissioning Bevilacqua family – probably Giovanni Bevilacqua and his wife Lucrezia – are featured in the altarpiece itself, while Veronese used workshop stand-ins for the sketch.

11 Veronese's parrots were rose-winged parakeets, imported from Africa, and often kept by leading families in Venice: see Gisolfi, *Paolo Veronese*, p. 59. In religious art, parrots often symbolized the Virgin birth of Christ. But they could also take on secular meanings relating to eloquence and artistic imitation, as they probably do in several of Veronese's subsequent paintings (see illus. 29, 41, 45).

12 A surviving pen, ink and wash drawing (Chatsworth House) is closer to the oil sketch than the painting, suggesting that this study preceded the sketch within Veronese's artistic process.

13 See Benjamin Paul, 'Ars Adulandi: Veronese and the Rivalry with Titian and Tintoretto', in *Paolo Veronese Giornate di Studio*, ed. Aikema, Dalla Costa and Marini, pp. 100–109. Veronese goes much further than his second master Caroto in his 'Pala dei Signori' (1544), who slavishly repeats Titian's saints.

14 For the influence of Parmigianino's drawings noted by Ridolfi see Salomon, ed., *Lives of Veronese*, p. 177; Beverly Louise Brown, 'The Genesis of Inspiration; Veronese's Early Look at Parmigianino', in *Paolo Veronese Giornate di Studio*, ed. Aikema, Dalla Costa and Marini, pp. 15–24.

15 The exclusion of donor portraits in the altarpieces commissioned for Sansovino's new church might also reflect concerns with religious reform among the Venetian patriciate in this period. Peter

Humfrey, 'La pala Giustinian a San Francesco della Vigna; Contesto e committenza', in *Nuovi Studi Su Paolo Veronese*, ed. Massimo Gemin (Venice, 1990), pp. 299–307.

16 See the similarly arranged seated foreground figure of St Margaret in Parmigianino's *Virgin and Child with Saints* (*c.* 1526–7, Bologna, Pinacoteca Nazionale).

17 Salomon, ed., *Lives of Veronese*, p. 123. Tintoretto copied the figure in his *St Louis, St George and the Princess* of 1552 (Venice, Gallerie dell'Accademia).

18 'He continued to use certain elements of their [Badile's and Dürer's] folds in the depiction of draperies, executing them, however, in an easier and quicker manner': Ridolfi in Salomon, ed., *Lives of Veronese*, p. 177.

19 Rembrandt Duits, '"Abiti gravi, abiti stravaganti": Veronese's Creative Approach to Drapery', in *Paolo Veronese: A Master and His Workshop*, ed. Brilliant and Ilchman, pp. 59–69.

20 For Veronese's 'fundamental respect for the integrity of the picture plane' see David Rosand, *Paolo Veronese*, ed. Mary E. Frank (London and Turnhout, 2023), p. 17.

21 The architectural structure shows 'a pictorial, rather than a tectonic, logic which will hold true throughout his career': ibid., p. 39.

22 His copy was still in the family palace in the late 1880s, but is now lost: Salomon, *Veronese*, p. 53.

23 Evidence for this can be found in Veronese's surviving depictions of the Holy Family at Oxford (Ashmolean Museum) and Amsterdam (Rijksmuseum), from circa 1551–2, both of which register the impact of Raphael's painting. In a third work, the *Mystic Marriage of St Catherine* (*c.* 1555–60, Yale University Art Gallery), the wicker-basket crib is taken from Raphael's *La Perla*.

24 The Cathedral itself had been rebuilt on a design by Giulio.

25 Veronese might also have drawn on a foreshortened figure of a soldier on a leaping horse by Pordenone, then visible on the facade of the Palazzo D'Anna on the Grand Canal in Venice, now known from a surviving drawing (*c.* 1531–2, London, Victoria and Albert Museum).

26 The painting has been reduced in size by 6 to 8 centimetres (2½ to 3 in.) meaning that these figures would originally have been more significant. See Marini and Aikema, *Paolo Veronese: L'illusione della Realtà*, cat. no. 1.10.

27 Giulio's octagonal ceiling painting in the Sala di Amore e Psiche of the Palazzo Te showing *Psyche Carried to Heaven by Zephyr* of 1526–8.

28 See Veronese's rearing horse in a near-contemporary pen and ink drawing showing *St George and the Dragon* (Florence, Gallerie degli Uffizi): an early example of Veronese's habit of transferring visual motifs between different subject-matters. See Marini and Aikema, *Paolo Veronese: L'illusione della Realtà*, cat. no. 1.11.
29 The portrait referred to here is the *Collaltino Collalto* (*c.* 1548–50, České-Budějovice, Castle Jaroměřice nad Rokytnou). See Marini and Aikema, *Paolo Veronese: L'illusione della Realtà*, cat. no. 1.9.
30 But see also the allegory discussed in Chapter Five in which a similarly clawed young blonde appears (illus. 51).
31 For Veronese's chiaroscuro drawings see Richard Cocke, *Veronese's Drawings* (London, 1984), cat. nos 17–42. John Marciari, *Drawing in Tintoretto's Venice* (New York, 2018), p. 39, notes that these highly finished drawings were 'the legacy less of Venice than of his native Verona'.
32 Salomon, *Veronese*, p. 61, sees it as a presentation drawing for the Mantua altarpiece. For the possible connections with reproductive prints see Bernard Aikema and Thomas Dalla Costa, 'Una Penna Particolarmente Felice', in Marini and Aikema, *Paolo Veronese: L'illusione della Realtà*, pp. 304–5.
33 See, for example, the reclining nude figure of Venus in a lunette of 'Winter and Spring' in the Sala dell'Olimpo at Villa Barbaro.
34 Salomon, *Veronese*, p. 61, sees it as 'somewhat disappointing'.
35 Salomon, ed., *Lives of Veronese*, p. 80.
36 Veronese did fresco Grimani's country villa at Oriago, and much later painted an altarpiece for his son in the family's chapel in Venice, in which he is featured in the guise of St Jerome (illus. 63).
37 Alessandra Zamperini, 'Veronese e l'arte classica riletture antiche e moderne', in *Paolo Veronese Gironate di Studio*, ed. Aikema, Dalla Costa and Marini, pp. 3–11.
38 Most art historians continue to believe that Veronese went to Rome with Grimani on one or other of his visits in 1559 or 1565. For a reconsideration of the evidence, and the proposal of an earlier date, see Vittoria Romani, 'Veronese e Roma: Fonti, Spunti Documentari, Indizi Stilistici', in *Paolo Veronese Gironate di Studio*, ed. Aikema, Dalla Costa and Marini, pp. 25–37.
39 Ridolfi noted that Veronese 'learned from good reliefs . . . the strength of the contours, the firmness of the muscles, the observation of the shadows . . . which cannot be practised so straightforwardly from life': Salomon, ed., *Lives of Veronese*, p. 177.

40 For some examples of Veronese's use of non-figural ancient reliefs he had seen in Verona in his paintings see Salomon, *Veronese*, pp. 45–6.

41 Manfredo Tafuri, *Venice and the Renaissance*, trans. Jessica Levine (Cambridge, MA, and London, 1995), pp. 1–13.

42 The patrons of Veronese's altarpiece (illus. 8) were relatives of Gritti through their mother and prominent members of his wider circle: Antonio Foscari and Manfredo Tafuri, *L'armonia e i conflitti: la Chiesa di San Francesco della Vigna nella Venezia del '500* (Turin, 1983).

43 Giustiniana, the daughter of Veronese's patron at San Francesco, Antonio Giustiniani, had married Marc'Antonio Barbaro in April 1543. Marc'Antonio's brother, Daniele, was responsible for the iconographic programme in the Rooms of the Council of Ten at the Palace.

44 Tintoretto drew on a print after Michelangelo's *Conversion of St Paul* (*c.* 1542–5, Vatican, Cappella Paolina).

45 A very similar effect of visual impossibility is conjured in Veronese's *St Luke* (1555) on the sacristy ceiling of San Sebastiano, in which the animal's horned head appears to grow directly out of the lower part of the saint's reclining body.

46 For Veronese's 'wit and humour' in his mythologies see Paul Barolsky, *Infinite Jest: Wit and Humour in Italian Renaissance Art* (Columbia, MO, and London, 1978), pp. 179–82. Richard Cocke, 'Wit and Humour in the Work of Paolo Veronese', *Artibus et Historiae*, XI/21 (1990), pp. 129–30, notes the playfulness of the foreground woman's two children without going further.

47 Gloria Gallucci, 'An Important New Sheet of Studies by Paolo Veronese from the Late 1550s', *Master Drawings*, XLVIII/3 (2010), pp. 327–40.

48 The drawings might relate to his ideas for a Rape of Europa seen from behind, perhaps based on a work by Giulio Romano. See Beverly L. Brown, 'The View from Behind: Veronese, Giulio Romano and the Rape of Europa', *Artibus et Historiae*, XXXVII/4 (2016), pp. 207–22.

49 For the relationship with the Villa Barbaro paintings see Gallucci, 'An Important New Sheet', p. 337. Salomon, *Veronese*, p. 228 n.46, has rejected this connection, but Marciari, *Drawing in Tintoretto's Venice*, pp. 40–42, notes that several further figures on the sheet were reprised in the frescoes.

50 Gallucci, 'An Important New Sheet', p. 335.

51 The drawing in the Kunsthalle in Hamburg of *c.* 1550 might be the first: see Cocke, *Veronese's Drawings*, cat. no. 3.
52 Thomas Dalla Costa, 'Drawings and Draughtsmanship in Sixteenth-Century Venice: Tintoretto and Veronese in Comparison', *Artibus et Historiae*, XXXIX/78 (2018), pp. 141–54 (p. 144), notes that Veronese took a 'variegated approach' with the initial pen-and-ink sketches followed by more detailed chalk studies for the important figures, culminating in a 'detailed model' close to the finished painting.
53 Marciari, *Drawing in Tintoretto's Venice*, pp. 42–4.
54 Marciari, 'The Drawings of Veronese', pp. 200–202.
55 For a useful contrast between Tintoretto's 'pragmatic' use of drawing and Veronese's more 'theoretical' or 'intellectual' approach see Dalla Costa, 'Drawings and Draughtsmanship'.
56 Tintoretto rarely drew in pen and ink, the preferred medium in the *terraferma*, while Veronese's more general graphic approach had little impact on other painters working in Venice.

2 San Sebastiano, Portraits, Villa Barbaro

1 See Xavier Salomon et al., *The Church of San Sebastiano in Venice: A Guide* (Venice, 2024).
2 Veronese's domination at San Sebastiano anticipates by some years that achieved by Tintoretto at the Scuola Grande di San Rocco, who only began painting there in 1564.
3 Terisio Pignatti and Filippo Pedrocco, *Veronese*, 2 vols (Milan, 1995), vol. II, pp. 554–5, docs 15 and 16 for Veronese's proactive contributions to the architectural decor of the presbytery.
4 For Bonifacio's role see Philip Cottrell and Peter Humfrey, *Bonifacio de' Pitati* (Treviso, 2024), cat. no. 187. Torlioni's nephew, Raffaele, also completed a painting there around 1550.
5 However, Veronese's paintings at San Sebastiano owe little debt to the older master, although he occasionally drew on his compatriot's ideas in other paintings (see illus. 40, 41). See also Chapter Three n.42.
6 For the nave ceiling Veronese drew on Giulio Romano's Sala di Psiche in the Palazzo Te, while the illusionistic balustrades and swags connecting the figures on the lower walls reprise Mantegna's frescoes in the Camera picta of the Mantuan Ducal Palace.
7 For the restoration of the ceiling panels see the essays in Giulio Maniera Elia, ed., *Veronese le storie di Ester rivelate*, exh. cat., Palazzo Grimani, Venice (2011).

8 For the scene as 'Esther Led to Ahasuerus' see Juergen Schulz, *Venetian Painted Ceilings of the Renaissance* (Berkeley and Los Angeles, CA, 1968), cat. no. 19, p. 76; and Richard Cocke, *Paolo Veronese: Piety and Display in an Age of Religious Reform* (Aldershot and Burlington, VT, 2001), p. 186.

9 Edward T. Cook, *The Life of Ruskin*, 2 vols (London, 1911), vol. I, p. 519.

10 Pignatti and Pedrocco, *Veronese*, vol. II, p. 554, doc. 9 and 10.

11 Deborah Howard, *Venice Disputed: Marc'Antonio Barbaro and Venetian Architecture, 1550–1600* (New Haven, CT, and London, 2011), p. 37.

12 Madlyn M. Kahr, 'The Meaning of Veronese's Paintings in the Church of San Sebastiano in Venice', *Journal of the Warburg and Courtauld Institutes*, XXXIII/1 (1970), pp. 235–47.

13 The repetition of the two martyrdoms – first shown in the monks' frieze in the upper nave – in the presbytery below probably reflects the non-visibility of the initial works for the congregation gathered in the lower part of the church.

14 Veronese was one of Tintoretto's rivals in the competition to paint the albergo ceiling at San Rocco held in 1564. Had he won the commission, he would have crossed the broadly observed dividing line that differentiated the two masters' main areas of artistic patronage, mentioned in the Introduction.

15 Veronese's three contrasting figures bring to mind the archers in Antonio and Piero del Pollaiuolo's *Martyrdom of St Sebastian* (1475, London, National Gallery).

16 David Rosand, 'Veronese at San Sebastiano: A Forgotten Fresco', *Burlington Magazine*, CXIV/830 (1972), pp. 325–6.

17 'The painter became a lens through which diverse individuals might see their respective personae re-cast in grander ways': John Garton, *Grace and Grandeur: The Portraiture of Paolo Veronese* (Turnhout, 2008), p. 12.

18 Veronese's portraits hung in the Palazzo Porto, built by Palladio, where he had also painted frescoes (now lost).

19 See the surviving *modello* for the portrait (Paris, Musée du Louvre), which, characteristically for Veronese, shows different sitters, probably members of his workshop, posing as the da Portos.

20 For a modern translation see Francesco Barbaro, *The Wealth of Wives: A Fifteenth-Century Marriage Manual*, ed. and trans. Margaret L. King (Toronto, 2015).

21 The families of both Livia and her husband had made their fortunes in Vicenza from trading in silks: see Garton, *Grace and Grandeur*, pp. 26–33.

22 In addition to the Barbaro portrait discussed in note 23 below, see the portraits now at Budapest, Szépművészeti Múzeum, and Cleveland Museum of Art (Barbarigo); Dresden, Gemäldegalerie (Contarini); London, National Gallery (Soranzo, and see illus. 64).
23 In his portrait of *Daniele Barbaro* (*c.* 1556, Amsterdam, Rijksmuseum), Veronese similarly adapted a court portrait design for a patrician sitter, reprising the seated position of Raphael's *Pope Julius II* (*c.* 1511–12, London, National Gallery), which he probably knew through Titian's copy of 1545 (Florence, Palazzo Pitti, Galleria Palatina). This reference may have been encouraged by the sitter's high position in the church as Patriarch of Aquileia.
24 'Black is more pleasing in clothing than any other colour': see Baldassare Castiglione, *The Courtier* [1528], trans. Charles Singleton (New York, 1959), p. 122.
25 See, for example, Moroni's *Portrait of Bernardo Spini* (*c.* 1573–5, Bergamo, Accademia Carrara), which may, however, have been influenced by Veronese's portrait in the Getty.
26 Similar painted bronze sculptures, seen at a sharp angle between columns, are featured in certain of the Villa Barbaro frescoes, suggesting a date for this portrait in the early 1560s.
27 Garton, *Grace and Grandeur*, p. 9.
28 Marco Boschini saw a portrait in the Nani palace in Venice in the late seventeenth century, but this is not identifiable with the current work. See Jean Habert, *Véronèse: un dame vénitienne dite la Belle Nani* (Paris, 1996).
29 Veronese's painting draws on Titian's *La Bella* (1536, Florence, Galleria Palatina, Pitti Palace), which probably also shows a young wife.
30 Garton, *Grace and Grandeur*, pp. 62–8.
31 'Even if I wanted to paint Virgil's Dido with her quiver of gold, her hair tied up in gold, her gown fastened with a golden clasp . . . and everything else resplendent with gold, I would try to represent with colours rather than with gold this wealth of rays of gold': Leon Battista Alberti, *On Painting*, trans. Cecil Grayson (London, 1991), para. 49, p. 85.
32 Garton, *Grace and Grandeur*, p. 61.
33 Xavier F. Salomon, *Paolo Veronese*, exh. cat., National Gallery, London (2014), p. 89, deftly notes that she less confidently occupies her role as a high-ranking aristocratic woman than her counterpart in Titian's *La Bella*, as if she were 'ashamed to be observed'.
34 Daniele Barbaro already knew Veronese's work very well, having provided the iconographic programme for the rooms of the

Council of Ten in the Ducal Palace in 1553, and sat for his portrait around 1556.

35 Donata Battilotti, 'Villa Barbaro a Maser: un difficile cantiere', *Storia dell'Arte*, XVIII/53 (1985), pp. 33–53, suggests a tension between architect and painter at the Villa, but see David Rosand, *Veronese*, ed. Mary E. Frank (London and Turnhout, 2023), p. 110, who doubts her reading.

36 For Daniele: Susy Marcon and Laura Moretto, *Daniele Barbaro 1514–70: Letteratura, Scienza e Arti nella Venezia del Rinascimento*, exh. cat., Biblioteca Nazionale Marciana, Venice (2015). For Marc'Antonio: Howard, *Venice Disputed*.

37 Denis Ribouillault, *The Villa Barbaro at Maser: Science, Philosophy and the Family in Venetian Renaissance Art* (London, 2023), pp. 62–71. For the woman as 'Divine Love' see Inga Jackson Reist, '*Divine Love* and Veronese's Frescoes at the Villa Barbaro', *Art Bulletin*, LXVII/4 (1985), pp. 614–35.

38 Mary Rogers, 'An Ideal Wife at the Villa Maser: Veronese, the Barbaros and Renaissance Theorists of Marriage', *Renaissance Studies*, VII/4 (December 1993), pp. 379–97.

39 Agostino Valier pronounced that it was the responsibility of the mistress of the house to stand as an exemplar of 'humility, obedience and subjection', and thus to serve as a model for her children and servants: see Agostino Valier, *Instituzione d'ogni stato lodevole delle donne Cristiane*. . . [Venice, 1575], ed. Francesco Lucioli (Cambridge, 2015), p. 119.

40 For these family portraits see Mary E. Frank, 'The Power of Portraits: Reuniting the Family at Villa Barbaro', in *Reflections on Renaissance Venice: A Celebration of Patricia Fortini Brown*, ed. Blake de Maria and Mary F. Frank (Milan, 2013), pp. 163–75.

41 These animals were household pets but probably also had symbolic meanings. As mentioned, the parrot might refer to Giustiniana's chastity, given its connection with the Virgin birth, while the dog would reflect her fidelity and the chained monkey the control of the growing boys' sexual appetites.

42 An unknown matronly woman arrives through a similarly multiplied framing doorway at the southern end.

43 The depiction of the servants makes the recent assertion that they disappear from view difficult to follow: see Diane Wolfthal, *Household Servants and Slaves: A Visual History, 1300–1700* (New Haven, CT, and London, 2022), p. 219. The brush and slippers that Veronese

playfully depicted in the Room of the Tribunal of Love should be taken as a further indicator of their constant presence in both the Villa itself and in Veronese's visual decoration of it.

3 Religious Paintings of the 1560s and '70s

1 The painting illustrates Luke 24:28–32. The earlier scene of the journey to Emmaus is depicted at the background left.
2 In his *Paralelle des anciens et des modernes* (Paris, 1688–97), the French academician Charles Perrault complained that the 'Venetian men and women pay almost no attention to the mystery that forms the subject of the painting' and was unhappy with the prominence of 'the little children playing with a big dog'. It 'would have been more reasonable for these three subjects to be featured in three different pictures rather than in a single composition to which they can impart no unity': translation from Charles Harrison, Paul Wood and Jason Gaiger, eds, *Art in Theory 1648–1815: An Anthology of Changing Ideas* (Oxford, 2000), p. 60.
3 Ruskin's 'sacred schools' were those of Florence and Umbria. See Edward T. Cook and Alexander Wedderburn, eds, *The Works of John Ruskin*, 39 vols (London, 1905), vol. VII, pp. 289–92.
4 For a more negative or hierarchical reading of the servant as blind to Christ's revelation see David Rosand, *Paolo Veronese*, ed. Mary E. Frank (London and Turnhout, 2023), pp. 149–50.
5 Nicholas Penny, *The Sixteenth Century Italian Paintings*, vol. II: *Venice, 1540–1600* (London, 2008), p. 229, identifies the family as Venetian patricians.
6 See the *Supper at Emmaus* (1513, Venice, San Salvator) attributed to Carpaccio, which includes a seated portrait of its patron, the patrician Girolamo Priuli, and might originally have hung in the family palace.
7 Monika Schmitter, 'The *Quadro da Portego* in Sixteenth-Century Venetian Art', *Renaissance Quarterly*, LXIV/3 (2011), pp. 693–751.
8 Blake de Maria, *Becoming Venetian: Immigrants and the Arts in Early Modern Venice* (New Haven, CT, and London, 2010), pp. 143–59, 203–7.
9 Paolo Veneziano's *Doge Francesco Dandolo and His wife Elisabetta Contarini* in the Frari (*c.* 1329–39) is one of the earliest.
10 This painting was one of four horizontally shaped works originally hung in the *portego* of the family palace and now in Dresden: see Christine Follmann, Marlies Giebe and Andreas Henning, eds,

Veronese: Der Cuccina-Zyklus (Dresden, 2018). Its composition owes a debt to the *Adoration of the Magi*, originally displayed directly opposite to it.

11 From left to right, the boys shown are Francesco, Domenico, Zuanne, Giroloamo, Marc'Antonio, Andrea and Giambattista: see Christine Follmann, 'Die Familie Cuccina und Veronese Gemäldezyklus' in *Veronese: Der Cuccina-Zyklus*, ed. Follmann, Giebe and Henning, pp. 24–35 (p. 30). For the maid as a Charity/*amor proximi* figure see Rose Z. King, 'Women in Sixteenth-Century Venetian Painting: Representation, Identity and Ambiguity', PhD thesis, University of Glasgow, 2022, pp. 209–16.

12 For the di Mutti family, also originally from Bergamo, see De Maria, *Becoming Venetian*, pp. 215–18. For Veronese's promotion of Zuanna see Andreas Henning, 'Der Cuccina-Zyklus von Veronese: Exzellenz, Prestige und Devotion', in *Veronese: Der Cuccina-Zyklus*, ed. Follmann, Giebe and Henning, pp. 12–23 (p. 15)

13 King, 'Women in Sixteenth-Century Venetian Painting', p. 190.

14 Penny, *The Sixteenth Century Italian Paintings*, pp. 206–35, suggests that the exclusion of women in Titian's painting reflects the legal fact of patrician family inheritance through the male line (p. 228).

15 Even if Daniele and Marc'Antonio are depicted in disguised fashion as Apollo and Bacchus in one fresco at the Villa, they are very much secondary in visual terms to Giustiniana and her children. For the identification of the brothers in this image see Denis Ribouillault, *The Villa Barbaro at Maser: Science, Philosophy and the Family in Venetian Renaissance Art* (Turnhout, 2023), p. 221 and fig. 219.

16 Hung prominently in their respective *porteghi*, they certain anticipate a viewership that extended well beyond the immediate family.

17 St George's nakedness symbolizes his purity and truth, according to long-established textual and visual conventions. The exposure of his flesh has powerful Eucharistic implications, given the role of the altarpiece in the Mass.

18 Peter Humfrey, *Titian* (New York, 2007), cat. nos 86 and 217.

19 Henry James, *Italian Hours* [1909], ed. John Auchard (London, 1992), p. 25.

20 For Titian's 'tragic' mode in his later paintings see Thomas Puttfarken, *Titian and Tragic Painting: Aristotle's Poetics and the Rise of the Modern Artist* (New Haven, CT, and London, 2005).

21 For Veronese's 'theatricality' see Rosand, *Veronese*, pp. 129–47. But see, too, the very pertinent doubts about the painter's wider reliance

on stage set designs for his depiction of architecture raised by David Hemsoll, 'Veronese's Painted Architecture: Vocabulary and Application', in *Paolo Veronese Giornate di Studio*, ed. Bernard Aikema, Thomas Dalla Costa and Paola Marini (Venice, 2016), pp. 175–87 (pp. 183–4).

22 Veronese's early altarpiece for Mantua (illus. 9) is the exception that proves the rule.

23 See Veronese's *Christ and the Centurion* (*c.* 1570, Madrid, Museo del Prado), in which the soldier may be shown falling to his knees before Christ as he asks him to heal his servant. But it is just as likely that we see the moment *after* the miracle, with the centurion opening his arms in a cruciform gesture in recognition of Christ's divine authority (that is, at the moment of his conversion).

24 Veronese would return to it repeatedly in his later sacred paintings.

25 Heather R. Nolin, 'A New Interpretation of Paolo Veronese's Saint Barnabas Healing the Sick', in *A Scarlet Renaissance: Essays in Honor of Sarah Blake McHam*, ed. Arnold Victor Coonin (New York, 2013), pp. 213–38.

26 The motif is featured in Tintoretto's *St Augustine Healing the Lame* (*c.* 1549–50, Vicenza, Musei Civici). See Tom Nichols, 'Saint Barnabé guérissant un malade de Véronèse et les images vénitiennes de la pauvreté et de la maladie', in *Venice and Paris, 1500–1700: La peinture vénitienne de la Renaissance et sa réception en France*, ed. Michel Hochmann (Geneva, 2006), pp. 63–82.

27 The building reprises Sanmicheli's architecture in Verona such as the Madonna di Campagna and (particularly fitting in a thematic sense) his Lazaretto. Sanmicheli had redesigned the dome of San Giorgio in Braida.

28 Richard Cocke, *Veronese's Drawings* (London, 1984), cat. no. 55.

29 Phyllis Pray Bober and Ruth Rubinstein, *Renaissance Artists and Antique Sculpture: A Handbook of Sources* (London and Turnhout, 2010), cat. no. 149.

30 Rosand, *Veronese*, p. 193, again interprets this marginal figure in more negative terms, seeing a symbolic contrast between his extinguished taper and the one lighting the Bible above. But Veronese's sensitive handling of the boy makes this narrowly iconographical reading seem too limiting.

31 Cocke, *Veronese's Drawings*, cat. no. 54; Paola Marini and Bernard Aikema, *Paolo Veronese: l'Illusione della Realtà*, exh. cat. Palazzo del Gran Guardia, Verona (Milan, 2014), cat. no. 2.5, p. 130.

32 William Roger Rearick, *The Art of Paolo Veronese, 1528–88*, exh. cat., National Gallery of Art, Washington, DC (Cambridge, 1988), cat. nos 50 and 51 for a detailed discussion of these two drawings.
33 Kate Lowe, 'Visible Lives: Black Gondoliers and Other Black Africans in Renaissance Venice', *Renaissance Quarterly*, LXVI/2 (Summer 2013), pp. 412–52.
34 Xavier F. Salomon, *Paolo Veronese*, exh. cat., National Gallery, London (2014), p. 46.
35 When shown as seated, the Virgin was conventionally understood as the 'Seat of Wisdom' in accordance with 1 Kings 10:18–20.
36 Ridolfi aptly noted how 'instead of courtiers, angels clad in precious vestments, embellished the work': Xavier F. Salomon, ed. and trans., *Lives of Veronese: Vasari, Borghini, Ridolfi* (London, 2014), p. 134.
37 For this tendency see Marie-Louise Lillywhite, *Reforming Art in Renaissance Venice* (Cambridge, 2025).
38 See Marini and Aikema, *Paolo Veronese: l'Illusione della Realtà*, cat. no. 2.12, p. 146.
39 See the three earlier versions of this theme in a devotional format now at Yale University Art Gallery, New Haven; the National Museum of Western Art, Tokyo; and the Hermitage Museum, St Petersburg. The patrons are unknown.
40 Salomon, ed., *Lives of Veronese*, p. 134.
41 Francisco de Hollanda, *Diálogos em Roma (1538): Conversations on Art with Michelangelo Buonarroti*, ed. Grazia Dolores (Heidelberg, 1998), pp. 76–7.
42 Veronese drew on Bonifacio de'Pitati's versions of this subject from the late 1530s and early 1540s, which feature a train of contemporary-looking courtly figures in the *terraferma* countryside, including a dwarf: see Philip Cottrell and Peter Humfrey, *Bonifacio de'Pitati* (Ponzano Veneto, 2023), cat. nos 97, 98, 136, 137.
43 Touba Ghadessi, *Portraits of Human Monsters in the Renaissance: Dwarves, Hirsutes, and Castrati as Idealized Anatomical Anomalies* (Kalamazoo, MI, 2018).
44 Naomi Yavneh, 'Lost and Found: Veronese's Finding of Moses', in *Gender and Early Modern Constructions of Childhood*, ed. Naomi Yavneh and Naomi J. Miller (London, 2016), pp. 51–66.
45 Claudia Terribile, 'Un figlio per due madri: Paolo Veronese e il tema del Mosè salvato dalle acque', in *Paolo Veronese Giornate di Studio*, ed. Aikema, Dalla Costa and Marini, pp. 79–88.

4 Biblical Feasts

1 In addition to the three feasts discussed in this chapter, Veronese also painted works of this type for the monasteries at San Sebastiano and the Servite church in Venice, both showing the Feast in the House of Simon (*c.* 1567–70, Milan, Pinacoteca di Brera and *c.* 1570–72, Versailles, Musée National); and for the Benedictines at Monte Berico, Vicenza showing the *Feast of St Gregory the Great* (1572, in situ).

2 These words are reported in Matthew 26:11, Mark 14:7 and John 12:8, but not in Luke. Veronese probably conflated these accounts in a way that did not pin him closely to any one of them: see Xavier F. Salomon, *Veronese*, exh. cat., National Gallery, London (2014), p. 72.

3 See Pordenone's *Sts Martin and Christopher* (1528–9, Venice, San Rocco). Philip Cottrell, 'Poor Substitutes: Imaging Disease and Vagrancy in Renaissance Venice', in *Others and Outcasts in Early Modern Europe: Picturing the Social Margins*, ed. Tom Nichols (Aldershot, 2007), pp. 63–85 (pp. 68–9).

4 The discolouration of the lower part of the column has not often been noted, with attention falling instead on the nail further up, which might symbolize Christ's wisdom via a passage in Ecclesiastes (12:11–13): see Michele di Monte, 'Le immagini in dettaglio: La pittura vista alla distanza giusta', *Venezia Cinquecento*, XXII/44 (2012), pp. 113–62 (pp. 135–53).

5 Responding to this effect in 1568, Giorgio Vasari especially commended Veronese's depictions of 'certain cripples, outstanding rendered': Xavier F. Salomon, ed. and trans., *Lives of Veronese by Giorgio Vasari, Raffaele Borghini and Carlo Ridolfi* (London, 2014), p. 30.

6 This arrangement broadly recalls Bonifacio de' Pitati's *Dives and Lazarus* (*c.* 1535–8, Venice, Gallerie dell'Accademia). But Veronese's sprawling leper is closer to one in Tintoretto's *St Augustine Healing the Lame* (*c.* 1549–50, Vicenza, Musei Civici), a work that he also drew on in the *St Barnabas* altarpiece.

7 Salomon, ed., *Lives of Veronese*, p. 75.

8 Veronese's interest in such outlandish figures might have been encouraged by the work of his father, Gabriele Bazaro, who sculpted a humorous grotesque of a man holding up a Holy water stoup for the church of Sant'Anastasia in Verona: see Salomon, *Veronese*, p. 24 fig. 4.

9 For Veronese's parrots see Diana Gisolfi, *Paolo Veronese and the Practice of Painting in Late Renaissance Venice* (New Haven, CT, and London, 2017), p. 59.

10 For the association of parrots with virginity see Erwin Panofsky, *Problems in Titian, Mostly Iconographic* (New York, 1969), p. 29.
11 The chaining of the monkey in the *Family of Darius before Alexander* (illus. 2) symbolizes the honourable intentions of the controlling men vis-à-vis the female family of Darius.
12 This figure reprises the lame man featured at the foreground left in the *Anointing of David* (illus. 13), as also the one at the lower centre of the drawing now in the Kasper Collection in New York (illus. 15).
13 T. J. Clark, 'Veronese's Higher Beings', in *Heaven on Earth: Painting and the Life to Come* (London, 2018), pp. 166–204 (p. 183).
14 For the role of servants in advertising the wealth and magnificence of their noble employers in Venice see Dennis Romano, *Housecraft and Statecraft: Domestic Service in Renaissance Venice, 1400–1600* (Baltimore, MD, 1996). For their visually marginalized depiction in much pre-Modern art, European and otherwise, see Diane Wolfthal, *Household Servants and Slaves: A Visual History, 1300–1700* (New Haven, CT, and London, 2022).
15 'When the ruler of the feast had tasted the water that was made wine, and knew not whence it was: (but the servants which drew the water knew).'
16 A firkin was equal to about 41 litres or 9 gallons.
17 The connection with the Holy pair was a flattering one for the patricians, even if the couple are arguably presented as generic types rather than individual portraits.
18 Salomon, ed., *Lives of Veronese*, p. 31.
19 On either side of Christ and his mother there are three disciples (probably Andrew, Philip and Bartholomew), similarly distinguished from the other guests by their non-contemporary appearance, and by the fact that they seem already to know that the miracle has occurred.
20 Few of these are now identifiable, although three on the right-hand side have been identified as officials of the monastery: Girolamo Scrocchetto (abbot), Alessandro da Bergamo (procurator) and Maurizio da Bergamo (cellarer): Jean Habert and Nathalie Volle, eds, *Les Noces de Cana de Véronèse: un oeuvre et sa restauration* (Paris, 1992), pp. 45–50.
21 He is sometimes identified as a disguised portrait of Veronese's younger painter-brother, Benedetto, though his action may also recall one of the dancers in Titian's *Andrians* of circa 1523–4 (Madrid, Musei del Prado), who similarly raises a glass of wine towards the heavens.

22 See Philipp P. Fehl, 'Veronese's Decorum: Notes on the Marriage at Cana', in *Art, the Ape of Nature: Essays in Honor of H. W. Janson*, ed. Moseed Barasch and Lucy Freedman Sandler (New York, 1981), pp. 341–65; and Richard Cocke, 'Venice, Decorum and Veronese', in *Nuovi Studi Su Paolo Veronese*, ed. Massimo Gemin (Venice, 1990), pp. 241–55.

23 Fehl, 'Veronese's Decorum', p. 347; see also Philipp P. Fehl, *Decorum and Wit: The Poetry of Venetian Painting. Essays in the History of the Classical Tradition* (Vienna, 1992), pp. 261–81.

24 Ridolfi described Veronese's feasts as 'regal banquets', rightly recognizing that their presentation is more reminiscent of the royal courts than of Republican Venice: see Salomon, ed., *Lives of Veronese*, p. 88.

25 Veronese did, though, draw broadly on Palladio's architectural language, quoting the red-pink Verona limestone of the two *lavabi* in the vestibule of the refectory in the foreground colonnades.

26 David Rosand, *Paolo Veronese*, ed. Mary E. Frank (London and Turnhout, 2023), p. 170, argues that Veronese sought to maintain a principle of 'structural decorum' by adapting his composition to the pluralistic views taken up in 'the room for which it is conceived'. But it is arguable that the painter's approach to pictorial space was more radically self-contained or subjective than that would allow.

27 Veronese's engaged auricular and haptic approach departs from the vision-obsessed idea of painting that had taken root earlier in the Renaissance. See Martin Jay, 'Scopic Regimes of Modernity', in *Vision and Visuality*, ed. Hal Foster (Seattle, WA, 1988), pp. 3–27.

28 Fehl, 'Veronese's Decorum', p. 357.

29 Antonio Casselli, 'Armonia: Seeing and Hearing in Paolo Veronese's "Le Nozze di Cana"', in *Experiencing Music and Visual Cultures: Threshold, Intermediality, Synchresis*, ed. Antonio Cascelli and Dennis Condon (London, 2021), pp. 179–82.

30 Veronese's approach recalls the habit of burying the sacred event in a crowded and contemporary-looking scene in certain earlier Venetian narrative paintings, such as those painted by Gentile Bellini, Carpaccio and others for the Scuola Grande di San Giovanni Evangelista (*c.* 1494–1510, Venice, Gallerie dell'Accademia).

31 Salomon, ed., *Lives of Veronese*, p. 183. An independent portrait of Titian by Veronese is recorded in the early sources, but cannot be identified today.

32 There is little evidence beyond Ridolfi's text to corroborate his claim that Titian awarded Veronese a gold chain following an

artistic competition for ceiling paintings at the Marciana Library in 1556, mirroring Charles's award of a similar object to Titian in 1533. Veronese did, however, contribute three roundels to the ceiling, including a panel showing *Music*, still in situ.

33 'All the sculptors and the painters come to admire it, two, four or six times': see Tracy Cooper, 'Un modo per la riforma Cattolica?: La scelta di Paolo Veronese per il refettorio di San Giorgio Maggiore', in *Crisi ed Rinnovamenti del Rinscimento a Venezia*, ed. Vittore Branca and Carlo Ossola (Florence, 1991), pp. 271–92 (p. 277).

34 Sheila Hale, *Titian: His Life* (London, 2012), p. 491.

35 Tom Nichols, 'The Master as Monument: Titian and His Images', *Artibus et Historiae*, XXXIV/67 (2013), pp. 219–38.

36 Salomon, *Veronese*, pp. 71–5.

37 The transcript of the interview was first published by Armand Baschet, 'Paul Véronèse appelé au Tribunal du Saint office, a Venise', *Gazette des Beaux-Arts*, XXIII (1867), pp. 378–82. Religious unrest (including reports of Protestant heresy) at the monastery may have attracted the Inquisition's attention.

38 Maria Elena Massimi, *La Cena in casa di Levi di Paolo Veronese: il processo riaperto* (Venice, 2011), pp. 179–81, for the most accurate transcript of the interview.

39 See, for example, Seneca's famous saying, 'there has never been a great talent without some touch of madness', from his *De Tranquillitate Animi* (*c*. AD 60), quoted in Rudolf Wittkower and Margot Wittkower, *Born Under Saturn: The Character and Conduct of Artists: A Documented History from Antiquity to the French Revolution* (New York, 1963), p. 99. For the classical *topos* of the mad poet more generally see Péter Hajdu, 'The Mad Poet in Horace's *Ars Poetica*', *Canadian Review of Comparative Literature*, XLI/1 (March 2014), pp. 27–41.

40 Marie-Louise Lillywhite, *Reforming Art in Renaissance Venice* (Cambridge, 2025), pp. 108–13.

41 Given the inquisitors suggestion of the addition of a Magdalene, some think that Veronese had originally depicted a 'Feast in the House of Simon': see, for example, Massimi, *La Cena in casa di Levi*, p. 181.

42 He may be a Jew, given his swarthy appearance and the yellow costume he wears. These visual characteristics were often used in antisemitic imagery of the period.

43 For the equivocal meanings of dwarves as both repellant and attractive in Renaissance imagery see Robin O'Brien, 'Grotesque

Bodies, Princely Delight: Dwarfs in Italian Renaissance Court Imagery', *Preternature: Critical and Historical Studies on the Preternatrual*, I/2 (2012), pp. 252–88.

44 Veronese had already included a very similar motif of almsgiving to the left in his recent *Feast of St Gregory the Great*, 1572, for Monte Berico in Vicenza. In both cases he drew on the similar imagery in Titian's *Presentation of the Virgin* (1534–8, Venice, Gallerie dell'Accademia).

45 Very few painters were summoned by the Inquisition in sixteenth-century Venice. However, Giambattista Ponchino (*c*. 1500–*c*. 1570), who had worked alongside Veronese in the rooms of the Council of Ten at the Ducal Palace, was similarly arraigned in 1554 regarding an altarpiece for his hometown of Castelfranco that included prominent Michelangelesque nudes. Some memory of this episode may lie behind Veronese's attempt to defend himself via Michelangelo's controversial use of nudity in the Sistine Chapel in July 1573.

46 The tribunal consisted of prominent Venetian patricians from the Trevisan, Foscari, Venier and Zorzi families, along with a Dominican from Brescia and the Apostolic Nuncio from Rossano: see Edward Grasman, 'On Closer Inspection: The Interrogation of Paolo Veronese', *Artibus et Historiae*, XXX/59 (2009), pp. 125–34 (pp. 128–9).

47 They were imagined as in the service of 'the owner of the house', who was 'a rich, important man'.

48 See note 29 above. A dwarf is depicted as an onlooker in Carpaccio's *Reception of the Ambassadors* (*c*. 1497–8, Venice, Gallerie dell'Accademia), for example, but he is made hard to pick out in the middle distance, and is allowed nothing of the prominence of Veronese's figure.

49 Michael Fried, *Absorption and Theatricality: Painting and Beholder in the Age of Diderot* (Chicago, IL, 1988), esp. pp. 107–60.

50 For the role of 'drolleries' in medieval manuscripts see Michael Camille, *Image on the Edge: The Margins of Medieval Art* (London, 1992).

5 Mythologies and Allegories

1 Malcolm Bull, *The Mirror of the Gods* (Oxford and New York, 2005).

2 Matthias Wivel et al., *Titian: Love, Desire, Death*, exh. cat., National Gallery, London, and National Galleries of Scotland, Edinburgh (London, 2020).

3 Thomas Dalla Costa, *'Venere e Adone' di Tiziano: Arte, cultura e società tra Venezia e l'Europa* (Venice, 2019), pp. 201–15.

4 Vienna, Kunsthistorisches Museum. In making this change, Veronese characteristically replaces Titian's quotation of a classical sculpture he had seen in Rome – the so-called *Bed of Polyclitus* – with a north Italian source.

5 A similar retreat from psychological tension and danger is evident in Veronese's small-scale furniture painting featuring *Diana and Actaeon* (1560–65, Boston, Museum of Fine Arts) that recalls Titian's *poesia* of the same subject (1556–9, London, National Gallery and Edinburgh, National Galleries of Scotland). Veronese features a relaxed hero who enjoys the view of exposed female flesh in contrast to Titian's anxious, compromised and tragic figure.

6 Titian's painting of 1559–62 is now in Boston at the Isabella Stewart Gardner Museum. Veronese's painting for Contarini is likely to have followed two smaller versions: see Nicholas Penny, *The Sixteenth Century Italian Paintings*, vol. II: *Venice, 1540–1600* (London, 2008), pp. 430–41. The date of the Contarini painting is indicated by that included on a preparatory drawing: Richard Cocke, *Veronese's Drawings* (London, 1984), pp. 154–7.

7 See Diane Wolfthal, *Images of Rape: The 'Heroic' Tradition and Its Alternatives* (Cambridge, 1999), pp. 9–12.

8 Comparison with Veronese's perhaps preparatory version of the subject (*c.* 1570, London, National Gallery) shows that he was at pains to conceal the bull's horns from view beneath the celebratory garlands.

9 His treatment of both these subjects was much emulated by painters in the following centuries in both Venice and elsewhere. See, for example, the *Rape of Europa* by the Roman painter Carlo Maratta (1680–85, Dublin, National Gallery of Ireland), which is closer to Veronese's painting than it is to Titian's.

10 The poet and critic Raffaello Borghini criticized Titian's departure from the text in his *Il Riposo* (Florence, 1584), pp. 64–5. In bringing the two lovers together at dawn, both painters probably followed Niccolò degli Agostini's vernacular edition of Ovid's *Metamorphoses* (Venice, 1522).

11 Ridolfi notes that 'Veronese brought the ultimate in grace and perfection so that they [his paintings] appear as those imaginary beauties that are formed in the mind': Xavier F. Salomon, ed. and trans., *Lives of Veronese: Vasari, Borghini, Ridolfi* (London, 2014), p. 131.

12 He might have known the edition of Marsilio Ficino's *Commentary on Plato's Symposium on Love* published in Venice in 1544. See Marsilio Ficino, *Sopra lo amore, o, ver' Convito di Platone*, ed. G. Ottaviano (Milan, 1973) in which we hear that 'God is Love, great and wonderful, as well as noble' ('Amore sia Iddio grande e mirabile: ancora nobile'), p. 42.

13 The dating proposed here is supported by the very similar two-handed embrace featured in the *Jupiter and a Nude* (1560–65, Boston, Museum of Fine Arts). See William Roger Rearick, *The Art of Paolo Veronese, 1528–88*, exh. cat., National Gallery of Art, Washington, DC (Washington, DC, and Cambridge, 1988), cat. no. 38, for a similar dating.

14 Veronese's painting is closer to the savagely parodic depiction of the two lovers with the cuckolded husband in Tintoretto's *Venus, Vulcan and Mars* (c. 1550–55, Munich, Alte Pinakothek).

15 For the rediscovery of Aristotle's *Poetics* in the sixteenth century see Brian Brazeau, ed., *The Reception of Aristotle's Poetics in the Italian Renaissance and Beyond: New Directions in Criticism* (London, 2020).

16 Aristotle's threefold description of the theatrical dramatis personae as better than the audience in tragedy, at the same level in comedy, and as lower in the so-called 'satyr plays', originally performed by actors dressed as goat-like followers of Dionysius, was well-known by Veronese's time.

17 In Tintoretto's *Venus, Vulcan and Mars*, Vulcan does just that.

18 Veronese's pointed marginalization of the male hero in this painting reprises an earlier painting in which Venus sits on the lap of a shadowy satyr (c. 1570, Switzerland, private collection).

19 The two works were probably not conceived as pendants.

20 The later *Mercury, Herse and Aglauros* (c. 1580, Cambridge, Fitzwilliam Museum) might be the only mythology by Veronese directly commissioned by the Holy Roman Emperor Rudolf II of Prague (r. 1576–1612), although a number of other works by Veronese ended up in his collection.

21 Xavier F. Salomon, *Veronese's Allegories: Virtue, Love, and Exploration in Renaissance Venice*, exh. cat., The Frick Collection, New York (2006), pp. 18–24.

22 See Cocke, *Veronese's Drawings*, cat. no. 106.

23 Anthony van Dyck saw these paintings in a Venetian palace in 1622–3 and recorded some of the figures in his Italian sketchbook: see Penny, *The Sixteenth Century Italian Paintings*, p. 421, figs. 4 and 5.

24 For these paintings as 'astonishing visual performances' see T. J. Clark, 'Veronese's Higher Beings', in *Heaven on Earth: Painting and the Life to Come* (London, 2018), pp. 166–204.

25 Louis-François Dubois de Saint-Gelais, *Description des tableaux du Palais Royal* (Paris, 1727), p. 377.

26 For a useful quick summary of the various modern proposals for the original arrangement of the four paintings on a palace ceiling see David Rosand, *Paolo Veronese*, ed. Mary E. Frank (London and Turnhout, 2023), p. 260 n.29.

27 Veronese drew on works such as Titian's *Triumph of Love* (*c.* 1545–50, private collection) in which the triumphant winged boy dances on the back of a lion.

28 Other than the woman with an ermine symbolizing innocence or purity in *Scorn*, and the figure of Fortuna or Venus in the *Happy Union*, Veronese avoided making his pictorial actors in this series appear as personifications of moral qualities or divine beings, showing them instead as contemporary 'people acting out scenes illustrating virtues or vices': Penny, *The Sixteenth Century Italian Paintings*, p. 422.

29 Carlo Ginzburg, 'Titian, Ovid and Sixteenth-Century Codes for Erotic Illustration', in *Titian's 'Venus of Urbino'*, ed. Rona Goffen (Cambridge, 1997), pp. 23–36.

30 Giorgione's painting mentioned here is now in Dresden, Gemäldegalerie. The best known of Titian's versions of 'Danaë', each with the raised knee motif, are in Naples, Museo Capodimonte; London, Apsley House; and Madrid, Museo del Prado.

31 For Veronese's ceiling see Jarrod Michael Broderick, 'The Myth in Image: Veronese's Ceiling in the Hall of the College', *Studi Veneziani*, LXXXI (2020), pp. 119–200.

32 For the Old Testament combination of Justice and Peace depicted in the Collegio ceiling panel see Psalms 85:10: 'righteousness and peace have kissed each other.' Veronese's painting closely reprises his recent *Venice with Hercules and Neptune* (*c.* 1575, Budapest, Szépművészeti Múzeum), painted for another ceiling of the Palace. But in that work semi-naked male figures adore the goddess.

33 For a recent analysis see Giorgio Tagliaferro, 'Reconsidering the *concorso* for the *Paradiso* in the Palazzo Ducale, Venice', *Römisches Jahrbuch der Bibliotheca Hertziana*, XLVII (2024), pp. 257–92.

34 For this and other paintings in the Palace from this phase see Wolfgang Wolters, *Storia e politica nei dipinti di Palazzo Ducale: aspetti*

dell'autocelbrazione della Repubblica di Venezia nel Cinquecento (Venice, 1987), pp. 273–9.

35 Giorgio Tagliaferro, 'Le forme delle Vergine: la personificazione di Venezia nel processo creativo di Paolo Veronese', *Venezia Cinquecento*, XV/30 (2005), pp. 5–158.

36 Rosand, *Paolo Veronese*, p. 301, notes that these columns symbolize the wisdom of the Venetian state, via their association with the biblical Temple of Solomon.

37 The programme devised by the Camaldolese monk Girolamo Bardi required Veronese to depict Venice dominating 'over various towers and cities in imitation of the goddess Roma, as she is seen in medals, seated above the world': *Dichiaratione di tutte le storie che si contengono nei quadri posti nouamente nelle Sale dello Scrutinio, & del Gran Consiglio, del Palagio Ducale della Serenissima Republic di Vinegia* (Venice, 1587), p. 63.

38 Veronese's substitutive approach calls to mind Italo Calvino's *Invisible Cities* (Turin, 1972), in which Venice is imagined by Marco Polo for the Chinese ruler Kublai Khan in terms of many other cities.

39 Venetia's 'court' includes personifications of the virtues of Honour, Peace, Security, Felicity and Liberty. The semi-naked female figure of Abundance with back turned more or less replicates one on the ceiling of the Sala dell'Olimpo at the Villa Barbaro (illus. 28).

40 See, for example, Matteo Pagan's woodcut showing a *Procession in St Mark's Square of Palm Sunday* of 1556–9.

41 A woman and her son do appear among the mêlée, perhaps serving to mitigate the prevalent gender arrangement.

6 Late Works

1 The pair are mentioned by Raffaello Borghini as among Veronese's very latest works. Borghini's text was written in 1582, so this year is the *terminus ante quem* for the paintings. See Xavier F. Salomon, ed. and trans., *Lives of Veronese: Vasari, Borghini, Ridolfi* (London, 2014), p. 42.

2 This was noted by Thomas Dalla Costa, *'Venere e Adone' di Tiziano: Arte, cultura e società tra Venezia e l'Europa* (Venice, 2019), p. 212 n.489. See also Veronese's version of the subject from the later 1570s (Vienna, Kunsthistorisches Museum) in which the lovers' uninterrupted engagement with one another is still more absolute.

3 Despite the persistence of the long-standing Homeric idea of sleep as the brother of death, it could also signify more positively, as an elevating sign of divine inspiration: see Maria Ruvoldt, *The Italian Renaissance Imagery of Inspiration: Metaphors of Sex, Sleep, and Dream* (Cambridge, 2004).

4 Expression gradually came to play a greater role in Veronese's paintings. See, for example, the heroine's face in *Scorn* (illus. 54).

5 The formal source for the dog-hugging motif was the well-known Hellenistic sculpture by Boethos of a *Boy Standing with a Goose*, perhaps known to Veronese through the similar figure included in the Nymphaeum at Villa Barbaro.

6 Her figure was based on the Hellenistic *Falling Gaul*, then on display in the Grimani collection in Venice, which Veronese had already quoted in the *St Barnabas* altarpiece (illus. 37).

7 See the *Resurrection* (*c.* 1578–80, Dresden, Gemäldegalerie) for a further example of a work of this type.

8 In the late 1570s Veronese himself had been asked to substitute a figure of the risen Christ for the more traditional one of St Mark that he had initially featured in an oil sketch for the *Allegory of the Victory of Lepanto*, destined for the Sala del Collegio in the Ducal Palace. The drawing is now in the British Museum, London, while the painting remains in situ.

9 For a comparison of the sacred paintings of these painters see Tom Nichols, 'Tintoretto, Bassano and the Rural Image', in *Tintoretto e il Paesaggio*, ed. Martina Frank (Venice, 2024), pp. 42–57.

10 See Paul H. D. Kaplan, 'Veronese's Last "Last Supper"', *Arte Veneta*, XLI (1987), pp. 51–62.

11 According to Mark 14:15 and Luke 22:11–12, it took place in 'a large upper room furnished and prepared'.

12 The rapid spread of the Scuole del Sacramento in the later sixteenth century reflects the gathering Catholicizing response to the Protestant attack on transubstantiation at the mass. See Maurice E. Cope, *The Venetian Chapel of the Sacrament in the Sixteenth Century* (New York and London, 1979).

13 The feeding of the poor rather than the dog might allude to Thomas Aquinas's Corpus Christi hymn pronouncing that the Eucharist, as the bread of heaven, should not be given to dogs: Kaplan, 'Veronese's Last "Last Supper"', p. 55.

14 He is also an outsider in a historical or temporal sense, since he belongs to the present day, rather than to the biblical past.

15 Thomas Martin, 'Grimani Patronage in S. Giuseppe di Castello: Veronese, Vittoria and Smeraldi', *Burlington Magazine*, CXXXIII/1065 (December 1991), pp. 825–33, who (mistakenly) thinks that the painting is largely by the workshop.
16 Veronese had already responded to Bassano's ruralizing imagery, especially when working for 'lesser' or non-patrician patrons. See, for example, the *Adoration of the Kings* (1573, London, National Gallery) painted for the Scuola di San Giuseppe active in the parish church of San Silvestro.
17 The drawing is now in a private collection. Richard Cocke, *Veronese's Drawings* (London, 1984), cat. no. 77. The areas of ermine are marked with a 'P' for 'pelo' or 'peliccia'.
18 A further example is the *Mary Magdalene in the Wilderness* (1580–85, Genoa, private collection).
19 Peter Humfrey, 'The Provenance of Veronese's "Martyrdom of St Lucy" in Washington', *Arte Veneta*, XLIII (1989–90), pp. 89–90.
20 Beverly L. Brown, 'Paolo Veronese's "The Martyrdom and Last Communion of St Lucy"', *Venezia Arti*, II (1988), pp. 61–8.
21 Thomas Dalla Costa, 'Paolo Veronese e la Bottega e le Botteghe dei Caliari', in Paola Marini and Bernard Aikema, *Paolo Veronese: l'Illusione della Realtà*, exh. cat. Palazzo del Gran Guardia, Verona (Milan, 2014), pp. 314–26.

Conclusion

1 Around two-thirds of Veronese's total output of paintings have religious subjects.
2 Admittedly, Veronese drew on Titian's strikingly informal depictions of children in works such as the *Ranuccio Farnese* and *Clarissa Strozzi* from the early 1540s in taking this approach. For these paintings see Peter Humfrey, *Titian: The Complete Paintings* (New York, 2007), cat. nos 134 and 135.
3 Barbara Babcock, ed., *The Reversible World: Symbolic Inversion in Art and Society* (Ithaca, NY, 1978).
4 'As the financial and symbolic value of the house and its possessions grew, women running the household required new management and social skills, which partly reversed the process of domestic seclusion': see Marta Ajmar-Wollheim, 'Housework', in *At Home in Renaissance Italy*, ed. Marta Ajmar-Wollheim and Flora Dennis (London, 2006), pp. 152–63 (p. 153).

5 Philip Sohm, 'Gendered Style in Italian Art Criticism from Michelangelo to Malvasia', *Renaissance Quarterly*, XLVIII/4 (1995), pp. 759–808.
6 The argument here is in some ways parallel to the idea that early modern still-life painting is essentially feminine because it is essentially non-narrative: see Norman Bryson, *Looking at the Overlooked: Four Essays on Still-Life Painting* (London, 1990).
7 Svetlana Alpers and Michael Baxandall, *Tiepolo and the Pictorial Intelligence* (New Haven, CT, and London, 1994), p. 21.

FURTHER READING

Aikema, Bernard, Thomas Dalla Costa and Paola Marini, eds, *Paolo Veronese Giornate di Studio* (Venice, 2016)

Brilliant, Virginia, and Frederick Ilchman, *Paolo Veronese: A Master and His Workshop in Renaissance Venice*, exh. cat., John and Mable Ringling Museum of Art, Florida (London, 2012)

Brugnoli, Pierpaolo, 'Nuovi documenti su Paolo Veronese e la sua famiglia', *Verona Illustrata*, XIII (2000), pp. 11–19

Clark, T. J., 'Veronese's Higher Beings', in *Heaven on Earth: Painting and the Life to Come* (London, 2018), pp. 166–204

Cocke, Richard, *Paolo Veronese: Piety and Display in an Age of Religious Reform* (Aldershot and Burlington, VT, 2001)

—, *Veronese's Drawings* (London, 1984)

Dalla Costa, Thomas, 'Drawings and Draughtsmanship in Sixteenth-Century Venice: Tintoretto and Veronese in Comparison', *Artibus et Historiae*, XXXIX/78 (2018), pp. 141–54

Fehl, Philipp P., 'Veronese's Decorum: Notes on the Marriage at Cana', in *Art, the Ape of Nature: Essays in Honor of H. W. Janson*, ed. Moseed Barasch and Lucy Freedman Sandler (New York, 1981), pp. 341–65

Follmann, Christine, Marlies Giebe and Andreas Henning, eds, *Veronese: Der Cuccina-Zyklus* (Dresden, 2018)

Garton, John, *Grace and Grandeur: The Portraiture of Paolo Veronese* (Turnhout, 2008)

Gemin, Massimo, ed., *Nuovi Studi Su Paolo Veronese* (Venice, 1990)

Gisolfi, Diana, *Paolo Veronese and the Practice of Painting in Late Renaissance Venice* (New Haven, CT, and London, 2017)

Habert, Jean, *Véronèse: un dame vénitienne dite la Belle Nani* (Paris, 1996)

Huber, Hans Dieter, *Paolo Veronese: Kunst als soziales System* (Munich, 2005)

Marini, Paola, and Bernard Aikema, *Paolo Veronese: l'Illusione della Realtà*, exh. cat., Palazzo del Gran Guardia, Verona (Milan, 2014)

Massimi, Maria Elena, *La Cena in casa di Levi di Paolo Veronese: il processo riaperto* (Venice, 2011)

Pignatti, Terisio, and Filippo Pedrocco, *Veronese*, 2 vols (Milan, 1995)

Rosand, David, *Paolo Veronese*, ed. Mary E. Frank (London and Turnhout, 2023)

Salomon, Xavier F., ed. and trans., *Lives of Veronese: Vasari, Borghini, Ridolfi* (London, 2014)

—, *Veronese*, exh. cat. National Gallery, London (2014)

Terribile, Claudia, 'La "Famiglia di Dario" di Paolo Veronese: la committenza, il contesto, la storia', *Venezia Cinquecento*, XV/29 (2005), pp. 63–107

Zamperini, Alessandra, *Paolo Veronese* (London, 2014)

ACKNOWLEDGEMENTS

Many thanks to Michael Leaman and François Quiviger for inviting me to contribute a second volume to the Renaissance Lives series. I could not have written it without the period of research leave kindly granted to me by the University of Glasgow, and the generous support of my immediate colleagues in the History of Art department. The comments on earlier drafts by Marie-Louise Lillywhite, Adam Flynn and Rose Zevos King proved very valuable, and I am grateful to Mark Tully for some useful suggestions regarding Veronese's interview with the Inquisition. Conversations about Veronese with my art-loving novelist sister, Tessa Hadley, and Steve Fitzpatrick were important to the framing of certain of the arguments presented here. As in my earlier books, nothing could have happened without the extraordinary love and support of my wife, Kerry Menzinger. Working on this book took me back to my time as a PhD student under the supervision of the Veronese scholar Richard Cocke at the University of East Anglia. Our many discussions about my then obsession – Tintoretto – were often framed by way of his supposed contrast to the 'elite' figure of Veronese. These two painters were, though, much more closely aligned with one another than I then allowed or understood.

PHOTO ACKNOWLEDGEMENTS

The author and publishers wish to express their thanks to the sources listed below for illustrative material and/or permission to reproduce it. Some locations of artworks are also given below, in the interest of brevity:

Chiesa di San Giorgio in Braida, Verona: 36; Chiesa di San Giuseppe di Castello, Venice, photo akg-images/Cameraphoto: 64; Chiesa di San Sebastiano, Venice, photos Matteo De Fina/Save Venice Photo Archive: 16, 17, 18, 19, 20, 21, 22; Duomo di Castelfranco Veneto, photo Mondadori Portfolio/Electa/Paolo e Federico Manusardi/Bridgeman Images: 4; The Frick Collection, New York: 51, 52; Galleria Sabauda, Turin: 41, 42, 49; Gallerie dell'Accademia, Venice: 39, 44, 45 (photo Scala, Florence – courtesy Ministero Beni e Att. Culturali e del Turismo), 46 (photo Cameraphoto/Scala, Florence); Gallerie degli Uffizi, Florence: 6 (photo Gabinetto Fotografico delle Gallerie degli Uffizi), 23; Gemäldegalerie Alte Meister – Staatliche Kunstsammlungen Dresden: 35; The J. Paul Getty Museum, Los Angeles: 25; Kunsthistorisches Institut in Florenz – Max Planck Institute (CC BY-SA 4.0): 28, 29, 30, 31, 32, 33; Kunsthistorisches Museum, Vienna: 10, 13, 14, 67; Kunstsammlungen und Museen Augsburg: 47; The Metropolitan Museum of Art, New York: 50, 57; Musée des Beaux Arts, Caen: 9; Musée des Beaux-Arts, Rouen: 37; Musée des Beaux-Arts, Strasbourg: 61; Musée du Louvre, Paris: 3, 5, 11 (photo © RMN-Grand Palais/Gérard Blot/Dist. Scala, Florence), 12 (photo © Peter Willi/Bridgeman Images), 26, 34, 38, 43; Museo di Castelvecchio, Verona: 7; Museo Nacional del Prado, Madrid: 40, 60; The National Gallery, London: 2, 53, 54, 55, 56, 65; National Gallery of Art, Washington, DC: 1, 68; Palazzo Ducale, Venice: 48, 58 (photo Didier Descouens/Wikimedia Commons, CC BY-SA 4.0), 59; Pinacoteca di Brera, Milan, photo Universal Images/SuperStock: 63; private collection: 15, 66; San Francesco della Vigna, Venice, photo Scala, Florence: 8; The State Hermitage Museum,

St Petersburg: 62; Villa Barbaro, Maser, photo Scala, Florence: 27; The Walters Art Museum, Baltimore, MD: 24.

INDEX

Illustration numbers are indicated by *italics*